Praise for *No Regrets*

"In *No Regrets Living*, Dr. Harley Rotbart offers a ~~step~~-by-step guide to approaching life with an attitude of gratit~~ude~~ ~~patie~~nce, and self-forgiveness, even in the face of adversity. ~~Us~~ing blend of scientific research and faith-based inquiry, Rot~~bart~~ shows how increasing our awareness of the 'everyday miracles' around us can move us closer to living a more conscientious and contented life. This is truly a fitting follow-up to his book of essays, *Miracles We Have Seen*. And, as an infectious diseases doctor, Rotbart reflects on the inexplicable origins and consequences of viruses like COVID-19 and offers coping mechanisms and lessons to all of us for moving forward."

—**Samantha Parent Walravens**, *Forbes* columnist and *New York Times*-acclaimed author of *Torn* and co-author of *Geek Girl Rising*

"I am absolutely stunned by Dr. Rotbart's wonderful and wise new book. His appreciation for the awe and majesty of the world around us—from the viruses under his microscope, to the graceful butterfly in his garden, the courageous patients he cares for at Children's Hospital, and the endless universe of stars and planets in the night sky—reminds us how much we have to be grateful for in our lives. His perspectives on life are truly unique, and his family's story is both heroic and humbling. From the issues of racism in America to recovery from the COVID-19 pandemic, this is a road map for moving forward in our lives without regrets."

—**Richard D. Lamm, JD**, three-term governor, State of Colorado, 1975–1987; co-director, Institute for Public Policy Studies, University of Denver; author of *Two Wands, One Nation: An Essay on Race and Community in America* and *Condition Critical: A New Moral Vision for Health Care*

"I love Dr. Rotbart's previous work, and I love this marvelous new book. In *No Regrets Living* he shares profound insights from his unique personal experiences to create a road map for a life of fulfillment and awe. This could not be timelier."

—**KJ Dell'Antonia**, former editor of the *New York Times* Motherlode blog; author of *How to Be a Happier Parent* and *The Chicken Sisters*

"No Regrets Living is a gentle book of practical wisdom from a man who speaks with an insider's insight into religion and science."

—**The Reverend Canon Mpho A. Tutu van Furth**, founder and CEO, the Tutu Teach Foundation; former executive director and CEO, The Desmond & Leah Tutu Legacy Foundation

"Dr. Rotbart, a physician and scientist, speaks a universal truth for people of all faiths and for people of no faith—contentment in life comes from reverence for the 'miracles' in the world around us, and from the humility to acknowledge we will never *fully* understand the source or substance of those miracles. You will be deeply moved, as I was."

—**Rabbi Joshua Hammerman**, spiritual leader, Temple Beth-El, Stamford, CT; author of *Mensch Marks* and *Embracing Auschwitz: Forging a Vibrant, Life-Affirming Judaism that Takes the Holocaust Seriously*

"Experts on aging often advise the elderly, who might be approaching the end of life, to find a way to eliminate or minimize regrets they've had and to come to peace with them. This book, however, gives those in much earlier stages of their lives a road map with various on and off ramps to achieve a lifetime goal of living with no regrets. Written in an easy style, the author gives wise advice on various ways of thinking, behaving, and believing to get there. With references to his own life experiences, family history, professional perspective, and scientific inquiry, Dr. Rotbart provides many moments of joy, chuckles, tears, and reflection. This is a book that should be read once and then read again at various life stages, and after significant life events, to keep things in perspective. Written in the face of the horrific COVID-19 pandemic, the author also intersperses commentary on the impact of the pandemic on his no regrets framework and offers many insights gleaned from this once-in-a-hundred-year set of events. An important book for any age, this book brings the wisdom and experience of a learned man who wants to pass on to others his lessons learned."

—**Jeremy A. Lazarus, MD**, past president, American Medical Association

"In this beautiful volume, Harley Rotbart, scientist and humanist, shares his profound vision of how to lead a deeper, richer life. You will regret not reading it and incorporating its wise and gentle teachings into your every day."

—**Samuel J. Rascoff**, professor,
New York University School of Law

"In *No Regrets Living*, Dr. Rotbart helps us bridge the gap between science and faith (meaning the belief in something larger than ourselves) with sage advice for finding contentment and wonder in a world filled with chaos and confusion. With beautiful examples from nature all around us, the book is interspersed with his *timeless* insights into life and his most *timely* insights on living in and moving forward from the COVID-19 pandemic—wisdom gleaned from his four decades as an infectious diseases physician and virologist. An indispensable book for our times. It will bring readers hope and resilience just when those are most needed."

—**Tovah P. Klein, PhD**, director, Barnard College Center for
Toddler Development; adjunct associate professor of psychology,
Barnard College; author of *How Toddlers Thrive*

"In a time of uncertainty, it is immensely reassuring to hear from a distinguished physician who offers both scientific understanding and heartfelt hope for humanity. *No Regrets Living* is crucial reading for all of us who seek to emerge from the pandemic with a deeper grasp of the wonders and blessings of our lives."

—**Ruth Behar**, author of *Letters from Cuba*,
and Victor Haim Perera Collegiate Professor of
Anthropology at the University of Michigan

"I found I could apply so much of Dr. Rotbart's sage advice in *No Regrets Living*. You really can change your way of thinking with the help of this book. So many of us dwell on the past: 'What if I hadn't done this?' or 'What if this hadn't happened?' *No Regrets Living* helps us focus and find wonder in our life today and look forward to the future, rather than looking back with regret at events we cannot change. *No Regrets*

Living will touch you deeply as it guides us through the life we live now and toward the one we hope to live going forward."

—**Erin Merryn**, author of *Stolen Innocence, Living for Today,* and
Bailey, No Ordinary Cat; People magazine's "Heroes Among Us"
and one of "15 Women Changing the World"; *Glamour*
magazine's Woman of the Year; force behind "Erin's Law"
for protection of children from child abuse

"No Regrets Living will bring hope and optimism to all who read it. Dr. Rotbart's perspective on the intersection of science, medicine, and faith is eye-opening, and a prescription for a life of contentment and joy."

—**Jeffrey J. Cain, MD**, past president, American Academy
of Family Physicians; chair, Amputee Coalition

"Wise and worldly guidance, from one of America's foremost physician experts, on coping with all the challenges daily living presents for us. Dr. Rotbart's seven keys for personal healing and growth are truly a gift, and his advice on transcending the COVID-19 pandemic couldn't be more timely."

—**Rabbi Daniel Cohen**, senior rabbi, Congregation Agudath Sholom;
author of *What Will They Say About You When You Are Gone?*
Creating a Life of Legacy; co-host of the nationally
syndicated radio show, *The Rabbi and the Reverend*

"Dr. Harley Rotbart has hit it out of the park again with *No Regrets Living,* just as he did with *No Regrets Parenting* and *Miracles We Have Seen.* As a physician, scientist, researcher, philosopher, spiritual guide, family man, heart patient, and veritable mensch, Dr. Rotbart has compiled a compelling seven-step prescription for living and loving well. Drawing from his unique combination of roles, Dr. Rotbart has created a roadmap for maximizing contentment and minimizing regrets by believing in something greater than ourselves; reveling in the miracles all around us; choosing healing over hurting; practicing gratitude and appreciation; promoting peace and kindness; living with a sense of purpose; and leaving a legacy of contribution. Wherever you are on your own life journey, this guide will take you to a higher pinnacle of fulfillment!"

—**Marianne Neifert, MD, MTS**, author of the *Dr. Mom*
parenting books and 2020 Colorado Women's
Hall of Fame inductee

"An infectious disease physician, Harley Rotbart is following the age-old advice: physician heal yourself. Part autobiography and part distilled wisdom of decades of helping patients, family members, and friends, *No Regrets Living* offers prescriptions for living life to the fullest. And this includes advice to humankind. Dr. Rotbart believes that evil can be eradicated like the many terrible diseases humans have conquered. This 'treatment' requires nurturing each new child in loving (not hateful, abusive) home environments, creating educations that encourage children to bring life-sustaining values home to parents, and political-social activism beyond donations and signing online petitions. Regret plagues many people throughout their lives and often at the end. There may be no sadder thought than 'it might have been.' *No Regrets Living* offers a way to avoid that fate."

—**Bernard Beitman, MD**, founder of the Coincidence Project;
author of *Connecting with Coincidence*; visiting professor of
psychiatry, University of Virginia; past chair, Department
of Psychiatry, University of Missouri-Columbia

"Uncertainty is the nature of life at any given time; especially so during a crisis like the horrific pandemic. Unlike other disasters that have a chronological beginning, middle, and end, COVID-19 is amorphous, invisible, with an ambiguous timeline lacking a clear endpoint. In *No Regrets Living*, Dr. Rotbart offers the reader information and insight for staying focused during critical times. His seven 'keys' provide the reader with actionable steps to build new values that are optimistic and solution-focused."

—**Laurie Nadel, PhD**, psychotherapist and author of
*The Five Gifts: Discovering Hope, Healing, and
Strength When Disaster Strikes*

"Dr. Rotbart extends his 'No Regrets' philosophy to everyone hoping to look back at their lives someday with a sense of fulfillment and satisfaction, without wishing things had turned out differently—a worthy goal for all of us. This is a truly inspirational book."

—**Christie Pearce Rampone**, co-author of *Be All In*;
three-time Olympic gold medalist and the most decorated
American professional soccer player of all time, and
Dr. Kristine Keane, co-author of *Be All In*; clinical and sports
neuropsychologist; assistant professor of psychiatry and
behavioral health at Hackensack Meridian School of Medicine

"Pediatrician Harley Rotbart's newest book, *No Regrets Living* outlines his seven-step prescription for living a fulfilled life, informed by his own personal journey growing up the son of a Holocaust survivor, pulling in lessons learned as a son and father, as a physician-scientist, and as one who has confronted and lives with a life-threatening heart condition.

"I consider the guidance shared by Dr. Rotbart on a very personal level as a daughter, wife, mother, and grandmother, who has navigated personal challenges. His 7 Keys speak to my own belief that the keys to life are embracing your purpose, recognizing what gives you joy and meaning, being grateful, and lifting up those around you."

—**Mary Anne Jackson, MD, FAAP, FPIDS, FIDSA**,
dean, University of Missouri–Kansas City School of Medicine;
professor, Department of Pediatrics, Children's
Mercy Hospital, UMKC School of Medicine

NO REGRETS LIVING

7 Keys to a Life of
Wonder and Contentment

✍

HARLEY A. ROTBART, MD

author of *No Regrets Parenting*
and *Miracles We Have Seen*

Health Communications, Inc.
Boca Raton, Florida

www.hcibooks.com

Other Books by Dr. Rotbart

Miracles We Have Seen
940 Saturdays
No Regrets Parenting
Germ Proof Your Kids
The On Deck Circle of Life
Human Enterovirus Infections

**Library of Congress Cataloging-in-Publication Data
is available through the Library of Congress**

ISBN-13: 978-07573-2394-2 (Paperback)
ISBN-10: 07573-2394-4 (Paperback)
ISBN-13: 978-07573-2395-9 (ePub)
ISBN-10: 07573-2395-2 (ePub)

Publisher: Health Communications, Inc.
        1700 NW 2nd Avenue
        Boca Raton, FL 33432-1653

Cover design by www.milagraphicartist.com
Interior design by Larissa Hise Henoch, formatting by Lawna Patterson Oldfield

Dedication

ℐ

As you'll read in the pages of this book, humans have given scientific names to phenomena in our universe for which we have little understanding. In that spirit, I dedicate this book to:

Sara for giving me the love, comfort, and *space-time continuum* to be able to write.

Matt and Nurit, Emily and Eitan, and Sam and Samantha for turning our *three-dimensional world* into six.

Gideon, Jeremiah, and Margalit for the *Big Bang* they bring to our lives.

My late parents, Max and Helen, and Sara's late mom, Ruth, who I *think* are sending us *cosmic signs* from above, but I *know for sure* provided much of the rich material and inspiration for the true stories in this book. And to Sara's engineer dad, Gene, who has his own *string theory* (pulleys are involved) and who insists I keep my geriatric skills sharp even though I keep reminding him that I'm a pediatrician.

And to the memory of child psychologist Dr. Louise Bates Ames whose kindness lifted me out of a parenting *black hole* and continues to inspire me.

And also to the memory of paramedic Paul Cary and the hundreds of others who, with galactic-size acts of courage, risked their lives to save others from COVID-19 only to lose their own lives.

"While I was sitting one night with a poet friend
watching a great opera performed in a tent under arc lights,
the poet took my arm and pointed silently.
Far up, blundering out of the night, a huge
Cecropia moth swept past from light to light
over the posturings of the actors.
'He doesn't know,' my friend whispered excitedly.
'He's passing through an alien universe brightly lit but
invisible to him. He's in another play;
he doesn't see us. He doesn't know.
Maybe it's happening right now to us."

—Loren Eiseley, American scientist, educator,
and philosopher (1907–1977)

♪

"I've had a wonderful life.
I wish everyone a life like mine."

—Aunt Helen on the occasion of her 100th birthday

Contents

ℐ

Acknowledgments

℘

I am grateful to Christine Belleris, my editor at HCI Books, for this second collaboration. She has added elegance and eloquence to my writing. I am also grateful to Christine's late father, Nick, who enlisted in the US Army after the bombing of Pearl Harbor, fought on two continents, and helped liberate the Dachau concentration camp; his courage and fortitude impacted the lives not only of the survivors of the Holocaust, but their children, like me, and generations to come.

Thanks also to Allison Janse, Larissa Henoch, Lori Lewis, Lawna Oldfield, Anthony Clausi, Camilla Michael, Lori Golden, Christian Blonshine, Peter Vegso, and all the other fine people at HCI Books whose publications touch readers deeply

This is the fourth book my agent, Lisa Leshne (The Leshne Agency, New York City), has represented for me. She is my advocate, my deal-maker, my debate opponent, and my friend.

My advance readers and dear friends, Danny Woodrow and Dennis Wolf, provided important feedback that greatly improved the manuscript. Liam O'Shaughnessy, age eleven, pushed me to publish another book and made me feel guilty whenever I saw him without having made enough progress.

I have been blessed to have accumulated a long list of special friends over the years. I'm especially grateful to Steve Shpall, who has stuck with me all the way since day one of kindergarten, and to Harvey Guttmann, who has stuck with me all the way since day one of medical school.

Introduction

℘

everal years ago I wrote a book called, *No Regrets Parenting: Turning Long Days and Short Years into Cherished Moments with Your Kids* (Andrews McMeel Publishing, 2012). The book guides busy parents in making the most effective use of their time during their kids' fleeting childhoods. My goal was to help parents act in the *present* to prevent *future* regrets about how they spent those precious years with their young children.

Acting in the present to prevent future regrets is my goal for all of us with this book as well. *No Regrets Living* is a proactive, seven-step plan to help us better appreciate what we have *in* our lives and take greater pride in what we've done *with* our lives—without spending precious time and energy wishing things had turned out differently. Of course all of us have had disappointments and lamentable moments. For some, those times have led to lasting unhappiness and a life that feels unfulfilled, even meaningless. Others have found ways to move past the downturns to find better ahead. The unique combination of roles I've had in my life—physician, scientist, child of a Holocaust survivor, and heart surgery patient—have led me to see the world through a lens of appreciation for the magnificence around me, which in turn has helped me accommodate those not-so-magnificent moments in my life.

The path I've taken toward *No Regrets Living* took many turns, each of which was formative in its own way and, collectively, have led me to a greater level of contentment in life. I hope to help you reach that level on your journey as well.

Of course there's no such thing as a life with absolutely *no* regrets (or, for that matter, parenthood with *no* regrets!), but the approach I propose seeks to minimize *future regrets* and, when possible, to find ways to correct the circumstances of *past regrets*—or at least find ways to grow from them and move forward. Perhaps my books should have been titled, *Parenting with* Fewer *Regrets* and *Living with* Fewer *Regrets*, but those titles aren't as catchy.

I'm a physician, a pediatrician specializing in infectious diseases to be more specific. The kind of pediatrician no parent would ever want their child to need. I've cared for the sickest kids at Children's Hospital Colorado—kids with HIV/AIDS, cancer, brain infections, and complications of bone marrow and organ transplants. Kids infected with exotic germs, and kids infected with everyday germs that became resistant and life-threatening. In the course of my training and career, I've had innumerable opportunities to look inside human bodies on the operating table. I've seen hearts beating inside chests, lungs expanding and contracting, urine forming in the bladder, stool forming in the intestines, and bile forming in the liver. I've seen deaths close up, and I've seen unexplainable recoveries from illnesses and near death. I've stood at the foot of the bed during dozens of baby births, held those babies in my arms, and handed them to their joyous parents. And I've experienced anguish with the parents of babies too sick to be held, and grief with parents whose babies wouldn't be going home.

One other unique perspective I've gained as a physician—I've collected miracles. A few years ago, because of a personal experience with a patient early in my training, I began asking esteemed colleagues if they'd had patients who had "miraculous" outcomes. The outpouring of responses resulted in my book, *Miracles We Have Seen: America's Leading Physicians Share Stories They Can't Forget* (HCI Books, 2016). It's impossible to read the remarkable essays in that book, written by the physicians who witnessed the events, without a sense of awe and wonder. I share a few of those vignettes in the pages that follow.

I'm also a molecular biologist and virologist, having done laboratory "bench" research for more than two decades at the University of Colorado School of Medicine. My research focused on the mechanisms of virus infections and ways to diagnose and treat them. I've watched in amazement the effect that viruses have on human and animal cells in the test tube, multiplying a millionfold or more until the cells cannot take it any longer and explode in death. I've also studied bacteria and fungi under the microscope, marveling at the elegance of their simple, single-cell existences, somehow able to contain everything they need to survive and multiply within the confines of an infinitesimally tiny edifice of their own making. And I've examined, with powerful electron microscopes, the tiny "organelles" within the cells of all species of plants and animals, including humans, which allow those cells to function. I've also studied unusual entities called phage, which are like viruses but infect bacteria instead of humans. Really, even bacteria get virus infections.

But here's the important part…I can't explain any of those things I've just described. Of course I know—and I teach—the medical and scientific dogma. And I believe those dogmas. I believe in those tiny organelles inside the cells of all living things and I believe those tiny organelles create the energy, and reproduce the genetic material, required to sustain life. I believe the cells, in turn, make up every living organism from germs, insects, plants, and animals to humans. Humans and other higher organisms are made up of organs and organ systems, and I believe that when organs and organ systems fail, organisms may die. Medical and scientific dogmas have been carefully studied and expanded since the beginning of humans' exploration of ourselves, and I believe the dogmas to be true. Proven and true. At least for now, until new facts are uncovered and today's truths either advance or are retracted. Indeed, the list of yesteryear's dogmas that have been *disproven* is long. Hippocrates's theory of the Four Humors and Four Temperaments, which sounds comical to today's doctors and scientists, persisted as dogma and influenced medical care for centuries.

I've faithfully and honestly taught today's medical and scientific dogmas to two generations of medical students and residents, to doctoral students and fellow physicians. Yet, the many centuries of study by scientists, physicians, and philosophers that have produced our current thinking about life and death haven't answered the fundamental questions: How did life happen? How did life start? Why can't we reproduce that beginning? Why can't we create, from scratch, even a single cell, to say nothing of an organ, organ system, or whole organism?

I'm also the child of a Holocaust survivor. I grew up in a home under the shadow of the most unspeakable evil the modern world has ever known, daily asking myself how something like that could happen to my father, his family, and millions of others. My father was arrested by the Nazis on August 6, 1941, at age seventeen, and transported to a variety of labor and concentration camps, finally ending up in Auschwitz two years later, on August 28, 1943. There, he was tattooed with the number 142178. This information is part of the precise and elaborate record-keeping by the Nazis known as *Häftlingspersonalbogen*, or prisoner registration forms, the bane of existence to every Holocaust denier in the world. These records, kept by the Nazis themselves and now magnificently archived in the United States Holocaust Museum in Washington, DC, prove, beyond any doubt, the unparalleled efficiency and evil of the Nazis. After his arrest, my dad never saw his mother or sister again; they were transported to concentration camps and killed. His father, Hersh, after whom I'm named, was arrested with my dad. Those like my father and his father, strong enough to be valuable as laborers, were not immediately sent to the gas chambers. As my dad's father became progressively weaker, my dad tried to do the work for both of them so the Nazis wouldn't notice his father's debilitation. Ultimately, they did notice and his father, no longer useful to the Nazis, was taken to the gas chamber.

I don't know much more about my dad's concentration camp experience—it's a known syndrome among survivors that they were hesitant to share those memories with their loved ones to spare them the pain. But it's also a known syndrome among survivors' *kids* that we don't ask enough, afraid of what we might hear and afraid of ripping open our parents' fragile emotional scars (the groundbreaking work on this subject is Helen Epstein's *Children of the Holocaust*.[1]) I regret not having asked more, and because my father died forty years ago, that's a regret I can't fix. After liberation from the camps and while working in an "underground railroad" helping to smuggle fellow survivors into Israel, Dad developed tuberculosis (TB) and was hospitalized in Czechoslovakia. His subsequent immigration papers sent him to Denver, probably because the high altitude and dry air were felt to be beneficial in recovering from TB.

Dad on arrival to America, author's personal collection

On arrival in America, penniless, without family, and not speaking a word of English, Dad's story of survival continued. He met Mom at a resettlement center where she served as a translator for the Yiddish-speaking immigrants. Needing to make a living, Dad began selling fruits and vegetables in a truck borrowed from my mom's uncle. Mom rode the truck as well, translating *kartoffel* and *tsibele* into "potatoes" and "onions" for dad's customers. Dad was the most brilliant fruit peddler in the history of fruit peddling, the smartest man I ever knew. My brother and I grew up very poor, but we never knew it. My dad's survival and entrepreneurial skills, and my mom's frugality and morality, taught us vital life lessons and the true definition of the word "rich."

Dad and his fruit truck, author's personal collection

Finally, I've been a patient as well, having had open-heart surgery to bypass four of my diseased heart vessels. I've also had lesser surgeries and a myriad of lesser ailments, each of which was frightening at the time. Through these encounters on the other side of the bed, I've had many hours to reflect on the human body (my body!) and its recuperative powers. The built-in mechanisms we each have to recover, from the tiniest paper cut to the "zipper" scar running the length of my chest wall, are impossible to fully appreciate without knowing the extraordinarily precise cellular processes involved—triggered into action automatically, without our thinking about them or even realizing they're happening. It's only when those processes go awry, when healing fails, that we become conscious of what's involved in our body's day-to-day maintenance. In fact, repair and recovery are going on every second of our lives even when there are no obvious injuries or illnesses. Our bodies are equipped with first responders, cells that scan for *potential* trouble and leap into action before a microscopic glitch can advance to something worse. We have cellular defenses and disposal systems for ridding us of defective cells and tissues, and they are acting while we sleep and while we're awake. Those are the things one thinks about as a recovering patient who has had medical training.

It's from those vantage points—as physician, scientist, child of a Holocaust survivor, and patient—that my prescription for the seven keys to *No Regrets Living*, and a life of wonder and contentment, has evolved.

In his 1972 book, *Natural History of Infectious Disease,* Frank Macfarlane Burnet, the Nobel Prize–winning Australian virologist, optimistically predicted, "[T]he most likely forecast about the future of infectious diseases is that it will be very dull."[2] That was before the epidemics and pandemics of HIV-AIDS, Ebola virus, Legionnaires Disease, SARS (Severe Acute Respiratory Syndrome), MERS (Middle East Respiratory Syndrome), Zika virus, Swine Flu, and, most recently, the novel coronavirus that causes COVID-19. So I hesitate, as an infectious diseases physician, to make predictions, but this is one I am certain of—the future of infectious diseases will *not* be dull.

The world is slowly recovering from a once-in-a-century pandemic. In response to the heartbreaking illnesses and unbearable death toll caused by COVID-19, societies across the globe came to a near standstill in efforts to halt the spread of the infection and, in so doing, caused unavoidable additional hardships to billions of people. However, within the tragedy of the pandemic, there are lessons to be learned and even silver linings to appreciate. As you'll read in the pages that follow, that is true for many catastrophic events—natural ones, like COVID-19, and even man-made ones like the Holocaust. The timing of this book's preparation and release has allowed me to weave my observations on the pandemic into the book's foundational *7 Keys to a Life of Wonder and Contentment.* My reflections on the pandemic, including coping mechanisms and paths for going forward, are offset in shaded boxes like this one.

While these shaded boxes deal with the pandemic in the context of our search for contentment in our lives, the essence of this book is not about infection at all. It's about discovering the joy of life with fewer regrets. I hope you'll agree that *No Regrets Living* is a timeless blueprint for reaching a fulfilling life now and long after the pandemic is relegated, along with past scourges, to the pages of history. When that happens, the shaded boxes will serve as a time capsule of sorts for future generations who I hope will never know anything like COVID-19 in their own lives but will still reap the rewards of the 7 Keys.

I invite you to embrace these 7 Keys with me:

Believe. Discover. Heal. Appreciate. Accept. Seek. Grow.

KEY #1
BELIEVE

THE FIRST KEY for *No Regrets Living*, and its true foundation, asks you to believe in something greater than yourself. Belief allows you to accommodate both joy and disappointment.

I would never attempt to tell you *what* you should believe, but I'm going to share a bit about what *I* believe as an example of the connection between belief and *No Regrets Living*. First, a spoiler alert. This is not going to be a "divine revelation" testimony. I haven't seen heaven; I haven't seen statues crying (not to disparage those who have—I just haven't); God hasn't spoken to me in a dream or elsewhere; and, despite being a scientist, I don't claim to be an expert about, or have special insight into, the

11

laws of nature. We all come to our beliefs and our choice of how to live by virtue of where we've been and what we've done so far, our experiences and background. I've been privileged to have had the roles in my life that I have, and I hope that my reflections on those roles and where they've led me will be helpful to you. Mostly, I hope that you will reflect on the many roles in your own life and the beliefs you have developed to derive your own formula for a life with more gratitude than regrets, a life of wonder and contentment.

Key #1 for *No Regrets Living* is not really about *what* you believe, but *that* you believe—in something greater than yourself, in an unknown and unknowable reality. Belief in something that can't be "proven." Indeed, *proving belief* is an oxymoron. Although there are other choices, let's start with two possible alternative belief systems: science and God.

SCIENCE

On May 20, 1964, two scientists listening to noises of the universe through a powerful audio telescope accidently stumbled onto an "echo" that, now knowing where to listen, could be heard at all times, continuously and uninterrupted. Turns out that echo, which can still easily be heard today by anyone on internet astronomy sites, is the remnant of the Big Bang. That faint echo changed science forever. Until then, many of the most esteemed scientists in the world believed that the universe always existed, that there was no "beginning." But now we know there was a beginning, and it occurred nearly 13.8 billion years ago in a most astonishing way if we are to believe the modern scientific dogma on the origin of the universe. According to that theory, which I believe to be true (until and unless proven otherwise), there was an infinitesimally small and unimaginably compact *singularity* containing every bit of energy and matter that would come to comprise our universe.

Let's tally what that means:

Astronomers had estimated that the observable universe has more than 100 billion galaxies. Our own Milky Way (galaxy) is home to around 300 billion stars, but it's not representative of galaxies in general. The Milky Way is a titan compared to abundant but faint dwarf galaxies, and it in turn is dwarfed by rare giant elliptical galaxies, which can be 20 times more massive. By measuring the number and luminosity of observable galaxies, astronomers put current estimates of the total stellar population at roughly 70 billion trillion (7×10^{22})[3]

Seventy billion trillion stars! And that's to say nothing of the inestimable number of quasars, black holes, planets, moons, asteroids, comets, and other "non-stars" in our galaxy and in the other 100 billion or more galaxies in the universe. And even that unimaginably high estimate of galaxies is undoubtedly low. The 2020 discovery of the South Pole Wall confirms that what we can't see or calculate is likely far greater than what we can:

The South Pole Wall, as it is known, consists of thousands of galaxies—beehives of trillions of stars and dark worlds, as well as dust and gas—aligned in a curtain arcing across at least 700 million light-years of space. It winds behind the dust, gas and stars of our own galaxy, the Milky Way, from the constellation Perseus in the Northern Hemisphere to the constellation Apus in the far south. It is so massive that it perturbs the local expansion of the universe.

But don't bother trying to see it. The entire conglomeration is behind the Milky Way, in what astronomers quaintly call the zone of avoidance...

"The surprise for us is that this structure...remained unnoticed, being hidden in an obscured sector of the southern sky..."[4]

And we know even less about "dark matter":

According to the prevailing theory of a confoundingly preposterous universe, the cosmos contains about five times as much invisible dark matter as luminous atomic matter.

Nobody knows exactly what dark matter is made of, but according to cosmologists it provides the gravitational scaffolding for the luminous structures in the universe—galaxies, galaxy clusters, superclusters, voids and chains like the South Pole Wall, all connected by spidery filaments in what's known as the cosmic web. The visible universe of stars and galaxies, cosmologists like to say, is like snow on mountaintops or lights on dark, distant Christmas trees.[5]

How can the puny bandwidths of our human brains grasp 70 billion trillion stars and their seemingly infinite accoutrements all initially packed into an infinitesimally, unimaginably, impossibly small space that scientists have called a singularity? And then it gets even more incomprehensible. For reasons unknown, and will likely forever be unknown, that singularity—containing all those cosmological behemoths *and* every molecule, atom, and subatomic particle of every species ever to populate the entire universe—ignited and exploded with a force greater than any we can imagine, releasing all that we know and all that we still don't know to move infinitely outward to become our still-expanding universe.

Yet for me, even *that* isn't the most perplexing of all the proposed phenomena surrounding the beginning of our universe—the most perplexing question, I believe, is what happened *before* the beginning? Where did the singularity come from and how did it contain everything that ever was and ever will be? My brain doesn't have the capacity to consider the eruption of this infinitesimally small, yet all-encompassing singularity, much less what existed before that eruption. Yet, science tells us that there was a singularity, that it erupted in a Big Bang (surely the most understated scientific term of all time!), and that we exist in a tiny, tiny, tiny corner of the resultant universe. Taken even further, the Big Bang origin of the universe brought with it an infinitely complex set of natural laws governing the universe, laws that themselves defy explanation without making further, often unprovable, assumptions. Those are the truths held by a belief system rooted in science, and as a scientist I accept them (until and unless proven otherwise).

GOD

Now let's consider an alternative belief system: God, a superior being or force with a hand in creating, and perhaps in still directing, the aforementioned universe. I won't try to summarize what a belief in God entails because there is no simple summary—the specifics can be found in millions of religious treatises written by authorities in thousands of different religions since the beginning of human communication. And, of course, the diverse profiles of God can be found in all the holy books of those religions. God is different for every religion and for every person who believes. Despite all the holy books and all the holy men and women throughout the ages, an omnipresent, omnipotent God remains unfathomable to most of us. Descriptions by even the most profound thinkers and scholars fall short. But, for the simple purpose of our discussion contrasting two belief systems to explain the universe, the "God theory" assumes that there was a Creator.

Now let's compare the incomprehensibility of the Big Bang with the incomprehensibility of God. For some, it might be easier to understand an infinitesimally tiny singularity that contained everything (EVERYTHING!) there ever was to be, which then, 13.8 billion years ago, exploded to create a universe guided by natural laws, a universe so vast that it contains everything we know and everything we can see with the most powerful telescopes and the most powerful microscopes, and everything we cannot see (the vast, vast majority of which we will never see). For others, it might be easier to understand an all-knowing Master Planner who had a hand in creating, and perhaps still has a hand in guiding, all that we know and see. And for many, belief in God includes belief that this Supreme Being hears our prayers and rewards and punishes.

Or, perhaps, the Big Bang, with its inherent natural laws, and God's creation and mastery over the universe are *equally* incomprehensible. Albert Einstein wrote:

> A knowledge of the existence of something we cannot penetrate, of the manifestations of the profoundest reason and the most radiant beauty, which are only accessible to our reason in their most elementary forms— it is this knowledge and this emotion that constitute the truly religious attitude; in this sense, and in this alone, I am a deeply religious man.[6]

If we can agree that an omnipotent God and an all-encompassing singularity are *equally* incomprehensible—impenetrable, to use Einstein's vernacular—does it really matter which is "true?" "Truth" and "belief" are also oxymorons, aren't they? And why shouldn't we be able to believe in both God and science. As I do.

There you have it—I'm outed as a believer in both the Big Bang *and* in God. How is that possible?

"THE MIRACULOUS EVENT" . . . .

There's a parable I have told my kids to help explain all we don't know, and the tiny bits we do understand, about the universe. In this little fable, an extraordinary event takes place on an imaginary planet that has only two dimensions, length and width. A flat planet. This is my updated take on Edwin A. Abbott's famous nineteenth century novella, *Flatland: A Romance of Many Dimensions.*[7] But in 1884, no one could have imagined the Big Bang, black holes, relativity, quantum particles, or any of the other scientific discoveries of the past century and a half. I created my modern-day version, called "The Miraculous Event," to help my kids understand why there is so much about our very existence we can't explain, and how silly we sometimes sound trying.

The story in a nutshell:

One day, on the two-dimensional planet known as Planar, where there was only length and width, no up or down, and all the people were flat geometric shapes, a dot appeared out of nowhere, right in the middle of Town Center. Within moments, the dot grew into a tiny circle and then a larger circle, and finally a gigantic circle so large it threatened to push aside everything in Town Center. But then, just as suddenly as it grew, the circle began shrinking, finally appearing again only as a simple dot before disappearing entirely.

This "miraculous event" caused great consternation on Planar, affecting every aspect of life for many years to come. Fanciful but heartfelt scientific and religious theories arose to explain the miraculous event. Although none of the denizens of Planar would ever understand what actually had happened, they all agreed that somehow, *"time"* was involved. For the flat beings of Planar, time was an intangible, a way of putting all occurrences into context as either before, during, or after this moment. A dot grew to a circle, to a very large circle, and then shrunk back to a dot again, all occurring over time. Of course, two-dimensional beings couldn't possibly fathom…a sphere. It was a simple three-dimensional sphere that touched down on Planar, first appearing as a dot and then, as it passed through the planet, a small circle, a large circle, and a giant circle at its equator before shrinking again to a dot as it completed its journey through the planet. The denizens of Planar could only explain the event in the two-dimensional terms they understood and within the limitations of their concept of linear time.

The moral of my little parable? There are things we may never understand because of the limitations of our existence, including our dimensionality and our concept of time. Perhaps there's a fourth dimension, or a fifth, out there where the unknowns of our three-dimensional world would be as easily understood as we understand a sphere. Perhaps. Fanciful but heartfelt theories have been proposed. String Theory, Super String Theory, and M Theory all propose multiple, ten or more, dimensions. Yet many physicists argue that, while useful for expanding our mathematical reasoning, none of those theories can adequately explain our universe or its natural laws. For now then, it's sufficient and safe to accept that there's much that occurs in our lives and in our universe that will likely forever remain a mystery, contradictions we will never resolve.

I can accept that because of my belief in something greater than me, greater than humans. In my mind, believing that the unfathomable singularity erupted in an unfathomable Big Bang, and that both were created by an unfathomable God, is perfectly syntonic. I see science as evidence (I won't use the word *proof*) of a higher power.

I've included the full version of my short story, "The Miraculous Event," as Appendix A to this book for those who would like to chuckle at how contorted and convoluted trying to explain the unexplainable can become. Or, alternatively, for a similar chuckle you can read any of today's most profound scientific attempts to reconcile the theory of relativity with quantum physics into a unifying Theory of Everything.

For that matter, let's consider how our three-dimensional world has tried to understand the COVID-19 pandemic. As in "The Miraculous Event" parable, over a very brief period of time the world watched as an event occurred. An outbreak of a flu-like illness spread, unlike any flu we have seen in over a hundred years, and caused a novel constellation of clinical findings the likes of which we've never seen. Hundreds of infected became thousands of infected, then tens of thousands, hundreds of thousands, millions. As a virologist, I have an understanding of the science of viral infections and of viral pandemics; I have studied them for nearly four decades. The magnitude of this pandemic was worse than some, not as bad as others. But what I, and the totality of the scientific community, cannot understand is so much more than we do understand. Beginning with the most fundamental question of all—what is a virus?

Like the dot that appeared on the two-dimensional planet in the parable, we use scientific tenets and vernacular to mask our ignorance of even that most basic precept. Yes, the coronavirus is an RNA virus encapsulated in a viral envelope that binds to cell receptors in our bodies, enters those cells, and takes over the protein manufacturing capacity of the cell to propagate itself into tens of thousands of progeny viruses that then spread to neighboring cells, ultimately resulting in profound tissue damage and destruction. Okay... but what is a virus? Why does it exist? What role do viruses play in the ecology of humanity, in our evolution as a species, and in determining our health and longevity? Do viruses have a purpose? Much more about viruses in the pages that follow, but for now let's appreciate that in combatting a viral pandemic, we are fighting an entity of unknown origin and unknown purpose. Like a sphere that touches down on a flat planet.

GOD AS SCIENTIST?

Here is a God concept I sometimes entertain—God as scientist. I have been a scientist for most of my professional life, and I practice the "scientific method," the process by which knowledge is advanced through meticulous experimental design. I've spent a lot of time looking at tiny organisms growing in test tubes in laboratory incubators. In research, we vary the conditions in our test tubes to explore how certain variables affect the growth of organisms. What helps bacteria and viruses thrive? More protein? More carbohydrate? More oxygen or more essential minerals? Higher temperature or more light? Which conditions or chemicals (or medicines) inhibit the growth of bacteria and viruses in the test tube? Can we find medicines that block germs but would not harm humans? From these types of experiments, we learn a great deal about bacteria and viruses and their ability to flourish and reproduce. We've also learned that microscopic organisms can be "trained," engineered to produce substances that can be very useful to us—like enzymes and antibiotics. In other words, by experimenting with different conditions in different test tubes, scientists discover what works best for microscopic organisms and how we can make those organisms work best for us.

Some clear nights, as I stare out at the dazzling and endless Milky Way, I picture the universe as a collection of trillions and trillions of test tubes, represented by the vast array of sparkling lights above me, in a Divine Incubator. Different conditions, different environments, different mixes of species and life forms—galactic-size experiments to determine which life pattern works best. Infinite variations on what we colloquially call "natural laws," laws that may not be the same in any two of the trillions of stellar test tubes.

The test tube analogy of God as scientist raises new questions for which I have no clear answers. Are humans on the Earth one of God's infinite experiments? Would a scientist create the conditions in our test tube and do nothing more than sit back and observe what happens, monitoring whether this iteration of life in the universe survives? Thrives? Are other test tubes scattered about the galaxies more successful, and is God simply monitoring those as well? While it's true that scientists do observe their experiments closely, they observe with a greater purpose. The outcomes of their experiments cause scientists to tweak the system, to modify the conditions, to *improve* the outcomes. Rather than being a passive observer, might God as scientist be frequently changing the conditions in each test tube based on those observations? As I might "train" bacteria to produce chemicals useful in medicine, might God be actively engineering us, responding to what we do and how we act? Scientists observe so they may respond. If God is a scientist, might God respond to our prayers, reward us for doing good and punish us for doing evil, thereby training us?

Of course, there are many problems with thinking of God as a scientist, tinkering in response to our choices and deeds. Shouldn't an all-knowing higher power already know how we will act, what we will pray for, whether we will deserve reward or punishment? Shouldn't a Master Scientist know the results of each experiment without even performing it? But if so, where is humans' free will?

I appreciate the contradiction in believing that humans have free will *and* that God knows what we will do with that freedom, but it doesn't bother me because the God I envision is in a dimension we will never understand, or only understand partially. In human scientist terms, an experiment proceeds linearly with new developments occurring in sequence and triggering the next investigations; that's the "scientific method" I mentioned earlier. But in a divine dimension where time may not be linear (see Key #5 to follow), it might be more akin to the sphere in our parable of the flat planet. Yes, God knows what will happen, but we still have free will to make it happen. Yes, God knows the choices we'll make, but we are still free to make them. And yes, God might intervene in our lives and, in that nonlinear time frame, the intervention might be interpreted by we humans as reward or punishment, miracle or tragedy. But those are merely terms we use within our limited human perspective, within our limited dimension and concept of time. In a frame of reference we can't imagine, and in a time frame that is nonlinear, those terms may be meaningless, as were the terms the two-dimensional inhabitants of Planar used to describe the miraculous event on their planet. Two-dimensional beings will never comprehend a sphere. The key to *No Regrets Living* is belief in something greater than ourselves—the natural laws of science, God, both, or something else entirely—and the acceptance of inevitable and unresolvable contradictions while making the best choices we can based on them.

To conclude Key #1, there are three reasons why believing in something greater than ourselves is crucial for no regrets living. By doing so,

1. We are humbled—the key words are "greater than ourselves."

2. We are forced to consider our actions in a larger context—what we think, say, and do potentially have significance beyond the immediate or obvious circumstances.

3. We are able to accept certain events, circumstances, and contradictions as beyond our understanding and control.

KEY #2
DISCOVER

THE SECOND KEY for *No Regrets Living* asks you to open your life to discovery. Discovery of the miracles around you and the messiah within you. Don't panic—as I promised earlier, I haven't had, and won't be sharing, divine revelation experiences or asking you to have them. Rather, I ask only that you sharpen your awareness of phenomena you already know well. This Key is an exercise in consciousness-raising.

MIRACLES

> "There are only two ways to live your life.
> One is as though nothing is a miracle.
> The other is as though everything is a miracle."
>
> —Albert Einstein

We all have a choice we can make in how we see the world. *No Regrets Living* asks you to discover the miracles around you. But to do that, first consider my definition of miracles: objects and events in nature and in our lives that, as with the inside of living human beings I have seen in the operating room or the human cells I have seen under a microscope in my laboratory, cannot be fully explained or re-created.

The Natural World

You needn't go to medical school to appreciate the ubiquity of miracles, as I've defined them. Rain is miraculous, so are flowers and trees and the extraordinary diversity of species on this planet. Huge whales and elephants are miraculous, and so are tiny guppies and insects. Dolphins talk to one another, so do whales, but it turns out ants and gnats do as well. Scientists and naturalists have documented intelligence and learning abilities in innumerable species of animals, and have also studied what appear to be their moral codes—for example, the care of hurt, disabled, or abandoned animals by others of their own species, and even by animals of other species; the grief shown by animals of many species for lost parents or offspring; and the shunning by members of certain colonies of others in the colony who play too rough or act cruelly. While we can easily anthropomorphize those human-like characteristics, what of Earth's nearly infinite species that have qualities *unlike* any human?

For example, how can we understand hummingbirds, one of my favorite species? Besides being gorgeous, they are gifted with some of the most extraordinary physical abilities in nature. They have the highest metabolic rate per body mass of any living animal, with wings that beat up to eighty times per second. Per *second*! They can hover in midair, fly at 35 mph, and dive at 50 mph. They recover their energy by slipping into a state of hibernation every night during which their metabolic rate slows to one-fifteenth of normal. Seriously, how cool (miraculous!) are hummingbirds? How can we explain their abilities, or even their existence?

And how about bats, one of my *least* favorite species (as an infectious diseases doctor, all I can think of when I see a bat is rabies! But maybe that's just me…). Numerically, bats make up one-fourth of all the world's mammals, but how many of us really appreciate their miraculous abilities? The saying, blind as a bat, belies their ability to feed on flying insects in total darkness by emitting sound waves and "hearing" the echoes of those waves on nearby insects—and then eating as many as one thousand mosquitoes a night! Although bats inhabit colonies of hundreds or thousands (one colony in Texas has more than a million members), a mother bat can find its infant by the pup's smell and sound.

Most people aren't crazy about spiders, and neither am I, but I also find them extraordinary. There are more than 45,000 species worldwide, most of which are harmless to humans, and all produce venom and silk. Spiders are carnivores, preying on insects they trap in their silk webs, injecting them with fluids that liquefy them, and then sucking up their remains. Really. And despite the yuckiness of that, I still can't kill a spider—I trap them in a plastic cup when they get in the house and relocate them outside. Because they, too, are miraculous.

Many animal species excel at travel—by air, water, or over land. Certain species of the Monarch butterfly migrate five thousand miles round trip each year, only to die shortly after their return—yet their *great*-grandchildren the next year (Monarchs have a short life span with several generations born in a year) take the identical route and even alight, *en route*, on the identical trees as their forebears. Not to be outdone, humpback whales also migrate more than five thousand miles, from the cold waters where they feed to the warm waters where they give birth. Caribou hold the record for land travel, migrating three thousand miles across North America each year.

Copperhead snakes (another of my least favorite species) have heat-sensing organs near their eyes that they use to detect small mammals in the dark to attack and eat. Certain frogs have adapted to forest environments and learned to fly, spreading their webbed feet as gliders to take them fifty feet or farther by air. There are seven hundred plant species that trap insects in their leaves and eat them. A single mushroom, or fungus, in the Blue Mountains of Oregon is the largest living organism on Earth, extending nearly two-and-a-half miles across. It was discovered because it is a parasite that envelops, kills, and eats whole trees.

And then there is the miracle of viruses, the objects of my research for decades. In the era of COVID-19, you might ask how viruses, which are so menacing, so threatening to all species and all societies, can be miraculous. Well, consider this. As I noted earlier, a single virus infecting a single cell can take over the machinery of that cell within minutes and, within a few hours, produce as many as 1 million progeny viruses, each of which can then spread to neighboring cells and do the same. No wonder we feel so miserable when we get the flu. But is that miraculous? Depends on your definition of miracle, but recall mine...objects and events in nature and in our lives that cannot be fully explained or re-created. No one yet has created even a single virus from scratch, yet each virus can create one million more of itself in a matter of hours, shutting down the cell it infects, and, as we have learned recently from COVID-19, virtually shutting down all of human civilization!

But we have also learned that viruses may have benefits for the world. They likely play a role in the evolution of species, transferring genetic material from one animal to another, and, over eons, some of those genes become permanent and inherited parts of human and other species' genetic makeup. Viruses also contribute to the development of our immune systems, with mild viral infections protecting us against more severe diseases. And scientists have been able to harness viruses for the production of new treatments and vaccines that have saved millions of lives. Viruses are being developed as Trojan Horses, vectors with which to deliver gene therapy to patients with inherited conditions such as sickle cell disease and cystic fibrosis. One of the approaches being used to develop a COVID-19 vaccine also uses a benign virus as a Trojan horse, carrying hidden COVID-19 genetic material into our bodies and triggering protective immunity.

My point? Humans can't create or even fully understand whales or guppies or dolphins or ants or gnats or hummingbirds, bats, spiders, butterflies, snakes, flying frogs, carnivorous plants, herbivorous mushrooms, or simple viruses. Someday we may come to a deeper understanding of these species, but I doubt we will ever be able to make one from scratch. Yes, we'll be able to clone some, but that's just making photocopies, not creating originals. And if we someday can create a single-cell bacterium in the lab, where did the raw materials for it come from? In my mind, the entirety of diverse flora and fauna on our planet is miraculous.

And what of the environment that supports those diverse species? I believe our atmosphere is a miracle, a perfect blend of gases that allow us to breathe while also allowing plants to breathe. So far, no one has found another atmosphere like it as far and as wide as we can see with our most powerful telescopes. That's not to say there aren't other planets and universes and atmospheres like ours—I'm certain there are, probably many—it's just that we haven't found them yet (and how exciting it will be someday far in the future to see the flora and fauna of those places!). The self-sustaining supply of water that has allowed waterfalls and rivers to flow unceasingly for millennia, and to fill our oceans and our lakes—and our cups from the faucet when we're thirsty—is a miracle. Imagine *humans* designing a system where clouds form from the mixing of gases, moisture occurs, rain falls, the fallen rain evaporates and goes back into the clouds, and the whole process starts over again and never stops. And there's enough water recirculating to supply billions of people and animals and trees and plants. How would we even start to create such a magnificent system? Brilliant human engineers have built spectacular damns, reservoirs, canals, power plants, and processing facilities to handle the abundance of water on our planet. But humans have yet to create a drop of water from scratch, without using the molecules that are already here. Yes, we can mix hydrogen and oxygen in a test tube and create water—but where did the hydrogen come from? Or the oxygen? Miraculous.

On a recent return to a beach I had visited thirty-five years ago, I found the ocean still there, pounding the shoreline as it always has for the nearly 4 billion years since it formed on Earth. I had been away thirty-five years, but the ocean never missed a beat. There was a new generation of surfers, the shoreline might have shifted a bit, but the ocean was still there, magnificent and miraculous. And what of the extraordinary biodiversity *under* the surface of the ocean? As with far-off planets yet to be discovered, how exciting it will be someday far in the future to fully appreciate the yet-to-be-discovered flora and fauna in our very own oceans! A remarkable documentary, *My Octopus Teacher*[8], chronicles the endearing relationship that develops between a human and a sea creature in a South African kelp forest—and will surely convince you of the underwater miracles yet to be discovered.

Our miraculous planet also produces enough food to feed every one of those exotic and not-so-exotic species and every one of us—if only humans could figure out how to distribute that bounty fairly and conscientiously to one another. Daily we are surrounded by modern manna—food that the Bible says dropped from heaven to nourish the Hebrews wandering in the desert. Our manna today comes from farm fields, ranches, and supermarket shelves but make no mistake—its ability to sustain all living creatures on this planet is nothing short of miraculous.

The COVID-19 pandemic gave the world a renewed appreciation for the miracle of our daily meals. Interruptions in the supply chain from farms and processing plants to grocery stores caused shortages of many of the staples we had become accustomed to. Even more disconcerting was the danger, actual or perceived, of even entering a grocery store, fearing that a fellow shopper or a store employee might cough in our direction. For some isolated in their homes, food was delivered to their doorsteps by family, friends, or shipping companies. We didn't starve, but we welcomed food in our homes with greater appreciation than in the past. In our developed part of the world, we learned to accept lesser quantities and fewer choices for our sustenance, and also learned we don't really need as much as we thought we did.

The inequities of our society were exposed as the pandemic exacerbated the daily struggle for food among the most vulnerable in our society—the poor, the homeless, the elderly, immigrants, and minorities. Families dependent on school meal programs to help nourish their kids were harmed by school closures and bureaucratic delays of government assistance. Those with low-income jobs, already struggling to put food on their tables, were hit the hardest by the lockdown and layoffs. And in less developed parts of the world, where famine and starvation are nearly constant plagues, shortages were profound and devastating. The pandemic taught us that we should no longer take the modern-day manna miracle for granted.

The BIG Ones

Speaking of manna, what about biblical miracles? You know, the BIG ONES. Did those really occur and why aren't they occurring in our time so we can witness them and reaffirm our faith rather than trusting Bible stories? Did the Red Sea (the proper translation is actually the Sea of Reeds) really split for the ancient Hebrews following a great wind, on Moses's command, as it says in the book of Exodus in the Old Testament? Or was there a natural phenomenon that occurred just as they arrived at the shore, making their timing the true miracle? Or did it happen at all? In 2014, the *Washington Post* published a piece on a scientist at the National Center for Atmospheric Research, the top US research center for atmospheric science in the United States. This scientist had developed and published (in a highly respected, peer-reviewed journal) a computer model proving the feasibility of the Sea of Reeds splitting during a dramatic windstorm, the type of windstorm that actually occurs in certain parts of the world like the Middle East (and Lake Erie!).

> What atmospheric phenomenon could make this occur? The (published) paper describes a coastal effect called a "wind setdown," in which strong winds—a little over 60 miles per hour—create a "push" on coastal water which, in one location, creates a storm surge. But in the location *from which* the wind pushes—in this case, the east—the water moves away. Such occurrences have been observed in the past in Lake Erie, among other places—and . . . also in the Nile Delta itself in the year 1882. "Wind setdown happens just as often as storm surge, but hardly ever hurts people, it just blows a harbor completely dry," says Drews. "So this water sloshes from one side of the body to the other and leaves a dry place."[9]

Versions of some Bible stories have survived for hundreds of generations and appear in so many sources that they probably did occur in some form, and science has supported some of these. A research paper published in May 2018 presented some pretty startling findings. Scientists at the prestigious Rockefeller Institute in New York and the University of Basel in Switzerland studied millions of DNA patterns, biological bar codes, which are located in the cells of all humans and animal species and give clues to relationships within and among different species. That research suggests that humans and most animal species appear to have been wiped out by a catastrophic event 100,000 to 200,000 years ago and then the diversity of life was started anew by a surviving few—perhaps even *two*—humans.[10] One of many apparent die-off events in Earth's history (more examples to follow), and no, this is not *proof* of Noah's great flood, Adam and

Eve, or the Bible, nor does it in any way *disprove* Darwinian evolution that resulted in animals and humans in the first place. But it does give one pause.

How about other BIG miracles? In the book of Numbers in the Old Testament, the people of Israel, wandering in the desert, had become tired of manna (humans are fickle—when manna first appeared, it was hailed as a miracle, but with time . . .). They craved the better variety and taste of food they had left behind in Egypt. They begged Moses for meat, and he in turn asked God for help. The story goes on to say that a great wind occurred, and quails fell from the sky, so plentiful that there was meat for all 600,000 Hebrews. Hard to believe that miracle, too, isn't it? But, in October 1984, this *New York Times* story raised the eyebrows of more than a few skeptics. Titled, "When Quail Come Back to Alexandria (Egypt)":

> Best of all, quail season in Alexandria is in full swing. From the end of September until early November, thousands of quail fly over Alexandria from central Europe *en route* to their winter habitat in the Sudan. The journey across the Mediterranean is long and tiring, so the birds fly in low over the water and land on Alexandria's shores in droves.

> Handmade cotton nets laid by Bedouin trappers await them . . . Thousands of quail are caught in nets or shot each day and shipped to homes and restaurants throughout Egypt.[11]

And it happens just like that *each and every year!*[12]

It's not just quail that return to Egypt. The eighth of ten biblical plagues, miracles the Bible says Moses brought to bear on Pharaoh, was locust swarms, which also occur with some regularity in Egypt, as recently as 2016,[13] and elsewhere on the eastern African continent and Asia as recently as 2020.[14]

I've already referred to the Laws of Nature or Natural Laws numerous times. Scientists and philosophers have waxed eloquently on how to define a law of nature. I use a simple definition: The laws of nature are those scientific principles that govern the phenomena we observe around us. Water has three forms: gas, liquid, and solid. The Earth rotates on its axis and revolves around the sun giving us a sunrise and sunset each day and 365 such days each year—day and year, two human constructs to explain the laws of nature. Humans and animals require oxygen to live, and they release carbon dioxide as a waste product; plants require carbon dioxide to live and release oxygen as a waste product. Most bacteria require oxygen to live, but some have developed the ability to live without oxygen. Cells divide to form twice as many new cells, and their DNA comprises the genes that allow life and uniqueness from one creature or plant to another. Progeny emerge from parents of every living species (a sterile, scientific way of expressing the awe we experience when babies are born). Winds blow, water flows, seasons change, and stars glow with light from explosions that occurred millions of years ago. Rivers rush toward oceans and seas where perpetual waves wash the shore. Quail migrate, and locusts swarm, over Egypt.

Science has tried to explain, at least to a degree, all of these observations, these natural laws. To do so requires assumptions that themselves raise more questions, but, for our purposes, let's consider the laws of nature to be those phenomena that are *expected* to occur and for which we have at least a partial understanding. We think of natural laws as perpetual, always obeyed, always in place. But when they appear not to be in place, when there is a deviation from the natural laws, observers are prone to call those events miracles. There are rare times in the history of the universe—the tiny part of its history

of which we're aware—when it appears to us that natural laws have
been violated. For example, the great flood, described in the story
of Noah in the Bible, finds support in numerous scientific treatises and in the opinions of many prominent scientists.[15] We know
floods occur, and they are within the natural laws as we understand
them. But could a massive flood, unlike any we have experienced in
recorded history, have wiped out much of life on Earth and resulted
in a new beginning? Miraculous, or just an exaggerated version of
the laws of nature?

And dinosaurs? Could they have simply been a failed experiment
within the natural laws of planet Earth, becoming ever more gigantic and more diverse, but not smarter, and ultimately destroyed by
a gigantic asteroid striking our planet 65 million years ago? Was the
destruction of every living dinosaur part of the universe's natural
laws? Or was this God as scientist tweaking a galactic test tube? Somehow, although all the dinosaurs appear to have been destroyed in a
single apocalyptic moment, enough mammals survived the crash to
populate the planet anew with a more sustainable set of life forms
having a greater capacity for intelligence. Was this just a random collision between two speeding masses within the natural laws of the
universe, laws we will never understand fully? Or was it a prehistoric
miracle? Until very recently, the period immediately following that
so-called "Cretaceous-Paleogene extinction," or "K-Pg event," was
a complete mystery because there was no fossil record. However,
extensive fossil discoveries in Colorado beginning in 2016 have shed
light on the post-asteroid period during which new mammal species emerged. Only small mammals survived the initial collision, but
over the ensuing hundreds of thousands of years, perhaps because of
the proliferation of new plant life documented in the same fossil bed

as the new mammals, larger mammals emerged and evolved, eventually leading to … us![16]

In addition to the dinosaur extinction event, there have been a handful of other mass extinction events in Earth's history, periods when remodeling of the entire biosphere of the planet occurred. Were the natural laws simply playing out, and, if so, where did those natural laws come from? How did they come to be natural? Or were these also examples of God as scientist?

The dinosaurs and other forms of life on Earth through the millennia have failed, but how will the human species do over time? And if there isn't a viable life system on this planet, maybe the universe's incubator will discover the perfect system in another galaxy, under different conditions. There are days when I read the news and fear the human experiment on earth is failing, but then I rally, invoke *No Regrets Living*, and regain hope for us. (More about that in Key #3)

Did the BIG miracles, the type described in the Bible where the natural laws appear to have been violated, really occur? Maybe, maybe not. I wasn't there. But I am here now, and I can no more easily explain how a sperm and an egg combine to make a human being than I can explain the miracles described in the Bible. I am here, now, and I can't explain a universe filled with trillions and trillions of stars and quasars, planets, moons, asteroids, and comets, 99.99999 percent of which we will never, ever see, even with the most powerful telescopes our best scientists can hope to design. I can't explain patients whose terminal diseases disappear on their own, or survivors of surely fatal car accidents. Are those miracles? But what about diseases that relentlessly progress despite our best medical interventions and our most fervent prayers, or fatal car accidents where good people die due to negligence of others? I can't explain the origins or existence of subatomic particles like protons, electrons, or neutrons. And if I can't explain subatomic particles, I certainly can't explain *sub*-subatomic particles (leptons, neutrinos, bosons, quarks…really, those are their names) or dark matter or dark energy or black holes or white stars. But I'm told they all exist, and they're critical to understanding our universe and how it formed. I have no more reason to doubt the scientific evidence for those phenomena, just because I can't understand quantum physics, than I do to doubt the scientific evidence I have contributed about the viruses I have studied for so many years. I am, however, absolutely confident that no matter how much we study and conjecture and hypothesize, and even if we really prove bosons and the other such things exist, we'll never understand the miracle of *how* they came to exist. That recognition is central to *No Regrets Living*, to the humility in believing in something greater than ourselves (Key #1) The belief in something greater than ourselves helps us appreciate the miracles around us and within us, and leads to acceptance of who we are, what our limitations are, and what might be out there that we haven't yet experienced and can't yet fathom.

On a recent plane trip, I sat next to a young divinity student named Julio who saw me working on this manuscript, and we started a discussion about miracles and other articles of faith. He suggested an interesting explanation for why we don't see the BIG miracles, of the kind the Bible speaks, today. He thought that maybe the people in biblical times needed more convincing of a single God than we do because, today, monotheism is much more widely accepted. I added that, maybe today, because of science, we're better able to appreciate the smaller, less dramatic miracles than were the ancients. Our sophisticated microscopes and telescopes have made visible what was previously invisible—miracles for those willing to accept them as such.

Medical Miracles

As I mentioned in the Introduction, I am a collector of medical miracles, a book project that began with a personal experience I had with a patient early in my pediatrics training. That child was a hero, saving his little brother from drowning in a freezing swimming pool in the dead of winter. But our hero succumbed to the cold, submerged, and slipped into what appeared to be an unrecoverable coma. Discussions of discontinuing life support and requesting organ donation had begun. This little boy's seemingly impossible recovery was one of the earliest influences on me as a physician and in my appreciation of all that I'll never understand in medicine. Dozens more stories like that formed the basis of the *Miracles We Have Seen*[16a] book, and a few of them are briefly retold in the Signs section to follow. But not all the endings in my collection of miracles were happy ones. Some of the most unforgettable essays describe heartbreaking clinical outcomes that, nevertheless, made a deep and lasting *positive* impact on those involved. Miracles which were more emotional than physical. Silver linings of forgiveness and resilience, children's wisdom, and families' generosity of spirit, all evoking salvation and triumph in the face of sadness and tragedy. Over the course of a medical career, those emotionally stunning events occur more frequently than, for example, a patient coming back to life, as my young drowning victim had, or recovering from a terminal disease after all hope had been lost.

So are the good clinical outcomes truly miracles? And if so, what do we call the bad outcomes? Much of what we do as doctors results in predictable outcomes; our ability to anticipate and influence outcomes has dramatically improved over the past century. But the unknowns in medicine will never disappear entirely. There will always be expected outcomes, miraculous outcomes, and tragic outcomes. I'm able to accept that, for the same reason I can accept everything else that we don't understand about our lives and our universe. Once we come to grips with Key #1 of *No Regrets Living*—believing there is something greater than ourselves, whatever that might be—we can accept those events over which we have no control, both the miracles and the tragedies.

There are also medical occurrences that may seem mundane but, when looked at more closely, can be better appreciated as miraculous. For one example, see Appendix B, "The Miracle" of Colonoscopy.

> The concept of a medical miracle has truly been tested during the COVID-19 pandemic. The families of patients who survived severe cases of the infection hailed their loved one's survival as miraculous, particularly when a ventilator (artificial breathing machine) was required during the illness or a new treatment was tried and appeared to save a life. Data gathered from COVID-19 patients early in the pandemic showed that the majority of those requiring mechanical ventilation succumbed to their disease. It was natural for those who survived, and for their families, to believe their prayers for recovery had been answered. But what of the *majority* of artificially ventilated patients, those who didn't survive? Were their prayers and those of their family not answered? Why were they not granted a miracle? Simplistic answers to these questions won't do. It's as unacceptable to say that those who died during the pandemic were less worthy than those who survived as it is to say that the victims of the Holocaust, like my father's family, somehow deserved their fate... If there was any doubt, the pandemic has confirmed how much we don't understand about our existence. And, as I've said before, I'm okay with that.

The Asymptote

When I started college at the University of Colorado, the upper-classman giving me and a dozen of my fellow incoming freshmen a campus tour walked us by a three-story building, proudly telling us that's where the campus's computer was located. In the subsequent forty-five years, technology has advanced so dramatically that the smart phone in my pocket has much more computing power than that three-story computer building ever had, and without the pro-gramming "punch cards" geeks of the day carried around (punch cards were the state-of-the-art at the time—you can Google it on your smart phone!). So, you may ask, with enough time and evolu-tion of our brains, and with the help of even more advanced com-puters and artificial intelligence that our brains will design, isn't it possible that someday humans will understand *everything* about medicine, about our lives, about the universe? Might not there be a day in the very distant future when all the miracles surrounding us are within our capacity to comprehend? Merely scientific and rational phenomena that can be re-created in our laboratories and technology centers? After all, the US Patent Office reports 300,000 new patent filings every year![17] Surely some combination of those will solve all the mysteries of the universe, right? And if not through innovations, perhaps through religion. It's estimated there are thou-sands of religions being practiced today.[18] Might not one of those discover all the answers?

No, I don't think so. There's a math entity known as an asymp-tote, a curve that approaches a line but never actually reaches it. It's depicted in the figure on the following page, where the horizontal line, U, is never actually reached by the asymptote (the upwardly curved line):

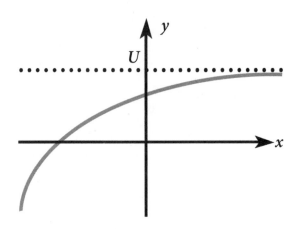

The asymptote is how I see the trajectory of human knowledge. The horizontal U line represents total understanding. Each day brings new discoveries and greater understanding of our lives and of our universe, bringing us higher on the arc and seemingly closer to the U line. But I don't believe we'll ever get all the way there. We don't even know where on the curve we are right now—how far away from understanding are we? Moreover, scientists well know that with each new discovery along the arc of knowledge, new mysteries arise, renewing our appreciation for how far from total understanding we truly are.

Scientists are taught to never say never (I can think it, though, can't I?). Although I have the utmost respect for what humans can accomplish, I don't believe all the great minds of science or religion will be enough for the asymptote to ever reach the U line. If a day does come when we believe we've solved it all, I hope a skeptical descendant of mine, many generations from now, will ask where and how we received the extraordinary mental capacity to have done it?

Finally, a cautionary note. There are hazards associated with our ascent up the asymptotic curve. As we seek greater and greater under-standing of ourselves and our universe, we risk developing technology that could lead to our destruction. While the world has recognized both the good and harm of *nuclear technology*, we have yet to be fully aware of the risks of *biotechnology* and *infotechnology*. Although our ascent up the knowledge arc has taught us, painfully, the tragic poten-tial of nuclear war, we haven't yet confronted the tragic potential of cyber war or cyber terrorism, the type of global conflicts that could be launched by a few computer geeks in their mothers' basements or by a few technocrats or terrorists in an enemy state. As we're sharing personal stories and photos on social media, social media is storing, sharing, and marketing our personal data, making social media out-lets today's fastest growing mega industries—and we are the com-modity they produce. Ditto search engines. As we google on Google, advertisers (and who knows who else?) purchase our interests and desires. So powerful are the data gathered about us by Google searches that the Centers for Disease Control and Prevention (CDC) has used the number and geographic origins of searches for the term "flu" and for the symptoms of flu as an early warning system for seasonal out-breaks of the disease. We've learned the potential benefits of genetic engineering in animals and plants and, as I mentioned earlier, even begun using gene therapy to cure heritable human conditions such as cystic fibrosis and sickle cell disease. But how do we prevent the use of the same genetic engineering techniques for creating designer babies, super athletes ("gene doping"), or artificially-intelligent human brains? Much as that three-story computer building from my college tour now fits in the smart phone in my pocket, talk has already begun of syncing human brains to computers which could, in effect, implant the equivalent of a smart phone on a chip inside my

head. Could human brains be hacked someday? Will future generations be more cyborg than human? The great challenge for us as we
ascend the asymptote of knowledge is to set enforceable boundaries
around the arc, lest we abuse our newfound understanding to our
own detriment.

Babel

One more Bible story to mention although it's not typically
thought of as representing a miracle. Quite the opposite—most
interpret it as a something of a curse. Shortly after the story of Noah
and the flood, the book of Genesis in the Old Testament tells of the
monolinguistic people of Babylonia building a tower to reach the
heavens. The story goes on to say that God punished them, or at least
halted them, by giving each of the workers on this Tower of Babel
a different language that the others couldn't understand, thereby
stopping the work in its tracks. The workers were then said to dis-
perse around the world, taking their personal languages with them.
The fact is that the Linguistic Society of America estimates there
are nearly seven thousand different languages spoken in the world
today, with perhaps thousands of others having become extinct over
the millennia.[19] Where's the miracle here? Well, isn't the fact that
the human brain is capable of effectively communicating in seven
thousand different ways a remarkable testimony to the extraordinary intellect and capacity for knowledge built into our nervous systems? To our climb up the asymptotic curve? Sure it would be nice if
we could all communicate better with one another, language being
only one barrier, but just focusing on our brain as the most powerful
computer ever created (and without even a single molecule of sili-
con!), our multilingual, multipotent brains are miraculous.

The COVID-19 pandemic illustrated in a most powerful way that, despite speaking seven thousand languages, we are truly one people sharing one home—human beings sharing the Earth. The masses of people infected with the virus included native speakers of most, if not all, of the world's languages. Yet it was the universal language of science that allowed people of every nation to finally tame the pandemic. Although the suffering brought by the pandemic was panlingual, the language of healing was singular. As every continent struggled to contain and recover from the outbreak, scientists overcame language barriers to share data and strategies with one another.

While scientists found common language, the pandemic tongue-tied political leaders across the globe who seemed more committed to assigning blame than to protecting their people. Although international health organizations acted quickly to name the virus (severe acute respiratory syndrome coronavirus 2, or (SARS-CoV-2)) and the disease it causes (COVID-19, standing for Coronavirus disease 2019), lest they be labeled with discriminatory terms (as was the misnamed Spanish Flu of 1918, which didn't arise in Spain), discriminatory names still became part of the harsh international discourse.

Locally, leaders had language difficulties as well, as they tried to explain to their communities the differences between lockdown, quarantine, shelter-at-home, and self-isolation; between incubation and transmission periods; and between aerosols and droplets. What makes a business "essential?" What makes a worker essential? Aren't "nonessential" workers and businesses really essential for the sustenance and survival of those labeled as essential? What curve are we trying to flatten? What is meant by "testing?" Testing whom and for what? What is "personal protective equipment?" What's the difference between N95 masks and surgical masks? Between cloth masks and bandanas? Are paper masks protective? The success of public health measures depends on terminology people can understand. Clarity cures confusion—but during the pandemic, there was little clarity, and confusion ran rampant. In turn, the confusion reduced compliance with recommended guidelines and mandates, undoubtedly contributing to the toll of disease and death. Adding to the confusion were disparate recommendations across county and state lines, often in variation from national guidelines as well. Which agency is more reliable when guidelines differ—the WHO? CDC? NIH? State health departments? Although it may have all been in English, people and organizations talked over and past one another, creating a veritable "tower of babble."

From the pandemic, we must learn that what's needed from those in charge of communicating to the public in times of crisis, and at all times, is transparency, cooperation, and carefully crafted language to bridge across all cultures. Language that speaks the truth from leaders who trust we can handle it. The extraordinary, really inexplicable controversy regarding use of masks became a political hot button issue as the pandemic evolved. But it all began with the earliest recommendations *not* to use masks—they are not helpful[20] we were told, and may even be harmful![21] As an infectious diseases doctor, having studied respiratory virus transmission for decades, I knew that to be nonsense. Of course masks are helpful, even life-saving—that's why doctors, nurses, and other providers wear them in the hospital when caring for our sickest and most vulnerable patients. Masks protect us from our patients, and our patients from us. Shortly afterward, public health officials corrected themselves and there was universal recommendation for the use of masks by everyone.[22, 23] This created a firestorm, an angry "tower of babble" of street protests, skirmishes on buses and in stores, even armed confrontations.

What happened? The early, and faulty, advice against masks was given for a noble reason—to preserve vital protective gear for healthcare workers and first responders. I get that. I, too, feared that my colleagues in the heat of battling the pandemic wouldn't have the masks they desperately needed—and in the earliest hot spots, that fear was realized. The news was replete with healthcare workers in beleaguered hospitals begging for more masks to be provided. But those shortages were due to insufficient stockpiles and distribution channels, not hoarding by a misanthropic citizenry. Rather than create a false narrative for the surreptitious purpose of conserving essential gear, the public should have been trusted with the truth. Homemade masks and other cloth face coverings would have saved lives. We should have been told that face coverings *are* helpful, but, for the benefit of our providers and first responders, we should use face coverings other than medical-grade masks. Our national heritage of patriotism and altruism would have been rekindled as it has been during other crises when we have been asked to sacrifice for the greater good. We could have handled the truth and we could have been trusted to do what's right. Inform us well so we can make well-informed choices. (Although, as an aside, I've worried a little bit about our educability and our ability to make good choices since passing a family of two adults and two kids biking opposite me on the bike trail; they all wore face masks but not helmets!)

Nowhere was the "tower of babble" more evident than in the media. Opinions were routinely presented as news, and the news varied with the network, newspaper, or website. Tainted by biased narratives and ulterior motives, the media aided and abetted the politicizing of the pandemic to the detriment of all of us seeking truth and guidance during the crisis.

How does discovery of the everyday miracles around and within us lead to *No Regrets Living*? If we are able to appreciate forests, rivers, and oceans and the extraordinary biodiversity they harbor as miracles, how could we possibly *not* protect them? Yet the news today is filled with stories of deforestation and man-made fires in the Amazon, Australia, and the western United States; toxic dumping into our rivers; plastics pollution of the oceans; and a dangerously fluctuating ozone layer above us. If we are able to appreciate the air we and all other living things need to breathe and survive as miraculous, how could we possibly *not* work toward reducing our carbon footprint and its impact on climate change? And yet, the controversy over whether climate change is man-made or natural has consumed us and prevented us from doing the right thing—what difference does it make *why*, or even *if*, the climate is changing? Shouldn't we be protecting our miraculous environment regardless of whether the earth is warming or cooling, or whether it's our fault or not? If we recognize the miracle of the human body (our bodies!), how could we possibly *not* cherish and protect them? Yet epidemics of obesity, drug abuse, alcohol abuse, and gun violence kill far more people every year than pandemics. And if we recognize the miracle of the nearly limitless capacity of the human brain for communicating (7,000 different languages!), innovating (300,000 patent applications every year!), and worshipping (thousands of different religions practiced today!), shouldn't that make us more willing to interact more thoughtfully and compassionately with one another?

I have hope that as we learn to discover the miracles that appear to us every day, we will strive toward a more conscientious life—without the regret that we didn't do our part to leave a better world for our kids and grandkids.

BUTTERFLIES

Key #2 for *No Regrets Living* also asks that you discover the Law of Sensitive Dependence on Initial Conditions, better known as the Butterfly Effect. The Butterfly Effect holds that a small action in one part of a system can have dramatic downstream effects in other—often far-off—parts of the same system. The eponymous example is that the simple flap of a butterfly's delicate wings in one part of the world could, with countless intervening and interconnected steps, cause a typhoon in another part of the world. In physics, the implication is that what appears to be a random or chaotic set of events or movements can be understood by examining individual actions that may have set those events into motion or contributed to them. In other words, order can be brought to chaos by understanding single participating factors.

Writers of inspirational literature have extended this to human interactions, arguing that any one individual's actions can have broad downstream effects, that a single person can potentially change the world by the decisions he or she makes and by his or her behavior toward others. More than ever, we are an interconnected world. A farmer using pesticides on his land may contaminate the ground water and nearby rivers, harming fish hundreds or thousands of miles away. Those dependent on the fish for a livelihood or for sustenance have never met the farmer, but his actions severely impacted their lives. A rancher feeding antibiotics to his cattle or chickens to improve their growth may be contributing to the growing problem of antibiotic-resistance in children.

But to make it more personal, let's take you as an example. You exist because your parents met. What factors led to their meeting? Who introduced them or convinced them to attend the event or workplace or restaurant where they met? And if there was a person responsible for your parents meeting, who was responsible for that person and for her parents who brought her into existence. And now that you exist, whom will you influence? What changes in the world will result from your existence, changes directly attributable to your parents meeting, and to their parents before them, and to the people

or events leading to all of them meeting. Who will look back someday and attribute their accomplishments and their impact to you?
Or, perhaps even more likely, how many people will your life impact
in ways you and they will never know. Untold numbers of people,
who may never know you existed, could have their lives changed
through your actions. Your charity and loving kindness may be paid
forward by those grateful for your actions, but so may your cruelty
and heartlessness be paid forward.

Act with care. Live your life so that at the end of each day you can
look back and know that you flapped your wings and improved the
world in some small way. Don't look back and regret the opportunities for good that you missed.

There isn't a greater example of the Butterfly Effect than the COVID-19
pandemic, beginning as a single event in a single location and spreading to
impact the lives of virtually every person on Earth. Our interconnectivity can
be our greatest strength, or it can be our greatest vulnerability.

Allow me one more butterfly analogy. As every grade school student
knows, caterpillars morph into butterflies. The process is actually quite
elegant and, as I suggested earlier for other features of the natural world,
quite miraculous. After binging on food and growing plump, molting several
times along the way, the caterpillar simply stops eating one day, spins itself
a silk cocoon, and becomes dormant. But it's a most unusual dormancy—the
caterpillar actually digests itself within the cocoon by secreting enzymes that
dissolve all but very specialized cells in its little body. Those specialized cells
grow into a fully formed, beautiful butterfly.[24] Incredible, right? But what's
the pandemic analogy? We sheltered in cocoons and experienced a most
unusual dormancy, at times feeling as if we were dissolving in loneliness,
despair, and fear. The cocoons served their purpose, but finally it was time to
emerge and flap our wings again. (I can sense you groaning. Sorry.)

SIGNS ·

Our family has its own version of the Butterfly Effect. Shortly after my grandfather died, our nephew, my grandfather's great-grandson, celebrated his Bar Mitzvah, the coming-of-age ceremony for Jewish children. It was a scenic outdoor ceremony with a pulpit set up facing east, as is the tradition. We were all missing Zadie, the name we called my grandfather, and knew how much joy he would have taken seeing his great-grandson reach this milestone. As our nephew began reading his portion from the Torah (the Old Testament), a giant yellow butterfly alighted on the red stone wall the pulpit was facing, mere inches from our nephew. Many of us in the audience noticed it, looked at one another with some amazement, which only grew as the butterfly stayed on that wall, just next to our nephew, for the entire ceremony. When our nephew finished his Torah reading and turned away from the wall to address the audience with his prepared speech, the butterfly flew away.

Since then, big butterflies have appeared at important times in our lives. Our oldest son's college graduation was in the university's giant football stadium, after which each school within the university separated into different venues for a more personal ceremony and the awarding of diplomas. Our son's school ceremony was under a big open-sided tent on the main quad. The graduates lined up alphabetically and marched past the podium to receive their diplomas as their name was called. Just as our son's name was announced and he started his walk toward the podium, a giant yellow butterfly entered the tent and flew past the podium, exiting the other side. The collective gasp from the small Rotbart contingent in the audience brought stares from those near enough to hear us, but we didn't care. We knew what had happened. Then, even more hauntingly, there was the very sad day my mom (Zadie's daughter) passed away and the funeral home came to her apartment to pick her up. As they were loading the gurney into the hearse, a big yellow butterfly flew over the gurney, right in front of all of us. Seriously eerie.

Another sign. My wife, Sara, tearfully asked her mother, who was dying, "How will I know you're watching over us?" Her mom answered, weakly and simply, "You'll know." Our daughter's wedding was over Memorial Day weekend, just twelve days after Sara's mom passed away. The sadness of Mema's absence was palpable as the wedding guests gathered in our backyard for the ceremony. Just before the service began, a beautiful blue jay landed on the birdbath in our backyard, visible to everyone watching the procession. The bird stayed there, quietly, during the entire service and appeared to be as transfixed by the proceedings as we were. For the next several weeks, the blue jay visited our backyard repeatedly. No longer quiet, it squawked at us, seemingly trying to grab our attention. It took over a nest high atop a pine tree overlooking our yard and dropped down to drink from, and splash in, the blue birdbath. Sara's mom loved blue and helped us pick the birdbath years before. For the rest of the summer and fall, even when we were out of town, we'd have blue jay sightings at propitious moments—when we were walking with our grandsons; after accompanying Sara's father for an important medical procedure; and, most recently, in the strangest of places. Our daughter and son-in-law, whose wedding the blue jay had watched six months earlier, boarded a Frontier Airlines plane to fly home after spending Thanksgiving with us. The crew announced that the plane had a computer problem. For safety reasons, the passengers would have to deplane and wait for another aircraft to arrive for them.

Frontier Airlines is known for the colorful designs on its planes' tails—each plane has a different giant animal painted on its tail, and each animal has a catchy name—Larry the Lynx, Flip the Dolphin, Carl the Coyote, Lance the Ocelot, Sally the Mustang, etc. More than one hundred different animals in all.[25] Well, it took a couple of hours, but the replacement plane arrived and…what were the chances? The iconic trademark animal on the tail wing was Skye the BLUE JAY, ready to fly my late mother-in-law's granddaughter and her new husband home safely! One hundred possible tail images and the safe replacement airplane was a blue jay! Coincidence, you say?

Photo credit: Our daughter, with permission, taken from the airplane window

My mom died seven weeks to the day after my mother-in-law. By then, the blue jay had moved on. The day after my mom's funeral, my wife and I were sitting on our back porch, trying to gather ourselves after yet another sad family event, and a dragonfly began flying back and forth, dozens of times, right in front of us. It was being followed by what looked like a baby dragonfly, as if the mommy was teaching the baby how to fly, how to be a dragonfly.

I looked it up and I now know that wasn't what was happening. It was much more likely a mating ritual with a male chasing a female. We sat there for nearly an hour, watching as the dragonfly flew its route, back and forth across the yard just feet from where we were sitting on the porch. Dragonflies typically hang out and mate over bodies of water—there was no such breeding ground in our backyard. Not long after the dragonfly and its suitor appeared and performed for us, at least ten other dragonflies began flying in the yard, orbiting around one another, an entire community of little flying helicopters. Thanks to an extraordinary National Geographic video I watched afterward, I realized we were witnessing an elaborate mating, chasing, and territory-defending ritual. The video reimagined for me what I thought I knew about dragonflies and reinforced, as such documentaries are prone to do, my appreciation for the ubiquitous miracles around us. Dragonflies are tiny miracles; watch the video for yourself and see if you agree.[26]

Okay, you ask, what's the point? No, I don't really believe my grandfather was reincarnated as a butterfly or that Sara's mom came back as a blue jay or that my mom is now a dragonfly fleeing male suitors (although ...). But the timings of those signs, so soon after we lost our loved ones, remind us of them in a beautiful way and gave us an ongoing way to remember them at spontaneous moments in the day, when we least expect it, and to feel their presence in our lives.

It's not impossible, of course, that in some afterlife my grandfather, mother-in-law, and mom are sending us those reminders, especially at times with special meaning to us, like when we're with our grand-children (their great- and great-great-grandchildren!)—I'd like to believe that. Along those lines, Sara absolutely believes that our late and beloved dog, Lizzy, a springer spaniel, sends Sara "memos," in the form of look-alike dogs, at important moments in our lives, like when two springers walked by us on our way to Mt. Sinai Hospital in New York to meet our first grandchild, or when a different pair of springers appeared down the block from our kids right after they moved into their new home—two different sightings, two springers each, two thousand miles apart. And I have no proof that it's not happening (sorry for the double negative) just as Sara believes it is.

Sara offers this as further proof: She had three beloved great uncles, her grandmother's brothers—Yudi, Yishi, and Yank (affec-tionately known in the family as the "Pep Boys"). Their lineages comprise much of Sara's family, which gathers for giant reunions every few years. The Pep Boys helped officiate at our wedding thirty-five years ago. They were larger than life individuals, both for their roles in the family and for their physical size. Big men in many ways. Several years after the uncles had all passed away, we and more than one-hundred of the uncles' other family members came together for one of our epic reunions in Rocky Mountain National Park. As we pulled up in our car to the reunion lodge, there were three giant bull elk, replete with huge antler racks, grazing outside the lodge, right in front of the entryway to the lodge. Draw your own conclusions.

I do believe that we can feel the presence of those we've lost, and mnemonics like butterflies, blue jays, dragonflies, springer spaniels, and elk help us feel an ongoing connection to our lost loved ones in unplanned and unexpected contexts, which makes those appearances poignant. Your mnemonics may not be of the fauna variety—perhaps certain words, smells, foods, images, songs, or dreams trigger your memories of those you've lost. Discovering the connection of these phenomena to the people who were important in your life can be powerful, especially if the memories of those you've lost are loving ones, deep relationships lasting beyond their passing. If during their lives, you hadn't loved and cared for them enough, respected and honored them enough, cherished your time with them, the reminders would not be pleasant ones. Jarred by memories of the shortcomings, theirs and yours, in the relationships, you will feel regret. The moments you have with loved ones are finite, but the memories are forever. Make the most of every moment with those you love.

COINCIDENCES

Everyone has experienced coincidences, but how we interpret them varies. For some people, coincidences are signs from above; for others, they are simply random, meaningless occurrences. Statisticians, who live by data rather than embracing the mysterious, explain coincidences by invoking the Law of Truly Large Numbers—inevitable occasional occurrences will occur in a busy world with infinite opportunities for overlapping events. The more spiritually minded see coincidences as evidence of a greater plan, a validation of fate. Analytical psychologist Carl Jung advanced the first attempt at a scientific approach to coincidences, introducing the term *synchronicity*, which he defined as "acausal parallelisms," or simultaneous occurrences without an apparent causal relationship. If the events had a meaningful connection to one another, he considered that to be a synchronicity. Jung's theory was criticized during his life and continues to be by many in the sixty years since his death. Because synchronicity cannot be scientifically tested, his critics argue, it cannot be proven to exist—rather, coincidences are merely…coincidental and without deeper meaning. In addition to being the father of analytical psychology, Jung was also fascinated with the paranormal, for example, extra-sensory perception. He saw meaningful coincidences as part of a greater unknown in the mental connectivity among people.

More recently, Bernard Beitman, the first psychiatrist since Carl Jung to systematize the study of meaningful coincidences, has further explored how synchronicity can be used effectively in people's lives—how to benefit by coincidences and even increase their frequency.[27] Beitman gives numerous examples of deeply meaningful coincidences he and those he interviewed experienced. He also introduces the concept of a *psychosphere*, a collective unconsciousness that surrounds us invisibly, much as the atmosphere we breathe visibly surrounds us—a very Jungian approach. Recognizing unconsciousness as the potential source of coincidences may help to make those chance occurrences less random seeming and more meaningful.

A running joke in our family has to do with a quasi-coincidence that began when I was in my residency training in Philadelphia. I lived in a neighborhood called Overbrook Park and shopped for clothes on the bargain rack at the Marshall's on City Line Avenue. Turns out Sara, whom I wouldn't meet in Denver for another five years, worked the cash register at that Marshall's during her summer vacations from school. I've told our kids that I'm sure their mom sold me the clothes she has been slowly purging from our closet for the past thirty-five years. I can't prove that, so the only true coincidence in that story is that we both were in the same store a long time ago. Not much there, I know. So for trivial coincidences like that, it's easy to dismiss them as meaningless—readily explained by the Law of Truly Large Numbers. I had to shop somewhere, Sara had to work somewhere, no big deal. But then the story of how we actually first met (in Key #4, to follow) was much more meaningful for us and feels much more like fate.

Clearly, science has a long way to go in understanding whether coincidences represent significant signs or simply random chance, but as you'll see in Key #5, I'm a proponent of fate and I try to glean meaning from coincidences in my life that impact me deeply. For a more comprehensive collection of meaningful coincidences, in addition to Dr. Beitman's book that I mentioned previously, the Small Miracles book series by Judith Leventhal and Yitta Halberstam Mandelbaum[28] details hundreds of coincidences that had profound significance for those experiencing them.

Medical Coincidences

I have had numerous experiences in my medical career when apparent coincidences became very significant events in the life of a patient. Lab tests ordered for one suspected diagnosis which revealed a different, more urgent diagnosis. A renowned surgeon who was in town to give a major lecture on the same day as a child with a complicated and life-threatening birth defect was admitted to the hospital; that surgeon happened to be the world's expert on surgical correction of that birth defect. He finished his lecture and stayed on to perform the life-saving surgery. A comatose child, my drowning patient described earlier, for whom imminent discontinuation of life support and organ donation were being considered, squeezed my hand while I was reading to him during one of my nights on call as a young trainee. Considered a coincidental involuntary muscle spasm by the senior physicians to whom I reported it, that squeeze was enough to delay "pulling the plug," and foretold a complete recovery.

As I mentioned earlier, my encounters with apparent medical miracles such as that one led me to ask eminent physician colleagues if they'd had similar experiences; the collection of those essays appear in the *Miracles We Have Seen* book. Many of those stories, witnessed by some of the most prominent physicians in the country, include remarkable coincidences and serendipity. A few examples:

Father Karl

A beloved priest finished rounds on his hospitalized parishioners in a suburban Boston hospital. He then got into an otherwise empty elevator, pressed the button for the lobby, and collapsed from a massive heart attack. But somehow the elevator didn't go to the lobby—instead the doors opened on the second floor, the floor housing the cardiac intensive care unit (CICU), where the cardiologist in charge of the unit was waiting at the elevator to go upstairs to make his rounds. This as the CICU staff was preparing to go home on a slow Saturday afternoon but had not yet left. The cardiologist described the scene: "The elevator doors opened, and to my utter astonishment and great dismay, a body rolled forward over the threshold. Gray hair, overweight, black suit. Entirely unconscious based on the roll. I turned the man over, face up. Others who were also waiting for the elevator helped me. Priest's collar, pulseless, sweaty, clammy—drenched, in fact—cold, pale." He went on to describe the pupils in the priest's eyes as fixed and dilated, a very bad sign for the condition of the brain. As if delivered exactly where he needed to be, Father Karl received immediate resuscitation from the cardiologist and the CICU staff. They could not restore his heartbeat, so while still performing CPR they dragged him to the procedure room, which was on the same floor. There he underwent a potentially risky procedure to open his blocked main heart artery. Although his heartbeat was restored quickly after the procedure, his brain function remained in doubt because of the long period of unconsciousness, which caused his pupils to be unresponsive. But, to everyone's amazement, Father Karl addressed his congregation from the pulpit, a mere four weeks later, thanking God and the doctors who saved his life. The cardiologist said that had the heart attack happened anywhere else, even in the same hospital, Father Karl would likely not have survived.

Jim

A seventy-five-year-old retired engineer was a regular volunteer at the University of Virginia School of Medicine as a standardized patient, part of a group of local community members who give of their time to help teach medical students. These volunteers serve as pretend patients, giving third year medical students the clinical history of a medical disease. The volunteers are briefed on the disease they are pretending to have and told which symptoms they should complain of when the students take their medical history. While monitored by closed-circuit TV, the medical students obtain the history from the patient and perform a physical exam, both of which are graded by the preceptor who watches the camera feed in the next room. It was Jim's assignment to pretend to have an abdominal aortic aneurysm, a potentially lethal ballooning of the main blood vessel in the body as it courses through the abdomen—the weakened wall of that vessel is prone to leak and burst, which can result in sudden death. Jim had already performed his act for, and been examined by, thirty-one previous medical students that week when Ryan, the thirty-second and final student to be tested, entered the examination room. After taking the made-up history from Jim, who of course actually had none of the symptoms he was complaining of, Ryan went on to the physical examination, expecting to find nothing in this pretend patient, just as the prior thirty-one medical students that week had found nothing. But Ryan did find something—he felt a pulsating abdominal mass and heard, with his stethoscope, a *bruit*, the characteristic whooshing sound in someone's abdomen with an aneurysm. Ryan was worried that this was just the power of suggestion—the pretend symptoms Jim gave suggested an aneurysm, and then Ryan found the physical signs classic for an aneurysm.

Hesitatingly, when the examination was finished and he went to present the case to his physician proctor in the other room, Ryan said that from the history given by the patient, he suspected an abdominal aortic aneurysm. And he went on to say that, even though he knew Jim was just pretending, there actually was a pulsating mass and a bruit. This is what Ryan's preceptor wrote about the interaction with her student: "Ryan did a nice job on both his history and physical examination and his presentation was also well done. But, when he told me that he had felt a pulsating mass and heard a bruit over the abdominal aorta, I admit to being a little peeved. *He's making that up or imagining it,* I thought. I challenged him, and asked if he was saying that to represent what he would have heard in a real patient. 'No,' he insisted, 'I really felt a mass and heard a bruit!'... Jim was already dressed and ready to leave but readily agreed to let me examine his abdomen. And there they were—an unmistakable mass and bruit. *Geez!* I couldn't believe I almost dismissed Ryan's findings as imaginary."

Further testing confirmed that Jim, the volunteer pretending to have an abdominal aortic aneurysm to help teach medical students, actually did have one. Thirty-one previous students had missed it. Had the final student, Ryan, not observed the signs of this real aneurysm, Jim might have died a sudden death. Instead, he was promptly taken to surgery where the aneurysm was repaired. Jim went on to make a full recovery.

Elli

A college freshman interning at the James Cancer Center of Ohio State University was initially supposed to work on another unit but, at the last minute, was reassigned to the surgical floor. For the previous five years, Elli had experienced increasingly severe, and mysterious, symptoms including dizziness, lightheadedness, face swelling, and occasional blackouts affecting her vision and hearing. Many doctors evaluated her over the years, each suggesting different simple and benign theories about what was causing her symptoms. She was treated with a variety of prescription and over-the-counter medicines for those diagnoses, and even had her tonsils taken out, but the symptoms persisted and were getting progressively worse. One day she noticed a lump in her neck and asked one of the surgeons on the unit where she was working what her chronic symptoms and the lump might mean. He looked in her throat and what he saw greatly disturbed him—the tissues on one side of the back of her mouth were displaced and bulging into her neck causing the lump. He ordered a CAT scan that revealed a baseball-size tumor at the base of her skull that was surrounding the main artery leading to her brain. The tumor was already cutting off some blood flow to her brain, causing the dizziness, lightheadedness, and other symptoms she had been having for years as the tumor continued growing; further growth of the tumor would be life-threatening. A seventeen-hour surgery, performed by the surgeon whom Elli had asked for help and two of his colleagues, was very complicated and risky because the tumor encased not only the major blood vessel leading to her brain but also the nerves controlling her facial muscles, vocal cords, and tongue. The procedure was successful, leaving her with only minor residual problems related to the nerve damage caused by the tumor. The tumor turned out to be one of the rarest of all cancers, occurring in less than one in five million people. Very few surgeons have received special training in removing this type of tumor. But of all the hospitals in Ohio where Elli might have worked, and on all the floors of the James Cancer Center where she might have worked—including the one she was initially assigned to—the surgeon Elli happened to ask in passing one day at work was one of the world's leading experts in just this type of tumor surgery. That question from Elli to that surgeon very likely prevented her from imminently suffering a major stroke and may also have saved her life.

Her surgeon wrote this: "Call this a case of good luck: being right where she needed to be, right when she needed to be there; doing the right job, with all the right people working beside her. Or call it serendipity, the alignment of all the stars to result in a wonderful outcome. Or call it a miracle. She and her family do, and so do I."

Daniel, Trevor, and Betiane

Medical teams from around the world began missions to Haiti following the devastating earthquake in 2010. One rural mountain clinic was even more desperate for help than others, with only intermittent electricity and no running water. The clinicians caring for patients there had to rely on their diagnostic abilities alone, as all but the most basic lab tests and equipment were unavailable. Despite many patients with heart conditions who came to that clinic, there was no EKG machine. On one particular mission, a donated EKG machine arrived with the clinicians, but it was broken. Daniel, a teen volunteer on that mission offered to take the machine back to his high school in the United States, where he was on the robotics team, and try to fix it, despite having no previous experience with an EKG machine. He and his team did fix it, and the EKG machine returned to the Haiti clinic with the next mission.

The teen volunteer on that next mission was Trevor, a star high school basketball player and the son of the cardiologist who was one of the clinicians on that next mission. The cardiologist himself only knew about the mission because he showed up at the wrong school to watch his son's game and sat next to another physician who had been on these Haitian missions. When this group arrived at the clinic, the first thing they wanted to do was try out the repaired EKG machine—Trevor volunteered to be the guinea pig. Shockingly, Trevor's EKG test found that he had a potentially fatal heart defect, probably since birth, the kind that can cause sudden death—and makes the news with some frequency when an athlete dies suddenly in the middle of practice or a game. Trevor returned to the United States for urgent heart surgery to repair his heart, made a full recovery, and went on to become a nationally recognized high school basketball star.

Through his father, who returned to Haiti for another mission, Trevor heard about a fourteen-year-old Haitian girl, Betiane, who had a different but equally lethal heart defect as Trevor's, diagnosed with the same EKG machine in the same clinic. But Betiane was an orphan with no resources or paperwork that would allow her to travel to the US for surgery—that is, until Trevor asked the surgeon who repaired his heart if he would be willing to do the same for a Haitian orphan if Trevor could figure out how to get the girl to the US. Of course he would, the surgeon said. That was only accomplished through heroic efforts on the part of the clinic staff, outreach to the US Embassy in Haiti, and, when the bureaucracies of the two countries seemed insurmountable and all else seemed to fail, the intervention of a newly elected US senator from the state where the surgery would be done.

The clinicians witnessing the remarkable chain of events wrote this: "So, to sum up, a donated but broken EKG machine was repaired by a teenage volunteer on a medical mission to Haiti. That machine returned to Haiti and diagnosed severe congenital heart disease on another teen volunteer (who had no symptoms of heart disease and) who was only there because his dad had gone to the wrong basketball game...That young athlete survived thanks to major surgery and...paved the way for lifesaving surgery for another teen who otherwise had no chance of survival. Three teens, who never met each other, saved each other's lives with the help of a miraculous little machine in a remote Haitian clinic. Today, the machine continues in use daily and is still the only EKG machine we've ever had there."

Are these examples of simple medical coincidence—patients and doctors each being in exactly the right place at the right time? Are they manifestations of Jung's collective unconsciousness or Beitman's psychosphere—mysterious connections among the parties involved that brought them together at precisely the right moment? Are they evidence of fate, part of a greater plan? Are they signs of divine intervention? For me, it's not nearly as important to answer those questions as it is to realize that there are signs everywhere, and that coincidences occur frequently, some more meaningful than others. By being conscious of those signs and coincidences, we discover how mysterious life can be and how much we may never understand. All of which leads me back to Key #1, belief in something greater than ourselves.

> The tsunami of clinical stories emerging from the COVID-19 pandemic has brought innumerable examples of medical coincidences that resulted in saved lives, and others that resulted in lost lives. How to interpret these events will forever remain a challenge for us. Those whose lives were saved because of fortuitous circumstances will believe a miracle occurred; those who mourn the loss of loved ones due to tragic circumstances will rue the cruel twist of fate that put their loved one in harm's way—perhaps in a nursing home or on a cruise ship—at the worst possible time. For each of those eventualities, our personal answers will come from what we believe about fate (Key #5, to follow) and how we accept the unknowns in our lives.

MESSIAH

Everyone has a different and very personal perspective on what the messiah means to them. For some, it's an imaginary construct, not rooted in reality; for others, it represents the very meaning and purpose of their lives. For some, the coming of the messiah means the first arrival of a savior; for others, the return of a savior. For me, I believe the coming of the messiah will be the result of an important discovery we each make within ourselves—the discovery of singular actions we can take that can have far-reaching downstream impact. The Butterfly Effect. I believe a small spark of the messiah is in all of us, and it will take all of us to save, or redeem, the world. Each of us flapping our wings to influence, imprint, and improve the lives of others. If the messiah is a single person, it will take all of us gently nudging our world closer to being deserving before the messiah will arrive or return. I believe in the coming of the messiah as a metaphor for an awakening deep within each of us of a divine spark. The gathering together of all those sparks from everyone in the form of focused and purposeful deeds of goodness toward one another. A collective movement toward a greater consciousness of our personal actions, the effect they have on us and others, all leading toward betterment of our world.

I see the messiah as an attainable state of being for humanity, if not in our lifetimes, perhaps in the lifetimes of our children or grandchildren. A state of being wherein our inner goodness and our good inclinations prevail over the evil inclinations we are all susceptible to. When that happens, I think we will be "saved," "reunited," and re-create "Eden." There's a long way to go, but we've also come a long way.

Earlier, I expressed some dismay about the direction humanity is headed—reading or watching the news each day lends serious weight to that dismay. Looking only at the microcosm of human existence—our society's daily experiences—it's easy to become discouraged. How will we ever be on the road to the messiah, to a time when humanity collectively finds its inner spark? But to see that we are, indeed, on the road, we must look at the totality of human existence. Are we closer to finding the messiah, the collective sparks within each of us, today than we were, say, one thousand years ago? Five thousand years ago? Sara and our kids are fans—addicts is a better term—of the Game of Thrones TV series. I personally can't understand why—I find it repulsive, which is the point I'm about to make. When the TV is on and I'm nearby, before I bolt from the room, I am stunned by the sheer horror of humanity's medieval existence as portrayed so vividly in that fictional show and I can't bear to watch it. Yet history books tell us that GOT fiction isn't far from the truth. The societies that preceded us by hundreds or thousands of years were, to repeat myself, repulsive. Aren't we, as a species, more compassionate, tolerant, civil, and purposeful than in eras past? And even within our own time, haven't we proven that people are educable and capable of betterment? Of igniting an inner spark, if only for a few moments in time?

As simple proof, let's take a most mundane setting. Look around you the next time you're at a busy city intersection and here's what you'll see: We drive safer and more environmentally friendly cars, obey traffic signals, use our car's turn signals, wait our turn at stop signs, wear seat belts and shoulder straps, and put our kids in car seats. When I was learning to drive, litter lined every city street; today's streets are mostly clean and when we see someone throw trash out their car window, we gasp—it's rare, isn't it? People can learn (stiff fines also help).

Beyond the intersection, every aspect of our society has proven that we can teach and we can learn; we can ignite the spark within us. Within the past ten years, our society has accepted gay marriage and transgender rights. Not that long before, at least not long within history's big picture, the United States passed the Civil Rights Act and women's suffrage. Laws alone don't define progress, but they are proxies for it, and they help society begin to accept needed reforms. As recently as my parents' generation, cigarettes were promoted as healthy and seat belts hadn't yet been invented. Today, we reuse and recycle; we disclose ingredients and expiration dates so we can eat and drink in healthier ways; we wait politely in lines and teach our kids to say please and thank you, imprinting them with politeness and civility. We have seen the value of charitable giving and taught the risks of drinking, smoking, and other excesses. We have made "designated driver," "safe sex," and "Amber Alert" part of our vernacular. The #MeToo movement exposed the prevalence of sexual harassment, and that awareness has helped to prevent more of it. We have recognized addiction as a disease and developed therapies, and we have stopped calling homosexuality a disease in need of a cure. We are rethinking the signs on our public bathrooms and the pronouns we use to describe ourselves. We adopt pets from shelters and children from foster homes and orphanages. Oh, and we invented democracy and the rule of law. Thanks to social media, people in the far corners of the Earth who otherwise might not have yearned for, or even known about, freedom and democracy are now rising up, taking to the streets, and demanding change. Although the process may seem glacially slow, society is educable.

Of course, not everywhere in the world has evolved to the same degree, nor has every corner of our country or even our neighborhoods. Large pockets of evil and insensitivity toward others still exist—at home and abroad. At the same busy city intersection, we may see road rage and drivers who, distracted by their cell phones or dashboard displays, are putting all of us at risk. Prescription drug abuse has become epidemic, and violence in the home and on our streets continues. E-cigarettes have become a new temptation and threat to our teens. And while litter on the streets may be less common, landfills and oceans are filling up with plastic and toxic waste.

For every two steps forward, sadly there always seems to be one step backward. History has a way of repeating itself. Anti-Semitism, sexism, xenophobia, and homophobia continue to rear their ugly heads despite what should have been defining moments in history. And how is it possible that, despite the lessons of slavery, the tragedy of the Civil War, and the vile Jim Crow laws, racism still pervades so many aspects of our society and of societies around the world? The recent murders of innocent African-Americans at the hands of police or vigilantes has ignited the most powerful reexamination of racial justice in the United States since the time of Reverend Martin Luther King Jr. Once again, I believe, we will advance as a civilization because of those tragedies and the courageous voices speaking out on behalf of the victims and on behalf of all who cherish decency and fairness. The price to pay for that advance has been high, but, if change for the good does occur, the legacy of the victims will be a powerful one.

Another sad step backward. Guns, the evil heir of the vile Valyrian Steel weapons from the Game of Thrones era (yes, I googled, "GOT weapons"), are a pox on all of us. It only takes one deranged and armed individual who does not cherish the precious life he has been given to ruin the lives of others. Mass shootings in places of worship and the targeted killings of police officers further highlight the persistent hatred in certain segments of our society, while seemingly random shootings in schools, malls, and movie theaters remind us that it's not just religion or authority under attack.

Clearly there are hiccups along the way, but overall the evidence suggests an upward trend line for humanity and that we are closer to discovering the messiah within each of us than we were generations ago. I believe we are slowly inching our way toward igniting humanity's collective spark. As long as we don't destroy ourselves before we get there.

Powerful images of the spark within us emerged during the COVID-19 outbreak. Heroic healthcare workers endured battlefield-like circumstances to provide comfort and save lives. Retired nurses and doctors came out of retirement to serve on the front lines. Truck drivers kept the nation's supply chain of food and other necessities flowing. Grocery store workers kept the shelves stocked as best they could and treated us graciously despite the risks they faced. Mail and package carriers and delivery workers also braved risks to make their appointed rounds, allowing the rest of us to avoid stores and malls. Factories converted their machinery to make ventilators, masks, and other protective equipment. Celebrities performed charity television concerts from their homes to raise hundreds of millions of dollars for those most in need as a result of the pandemic. Neighborhood restaurants served takeout while wearing protective gear and donated leftover food to shelters. Households turned their sewing machines into face-mask factories to donate to hospitals and nursing homes. Automakers and other manufacturers converted their assembly lines to make ventilators. Volunteerism reached the highest levels since World War II. Neighbors helped neighbors in every neighborhood in the country and across the globe. If we can find a way to keep the spark within us burning long after the pandemic, we will come closer to the coming of the messiah by whatever definition you hold.

The pandemic also proved, again, how educable society can be. In contrast to the glacially slow changes I cited earlier, people across the globe heeded the recommendations of public health experts and changed their behaviors, literally overnight. Although the messages were often mixed or controversial, for the most part, we used our best judgments and responded conscientiously, with appropriate concern for ourselves and for our communities. We closed our schools, churches, offices, and businesses, maintained social distance, wore masks, and self-isolated when necessary. A mass education like none other in history, reaching even a most unlikely corner of the population—ISIS leaders advised their terrorist network not to travel to Europe during the pandemic because of high infection rates there;

to use frequent handwashing; and to cover their mouths when yawning or sneezing![29]

Time will tell if the measures we took and taught were as effective as we hoped they would be. As the pandemic progressed, people became increasingly weary of the restrictions and wary of their necessity. Pandemic fatigue caused people to become more lax in their precautions, resulting in inevitable surges of cases. Those lapses notwithstanding, the rapidity of our education, under fire from COVID-19, gives me hope that if we can educate ourselves equally well to the other existential threats the world faces—threats as grave and life-threatening as a virus outbreak—our inner sparks will ignite with much more urgency.

There is dramatic evidence of the emergence of a collective inner spark in my own field, medicine. Health care in virtually every corner of the globe now reflects the progress and methodology of the most advanced medical systems here in the United States and in other developed countries. Surgical techniques, therapeutics, medical equipment, and even the design and staffing of clinics and hospitals are all approaching a global uniformity—a very high standard of practice absent in much of the world as recently as a hundred years ago when the greatest determinant of survival from intensive care or surgery was where in the world you received your care.

The COVID-19 pandemic is the latest example of today's standards of medical care crossing virtually every international boundary. Approaches to, and implementation of, vaccines, antiviral therapies, and supportive measures like ventilators were nearly identical in every country on every continent. Of course, developing countries lagged in their ability to implement some of the advances, but only because of lack of resources, not lack of shared knowledge or skill. COVID-19 hospital wards and intensive care units in Viet Nam, Vienna, and Vermont were almost indistinguishable in the care they offered—high quality care of the kind only made possible by the sharing of information and by profound compassion for our fellow humans—the awakening of millions of inner sparks.

KEY #3
HEAL

"What's true of all the evils in the world
is true of plague as well. It helps men
to rise above themselves."

—Albert Camus, *The Plague*

KEY #3 FOR *No Regrets Living* reso-
nates deeply with me as a physician—
our obligation to heal. But you don't
need a clinic or patients to accomplish
this goal. There are countless opportunities for heal-
ing available to everyone. The world's history is filled with the tragedies befalling masses of innocents, and the daily news is filled with
tragedies befalling blameless individuals. Tragedies resulting from
acts of evil, incurable diseases, pandemics, and natural and man-
made disasters. But, as you'll read in the pages to follow, humankind

is imbued with the antidote to all of those scourges, a secret weapon: our *prepared minds.*

EVIL

Let's examine evil from the two initial vantage points in Key #1 of *No Regrets Living,* the belief in something greater than ourselves: God or science. Good people like my father and his family, and the millions of other victims of the Holocaust, serve as evidence for many that there can be no beneficent God. What kind of God allows the Holocaust, the pogroms that devastated my grandfather's family (Appendix C), the ethnic cleansing of Muslims by Serbs in Bosnia, the genocide in Rwanda, the Crusades, the persecution of Christians by the Romans, or the hate crimes against racial, religious, and other minorities in the United States of America? What kind of God allows the al-Qaeda terrorist attacks of September 11, 2001 that slaughtered nearly three-thousand people at work that day earning a living for their families, or the mass beheadings of innocents committed by ISIS? *Where is God? There is no God! God is dead!* Others might accept evil as simply another phenomenon that can *only* be understood by God, proof of a truth beyond our ability to comprehend, and that we must accept with blind faith. For still others, the existence of evil might be considered an unfortunate reality of human nature, pro-scribed by science and the natural laws of the universe, witnessed and experienced since the beginning of time.

Whether God, science, or both, I take shelter and comfort in know-ing we will never understand most of what happens in this life— recall the diagram of the asymptote, the upward arc that approaches but never actually reaches its goal line. Key #3 for *No Regrets Living* allows me to be saddened and horrified by what I see as injustices in the world, accept that I will never understand how or why many of them could happen, yet work tirelessly to stop them, to heal the world of them.

Hitler was by no means the first face of unspeakable evil that human civilization has endured. The staggering killing and suffering inflicted by Nero, Charlemagne, Genghis Khan, Torquemada, Ivan the Terrible, Vladimir Lenin, Talaat Pasha, Mao Tse-tung, and Hitler's contemporary, Joseph Stalin, are among the darkest stains on human history. Sadly, the list is far longer than just those and dates back much further. We sometimes speak of "biblical evil," for example, in describing the horrific actions of the ISIS terrorist group. Indeed, the Bible is filled with the perpetrators and the victims of evil, beginning with the murder of one brother by another.

It doesn't take great insight to learn the most important lessons of the Holocaust: evil exists, has always existed, and eternal vigilance is required to prevent such evil from growing and destroying all in its path. Unfortunately, humans didn't learn that lesson from the innumerable examples of horrendous evil that *preceded* the Holocaust in history. But most disturbingly, what did the lesson of the Nazis teach us going forward? How could our *post*-Hitler world allow Pol Pot, Saddam Hussein, Idi Amin, Fidel Castro, Osama bin Laden, the genocide of Tutsis by the Hutus in Rwanda, or the deaths of innocent children due to gun violence on the streets of American cities?

I'll foreshadow Key #5 by noting that the pandemic evoked new and inspirational forms of giving and kindness in a society beleaguered by the worst plague of our times. But, sadly, the pandemic also elicited new and dangerous forms of evil. Those who would discriminate against ethnic groups and immigrants found new excuses to do so. Domestic violence increased during the lockdowns. Political anger spilled into violence at demonstrations in support of, and against, public policies. Some sought to profit from the pandemic by price gouging scarce supplies. Scams and snake oil salesmen emerged to take advantage of the most vulnerable and desperate. Social media posts appeared, some proudly, showing people spitting on food in grocery stores and on workers in subways and on buses.

And two more subtle forms of evil also emerged during the pandemic: Countless gatherings of large numbers of people during the height of the pandemic defied public health measures of social distancing and wearing masks, thereby putting not only those in the crowds but everyone they subsequently came in contact with at risk of infection and, potentially, death. Finally, people hoarded essential items like hand sanitizer, cleaning products, and, most perplexingly, toilet paper. Hoarding says, "I am more important than you," and isn't that at the root of most acts of evil? As you'll read in Key #5, the good deeds during the pandemic greatly outweighed the bad, but even during unprecedented crises, we need to innovate ways to prevent evil. And we will—read on.

So, what are we to make of monstrous, and even of subtle, evil? Do we think: 1) There is a God who allows evil for a purpose beyond our comprehension; or 2) Evil is part of a system of natural laws, most of which is also beyond our comprehension? On the one hand, what kind of God could that be, and, on the other, what does that mean for the future of our world if evil is an indelible part of natural law?

Again, unanswerable questions. But I am certain of one thing: We must not accept the inevitability of evil. As futile as it might feel at times, we can work to stop evil from occurring and recurring and, someday, I believe we will succeed. We will heal the world of evil, and eradicate it. And I'll *prove* it to you.

Let's start with other seemingly impossible "eradications" our society has already accomplished in just the past 150 years. For that, I'll again don my infectious diseases hat and use the examples of germs.

INCURABLE DISEASES
AND PREVIOUS PANDEMICS

As many as half of all Europeans living during the four-year period between 1347 and 1351 died—75–200 million people—due to the Black Death, known today as bubonic plague. The 1918 Spanish Influenza pandemic (misnamed because it probably didn't arise in Spain) is estimated to have killed 50 million people, 675,000 in the United States alone. Since 1918, there have been recurrent influenza pandemics, each due to a different strain of the virus: the Asian Flu pandemic (which actually did arise in East Asia) in 1957–58 killed 1.1 million people worldwide and 116,000 in the United States; the 1968–69 Hong Kong influenza pandemic killed an estimated 1 million worldwide and 100,000 in the US; and the 2009–2010 Swine Flu pandemic was estimated to have killed between 150,000 and 575,000 worldwide and nearly 13,000 in the US.[30] The World Health Organization estimates that 35 million people have died of HIV/AIDS since the first reported cases in the early 1980s. Cholera has killed countless millions in outbreaks through the centuries.

Each of those devastations brought out the best and worst in people. At our best, we joined together to fight the diseases, support the victims, and protect the vulnerable. At our worst, we invented stereotypes and sought scapegoats. But most of all, those unimaginable tragedies gave us a vision for the human capacity to heal the world. How? It's all about *prepared minds*. I'll begin with the story of a little-known Hungarian physician, Ignaz Semmelweis.

From the 1600s through the 1800s, death of women in childbirth approached 25 percent, with most of the fatalities due to an infection known as "puerperal fever." In 1847, Dr. Semmelweis made the startling observation that the death rate among women under the care of physicians in lying in hospitals (obstetric facilities) was many-fold higher than the death rate among women cared for by midwives at home or on midwife wards. His even more astonishing finding was that midwives routinely washed their hands between patients whereas doctors didn't. When Semmelweis instituted anti-septic techniques in lying-in hospitals, the infection and death rate among women in labor fell by 90 percent. Prior to Semmelweis, the need for sterile techniques in hospitals was unknown—doctors routinely moved from one patient in labor to another, performing frequent pelvic examinations, without washing their hands. It took more than 99.999 percent of human existence before hand washing became a known preventative of disease. And yet, finally, we got it. Although it should be mentioned that the physicians of the day didn't get it. They rejected and ridiculed Semmelweis, refusing to believe they were themselves responsible for their patients' deaths, not understanding how hand washing could possibly make a difference. It wasn't until Louis Pasteur proved the germ theory of infection, fifteen years after Semmelweis proposed hand washing, that the medical community belatedly accepted Semmelweis's theory about the need for sterile technique and antisepsis to prevent transmission of germs from one patient to another. Semmelweis died in a sanitarium, driven to madness by his colleagues' derision and renunciation of him. As I wrote earlier, I believe we are educable, but it isn't easy.

At the turn of the twentieth century, tens of thousands of workers died during the construction of the Panama Canal and Panama railway. In 1904, Dr. William C. Gorgas was appointed head of the Canal Zone Sanitation Commission and was among the first to recognize that it was mosquito transmission of Yellow Fever and malaria that was the main cause of the workers' deaths. For his achievements, saving many thousands of lives by instituting dramatic hygienic measures—including draining the massive mosquito breeding swamps surrounding the Canal Zone, fumigation, installing fresh water systems, and introducing mosquito netting—he was named surgeon general of the United States in 1914 by President Woodrow Wilson but not before enduring widespread criticism and scorn by those who didn't accept his mosquito theory.

On September 28, 1928, Scottish physician-scientist Alexander Fleming made an unlikely discovery, due to a laboratory accident, that would change medicine and the course of human history forever. He noticed that mold spores, which apparently blew into his lab from an open window, had taken hold and grown on petri dishes (flat round test tubes) where he was conducting experiments on bacteria. The bacteria colonies nearest the mold spores died, whereas the bacteria farthest away from the mold continued to thrive. Fleming hypothesized that something secreted by the mold had killed the bacteria. He subsequently identified that substance as penicillin, named such because the mold was a *Penicillium* species. That chance discovery was truly a modern medical miracle. Prior to penicillin, for example, more soldiers died of infection in World War I than of battlefield injuries. In the decades since the discovery of penicillin and newer antibiotics, infection deaths in every venue have plummeted. How fortunate (miraculous?) that Fleming, like Semmelweis and Gorgas before him, had the intellect and intuition to observe, interpret, and respond to the circumstances confronting him.

Seventy-five years before the fateful gust of wind and before Alexander Fleming was even born, Louis Pasteur, the "father" of microbiology who introduced the germ theory of disease, predicted how miraculous discoveries of the future would be made. In a speech given in 1854, Pasteur famously said, "In the field of observation, chance favors the prepared mind." That is the "antidote" I mentioned earlier—the *prepared mind*. The fortuitous discovery by Fleming, a man with a prepared mind, changed human history and, literally, helped heal the world. Eloquently exemplifying Key #1 *No Regrets Living*, Alexander Fleming deferred to powers greater than his, simply saying, "I did not invent penicillin. Nature did that. I only discovered it by accident."[31]

One final vignette. The disease known as paralytic poliomyelitis (polio) has been recognized as early as ancient Egyptian hieroglyphics. Outbreaks of polio first occurred in the early twentieth century, but it wasn't until President Franklin Roosevelt developed the disease in 1939 that public awareness, and fear, of the disease also reached epidemic proportions. In 1952, the polio epidemic in the United States numbered nearly 58,000 cases, of which 3,145 patients died and 21,269 were left with permanent paralysis. Although limited use of immunization against other diseases, such as smallpox, began as early as the eighteenth century, a large-scale immunization program wasn't possible until scientists at Boston Children's Hospital developed a technique for growing viruses in test tubes filled with cells. This cell culture technique allowed for the development of polio vaccines by Jonas Salk and Albert Sabin. The last reported case of poliomyelitis in the United States, following years of mass immunizations, occurred in 1979. Years earlier, Debbie, a middle school friend of mine, was one of the last children in Colorado tragically paralyzed by the polio virus; she became infected just before the oral vaccine, given as a small red drop on a sugar cube, was available for millions of children across the country.

One of the unfortunate and unforeseen, but understandable, effects of the COVID-19 pandemic was the decline in numbers of patients obtaining routine health and dental care and undergoing elective surgical procedures. Patients avoided clinics and hospitals for fear of increased exposures to the coronavirus. A number of studies even found the incidence of heart attacks fell by almost half during the pandemic—perhaps also due to avoidance of medical facilities by patients who otherwise would have sought evaluation (although a more sanguine explanation offered by some was that isolating at home reduced stressful triggers of heart attacks).

Most ironic of all, as the world desperately awaited the development of an effective vaccine to protect against COVID-19, routine childhood immunizations for polio and other preventable diseases dramatically decreased as parents shunned doctors' offices. The result: half or more of all young children fell behind on their vaccination schedules. The value of a vaccine for COVID-19 should remind all parents of the value of vaccines for all the diseases we have successfully prevented for decades.

During the pandemic, COVID-19 vaccines were developed faster than any other vaccines in history and, sadly, like so much else during the pandemic, became a political issue. Politicians undermined the safety and efficacy of a COVID-19 vaccine even before clinical studies were complete and a vaccine approved for use. The effect was profound—early surveys showed that fewer than half of the population would take a vaccine when it became available.[32]

Even worse, undermining the COVID-19 vaccine for political gain threatened the acceptance of *all* vaccines—if a COVID-19 vaccine can't be trusted, why should other vaccines be trusted? Why should the FDA or CDC or WHO be trusted—maybe they have political motives? Vaccines have saved millions of lives for the past seventy-five years. They are a miracle of modern medicine, a vital matter of health and safety, and must never again be turned into a political issue.

Polio has now been eradicated in most of the world. Once again, it took more than 99.999 percent of human history before we learned the technique of vaccination to prevent deadly diseases. But we did finally learn. Again, as in the era of Semmelweis and Gorgas, there are those who today refuse to accept medical advances, in this case the safety and efficacy of vaccines. So called anti-vaxxers refuse to have their kids vaccinated, hence the resurgence of measles and other preventable life-threatening diseases. But don't get me started . . .

The COVID-19 pandemic, caused by a novel coronavirus, is the most recent example of humankind's ability to heal. Coronaviruses are well known—they are one of the leading causes of the common cold. But the COVID-19 coronavirus strain is much more potent than those causing common colds, particularly for the elderly and those with underlying medical conditions. COVID-19 has taught us much about the power of our prepared minds. Within days of the first reports of widespread cases, diagnostic tests were already being developed and quickly distributed across the globe. There were criticisms that the development and distribution could have been even more efficient, and the early versions of the tests had flaws, but, for perspective, consider this: Following the recognition of the first cases of HIV-AIDS in the early 1980s, it took years for the virus cause to be identified and the first reliable diagnostic test to be developed. Years! (See the story of Jonathan in Key #7.)

But AIDS prepared us for COVID-19, just as polio and other virus battles helped prepare us for AIDS. It's because of what we painfully learned from AIDS that not only were COVID-19 diagnostic tests available in mere days, candidate vaccines and potential treatments for the virus were in development mere weeks after the first cases were recognized. AIDS schooled us about identification, diagnosis, prevention, and treatment of all virus infections. As a result, our handling of subsequent virus crises has been dramatically improved. Thought of another way, the tragedy that was, and continues to be, HIV-AIDS has guided the prepared minds of science and medicine toward protecting society from the worst case scenarios that could have resulted from Ebola virus, SARS (also caused by a coronavirus), MER (caused by yet another coronavirus), Swine Flu (H1N1), and now COVID-19. And the same science that we learned from HIV-AIDS directly led to a cure (CURE!) for hepatitis C, the first chronic virus infection ever to actually be completely eradicated from infected patients. When all is said and done, and as we continue to improve our handling of viral epidemics and pandemics, the lessons from HIV-AIDS will surely have saved more lives than the disease has taken. Let me repeat that, ultimately, although at a catastrophic price, HIV-AIDS will have resulted in more lives saved than it has taken. Again, from the most immediate experience, the death toll from COVID-19 would have been immeasurably higher were it not for the lessons in diagnosis, prevention, and treatment learned from HIV-AIDS. Prepared minds in action.

History has also taught us that pandemics always end—either because of human actions to limit them or because the germs lose steam, run into unfavorable seasonal conditions, or run out of susceptible humans. Pandemics end, but so far, the world, thankfully, hasn't ended due to any pandemic. And as with HIV-AIDS, humans have gotten smarter as a result of each pandemic. What will be the most important lessons learned from this pandemic? COVID-19 must teach us the importance of preparedness, of anticipating worst case scenarios. Not only must we be better prepared for the next pandemic, and there will be one, but, importantly, this experience must also teach us to be better prepared for any potential bioterrorism attack. Had this been a bioterrorist attack, with intentional and simultaneous release of virus in multiple places across the world, the devastation would have been unimaginable.

COVID-19 was a painful teacher. But if we learn from it to better prepare ourselves for future crises, the pain will not have been for naught. During the early weeks of the pandemic, the difficulty ramping up with needed personal protective equipment (masks, gloves, face shields), ventilators, and hospital beds, particularly in the hardest-hit and most populous parts of the country, will be a reminder for all future governments to be proactive rather than reactive in protecting the health of their countries and communities. But I hope we will also have learned crucial economic and societal lessons. More about those to follow.

I believe those same prepared minds, which Pasteur so eloquently described as having the capacity for profound discovery, are ultimately the route to preventions and cures of *all* medical *and* societal diseases. Take clean water, for example. Within the past 150 years, the United States and the developed world have learned the benefits of water sanitation systems to provide safe drinking water. Yet in much of the developing world, safe drinking water is still lacking. The World Health Organization estimates that safer water could prevent 1.4 million child deaths from diarrhea, 500,000 deaths from malaria, and 860,000 child deaths from malnutrition each year around the world. An additional 10 million people could be protected from incapacitation by parasitic diseases. The horrible example of lead-contaminated water in Flint, Michigan, brought the issue very close to home. We know what's needed; now, we must apply our prepared minds to determine how to overcome the geopolitical and financial obstacles to provide it. The same minds that have evolved to communicate in nearly seven thousand different languages must now learn to communicate with one another toward the common global good.

I'm an infectious diseases doctor, hence, the selection bias in the examples I have given of the human capacity for curing and eradicating disease, but let that not be to the exclusion of the astounding advances in the treatment and prevention of heart disease, cancer, and genetic, metabolic, and other once seemingly incurable diseases, also within the past century.

Many of the most impactful advances in healing have come, not from the laboratory or the clinic, not from clinicians caring for individual patients, but from brilliant epidemiologists, experts using their prepared minds to analyze entire populations of people. Epidemiologic studies have taught us, among a panoply of other discoveries, that: smoking causes cancer; high cholesterol is a risk for heart disease; aspirin during certain childhood infections causes Reye's syndrome (severe brain damage); sleeping on their bellies increases babies' risk of Sudden Infant Death Syndrome (SIDS); air pollution worsens respiratory diseases; asbestos exposure causes lung cancer and other pulmonary diseases; radiation causes skin, bone marrow, and other cancers; lead pollution causes brain damage in children; the drug thalidomide used in pregnancy causes birth defects as does drinking alcohol, whereas folic acid prevents birth defects. Those discoveries, by prepared minds using statistical analyses of huge collections of health data, have resulted in dramatic changes in how we live and how long we live.

The COVID-19 pandemic raises new epidemiologic questions and highlights older mysteries of medicine that have yet to be solved. What determines vulnerability to the coronavirus infection? Why are some demographic and socioeconomic groups so much more susceptible to infection and severe disease? Why do underlying diseases like obesity, high blood pressure, and diabetes predispose patients to more severe COVID-19 disease and death? How can we reduce the number of people with those underlying diseases? Is access to adequate healthcare actually the greatest determinant of outcome to COVID-19?

At the root of these epidemiologic questions is the need for determining the co-factors that underlie disparities in disease and death. That knowledge will lead to much more than simply a better understanding of pandemics and viruses—it will lead to greater insight into all of medicine, propelling us further upward along the asymptotic arc I described earlier. Toward healing the world.

Whence came the ingenuity and creativity to recognize health challenges and crises and respond with reasoned, methodical approaches to solving them? Humans have pushed the boundaries of medicine further in the past few generations than any of our great-great-grandparents could have imagined. How did that happen? And what does the future hold for new advances. How great is our capacity to prevent, heal, cure…and eradicate? How magnificent will the discoveries of our children's and grandchildren's generations be? And if that's true for medicine, what of other societal imperatives? Don't we have the capacity to prevent death and destruction from other causes?

Because of HIV-AIDS, the research funding for virus diseases, their prevention and therapy, dramatically increased, as did our scientific knowledge. But the lasting lessons learned from the HIV-AIDS pandemic went far beyond simply the scientific and clinical ones. We learned about the destructive pain caused by discrimination, about unfounded fear, about false narratives claiming causes and cures. HIV-AIDS taught us about the need to improve our delivery of healthcare, especially to the underserved. And AIDS also taught us new ways of thinking about marriage and family.

So, beyond the medicine and virology, what lasting societal and social lessons will we have learned from the COVID-19 pandemic? Here's what I hope we will have learned:

- There is no more important role for government than protecting the health, safety, and welfare of its citizens.
- Coordination among federal, state, and local governments is critical and must be systematically improved.
- Government must be more transparent and less political in managing a crisis.
- Childcare and eldercare are among the most at-risk necessities during a crisis, any crisis, and we need enhanced safety nets for them.
- The most vulnerable in our society must be protected, not just from pandemics, but from what Pope Francis called our "throwaway culture" mentality, our disregard and disrespect for those felt to no longer be useful: the homeless, the mentally ill, the disabled, and the elderly.
- Vital government systems for a stable economy—including unemployment insurance, payroll protection, and small business loans—must be modernized and better funded.

- Internet capacity, capability, and access must be upgraded to better handle the needs of all members of society during a crisis.
- Voting rights and the integrity of the voting process must be protected at all times, but especially when going to the polls may be dangerous or impossible.
- Our national budget must be re-prioritized; among our highest priorities should be:
  - ✓ Creating an emergency response paradigm for future pandemics or bioterrorism attacks
  - ✓ Funding for basic research into: treatment of infectious diseases; determinants of the resistance of germs to treatments; novel immunity-boosting approaches
  - ✓ Building stockpiles of equipment and supplies by creating a Strategic Health Reserve similar to our Strategic Petroleum Reserve
  - ✓ Improving lives in our underserved communities
- Increase appreciation and respect for quality, peer-reviewed science and the scientists who do it (while disregarding the scams and purveyors of snake oil).
- Incentivize private industry to develop treatments and vaccines for which there may be no profit motive, yet great public need.
- When people act in unity and solidarity for the common good, lives are saved.

Although the proverbial cow is out of the barn for *this* pandemic, there will be other cows and other barns in our future. As with HIV-AIDS, with the time to reflect and be proactive rather than reactive, we should find ways for the COVID-19 pandemic to move us forward as a society. Time to again mobilize our prepared minds and keep the trend line of society's progress moving upward.

NATURAL DISASTERS

In 2004, one of the largest earthquakes ever recorded occurred in the Indian Ocean, triggering a monster tsunami that killed more than 225,000 Indonesians. That horrific number is dwarfed by the 3 to 4 million people killed in the Yangtze River floods in China in 1931. The same river flooded again four years later, killing yet another 135,000 people. The 2010 earthquake in Haiti killed an estimated 160,000 people. Since the beginning of recorded history, earthquakes, cyclones, hurricanes, tsunamis, and floods have killed tens of millions of people. Between 1958 and 1961, 15 to 45 million people were killed by famine in China, and tens of millions more killed by famine throughout the world in the past century alone. Tens of thousands more by wildfires, landslides, avalanches, blizzards, heat waves, tornadoes, and volcanoes. Are these events simply the manifestations of natural laws or are they aberrations of them?

Eons of history have proven that natural disasters are embedded into the fabric of our planet. Like the flow of rivers to the oceans and the rise of mountains from tectonic shifts, natural disasters follow natural laws, laws established at the very beginning of our universe. Laws that scientists have studied and proven and upon which all modern scientific theory is based. In a planet with geology and a weather system like ours, earthquakes, tsunamis, floods, and all of the other natural sources of such great anguish are to be expected. However, over the past century, we have proven that humans' prepared minds have been uniquely empowered to predict and even prevent many of those disasters.

The impact of natural disasters on lives and property has decreased because we have gotten much better at responding to them and protecting against them. In 2012, China completed construction of the

Three Gorges Dam, the largest hydroelectric power generator in the world—and also a receptacle of Yangtze River flow. The dam is projected to prevent the tragic types of flooding that occurred on that river in the past (albeit at the cost of more than one hundred lives lost during the construction and hundreds of thousands of people displaced by the project). It is estimated that more than 15 million people (and 1.5 million acres of farmland) will be protected by the dam. On another front, the Pacific Tsunami Warning Center uses seismic data from earthquake recording to predict the possibility of tsunamis and issue alerts, which save lives. (Notably, although far advanced from just a few years ago, it's not a perfect system—the Indonesia tsunami of October 2018 occurred after a warning had been lifted following an earthquake that was not thought to pose a significant risk for tsunamis.) There is no reliable method of predicting major earthquakes—yet. And the US Geological Service does not foresee a breakthrough in earthquake prediction anytime soon.[33] Yet, once again, human ingenuity and prepared minds have come to the rescue. A massive 7.0 magnitude earthquake hit Anchorage, Alaska, on November 30, 2018. As a result of prior implementation of strict building codes, there was no loss of life, collapsed buildings, or widespread infrastructure damage. It is on that strategy that the USGS bases its earthquake mitigation work. In contrast, hurricane tracking systems have been very successful in saving lives of coastal and island dwellers over the past several decades, as have avalanche and tornado warnings. And, as with earthquakes, improved construction strategies have protected populations in high-risk hurricane areas that are socioeconomically able to implement them; less-developed countries lag behind, as evidenced by hurricane devastations in Haiti and Indonesia.

MAN-MADE ACCIDENTS

Every area of society is safer from man-made accidents today than it was a generation ago. Construction safety and building codes have reduced the risks of fire and structural failures, as previously noted. Seat belts, shoulder harnesses, airbags, rear and side cameras, and stronger car chassis have saved untold numbers of lives on the roads. The National Highway Traffic Safety Administration reports more than 300,000 lives saved by seat belts since 1975 (15,000 lives saved in 2017 alone), more than 10,000 young children's lives saved by car seats in the same period, and 50,000 lives saved by frontal airbags since 1987.[34] Commercial air travel is safer than ever before. The Aviation Safety Network reports that 2017 was the safest year for air travel ever, with fewer fatalities than both 2015 and 2016, which were the previous safest air travel years.[35] Sadly, within a five-month period from late 2018 to early 2019, 346 people were killed in twin tragedies resulting from crashes of the 737 MAX airliner, hopefully aberrations in an otherwise greatly improved air travel safety record. Our prepared minds have seen the harm that accidents cause and have tackled it with creative technological approaches. Yet technology has also brought new risks for accidents that must now be confronted by those same prepared minds—there are more opportunities today for distracted driving than in the days before cell phones and dashboard entertainment consoles. Perhaps driverless cars will someday eliminate those distraction risks, as well as accidents caused by speeding and DUIs. All told, we have more reason for hope than fear.

EVIL, AGAIN

Now, let's return to the question of evil and those who commit heinous crimes against humanity. I believe, like diseases, disasters, and man-made accidents, evil is preventable, perhaps even curable. Eradicable. The root causes of evil, like the root causes of heart disease and diabetes, will, I believe, be determined and addressed by society using our prepared minds. As a pediatrician, though, I can offer a head start in our search. Virtually every societal malady can be traced to childhood. The environment in which a child is born and raised is the single greatest determinant of that child's future as an adult—and his propensity for choosing to do good or evil. Of course there are exceptions, but, as a general rule, a child raised with love and kindness, a child taught tolerance and acceptance, a child witnessing ethical and charitable role models does not turn into Adolf Hitler. Our focus for scientific advances to heal the world, to prevent and someday eradicate evil, must start in the home where that disease starts and spreads from adult to child.

One of the essays in my *Miracles We Have Seen* book is the story of two three-year-olds, told by one of the foremost authorities on child abuse in the country, Dr. Richard Krugman. A brief excerpt:

> The lead story on the evening news was about a missing three-year-old. She and her four-year-old brother had been playing in their front yard on a warm August day when a car pulled up, the side door opened…and [she] got into the car. Her brother raced inside their home to get their parents, but by the time they all got back outside, the car and the little girl were gone. The police were called and for the next two days, they, her parents, and the community frantically searched for her.
>
> Two days later, the morning television shows were interrupted with breaking news. The girl had been found alive! Two birdwatchers walking in the foothills west of town—twenty miles from the front yard— heard what sounded like a child crying nearby. They followed the sound

to an outhouse in a campground and opened the door. Down at the bottom of the outhouse, in the waste well, a little girl was crouched in a corner, shivering. Miraculously, this particular outhouse had a leak and there was no fluid in the well. Had it not leaked, she surely would have drowned.

Now, more than thirty years after her kidnapping and attempted murder, this little girl is a happily married mother of three. She has her master's degree in counseling and a successful practice helping others. Many believe that if you were abused as a child, you will be an abuser. That turns out to not be true. More than two-thirds of abused children never repeat the cycle and many, like this remarkable three-year-old, do very, very well. However, in our experience, it is true that all abusers have themselves been abused in childhood. Our center psychiatrist interviewed the kidnapper. When he described his childhood…it was almost certain he was abused. Neighbors who lived on the same cul-de-sac he lived on told us that they recall him wandering from yard to yard as a little three-year-old, seemingly lost or looking to get away from his house. They told me they wished they knew then what they know now about child abuse and neglect so they could have reported the family in hopes of protecting the child.

The life trajectories of these two abused three-year-olds, who grew up a generation apart in our community and crossed paths one day in August, took them in very different directions. One went to prison, the other to a productive life helping others. One was lost to the vicious cycle of child abuse, the other miraculously saved by an unlikely convergence of Good Samaritans walking near a leaking outhouse.

These three-year-olds remind us of the fragility of childhood, and our collective obligation to work toward building a society that can better protect children from harm.

While evil is surely spread from adults to children, the converse can also be true—good can spread from children to adults. Here's yet one more infectious diseases analogy. Many severe infections in adults are caught from their kids who often don't get as ill as their parents with the same germ. Kids often contract these infections in schools (which is why school closures are among the first steps in containing a pandemic). For example, adults typically get sicker with chicken pox, hepatitis A, fifth disease (parvovirus), and coxsackievirus—infections that usually start with kids but affect adults more severely. Even common colds and flus are often worse in the adults who catch them from their kids.

So...what's the point? Goodness, kindness, compassion, and understanding can also potentially spread from kids to their parents—through education. Wisdom and values transmitted to kids in school can have a vital role in teaching parents via their kids. An extraordinary example:

In 1998, the middle school in a tiny mining town in Tennessee developed a program to teach its students about tolerance, focusing on the Holocaust. The kids learned that during the Holocaust many Norwegians wore paper clips on their lapels as a silent protest against the Nazis. The middle school students began a project to collect 6 million paper clips to better understand the magnitude of the Holocaust's devastation on the Jewish communities of Europe. The students in Whitwell, Tennessee (population approximately 2,000), were deluged with paperclips, including from Presidents George W. Bush and Bill Clinton, from countless celebrities, and from supporters and admirers around the world. Accompanying the paper clips, more than 30,000 letters of support and personal testimonials poured into the school; the counting of paper clips stopped when it reached 30 million! The project's impact was profound, with a book,[36] a documentary film,[37] an educational curriculum entitled "One Clip at a Time," which is taught around the world to fifth grade and higher students, and a unique monument to the 11 million victims of the Holocaust—Jews, gypsies, gays, and others—located, improbably, in Whitwell, Tennessee. Why improbably? Because at the time of the project's beginnings, there wasn't a single Jewish student in the Whitwell Middle School, nor a single Jewish resident of Whitwell (and by reports, there still isn't!). The monument includes, in addition to hundreds of artifacts of the Holocaust that have been donated, an actual Nazi railcar that had been used to transport prisoners to the extermination camps, into which the children poured 11 million paperclips. The project and its lesson of tolerance, like the infections I mentioned earlier that spread from kids to adults, spread like wildfire to the adult community of Whitwell and to adult communities throughout Tennessee, the United States, and the world. Children teaching tolerance and compassion to adults. Education spreading, like the flu, from the classroom to the kitchen table.[38]

While it is true that schools are often incubators for infectious diseases and school closures are among the very first steps in response to a pandemic, the COVID-19 pandemic reminded us not to take that measure lightly. In addition to the gap in kids' educations caused by school closures, it was clear that gaps in kids' nutrition, socialization, and overall health also occurred. School meal programs lapsed in many areas; the lack of home internet made even the admittedly inadequate opportunity for online socialization impossible for kids in the most vulnerable households; and studies showed increased incidences of domestic violence and decreased attention to kids' illnesses and to childhood vaccines. The partnership between parents and schools in providing for kids' needs was disrupted by the closing of schools. As a result, many experts in child education and child health urged reopening of schools as quickly and as safely as possible. In mid-summer, 2020, at one of the peaks of the pandemic, a joint statement from the American Academy of Pediatrics, the American Federation of Teachers, the National Education Association, and the School Superintendents Association noted:

"We recognize that children learn best when physically present in the classroom. But children get much more than academics at school. They also learn social and emotional skills at school, get healthy meals and exercise, mental health support and other services that cannot be easily replicated online. Schools also play a critical role in addressing racial and social inequity. Our nation's response to COVID-19 has laid bare inequities and consequences for children that must be addressed. This pandemic is especially hard on families who rely on school lunches, have children with disabilities, or lack access to internet or health care.

"Returning to school is important for the healthy development and well-being of children, but we must pursue re-opening in a way that is safe for all students, teachers and staff..."[39]

We have proven that the challenges posed by once-incurable diseases, pandemics, natural disasters, and man-made accidents are indeed surmountable by prepared minds with the capacity for scientific inquiry and profound discovery. We can work to heal the world. What exactly can each of us do?

ACTIVISM AND ADVOCACY

We can turn anxiety into activism. If we are not personally involved in research or implementation of steps to understand and solve the considerable remaining obstacles to a better world, we should support those institutions, charities, companies, and individuals that are. The options are endless because the needs are so great. More about giving and volunteering in Key #5 to follow, but as important as it is to give of our money and time, it isn't enough. The world needs us to become activists for the causes most important to us. Activism requires us to become knowledgeable enough about our "hot button" issues to know what kind of help is most needed, to provide that help, and to spread the word to others. The environment, homelessness, poverty, world hunger, voter rights, immigration, racism, childcare and education, minimum wage, equal pay, nuclear proliferation, child and domestic abuse, gun control, addiction, adoption, animal cruelty, capital punishment, women's rights, LGBTQ rights—what gets you most animated and motivated? Or maybe it's politics—getting the person or party elected that best speaks to your priorities and needs (or running for office yourself!). Do you feel strongly enough about your religion to be more involved in your house of worship or in national religious movements? What might you do to improve the quality of life in your city or your neighborhood? Are the national parks important to you, or perhaps your local parks, museums, and theaters? Raise money for your cause, march for your cause, lobby Congress for your cause. But whatever your cause, and, however you've determined is the best way to advocate for it, don't contribute to the troubles in society by advocating in a nonproductive or harmful way. Getting arrested makes for great headlines but doesn't accomplish much. Discourse and dialogue rather than disruption and disturbance. In the words of Reverend Martin Luther King Jr: "Nonviolence is a powerful and just weapon, which cuts without wounding and ennobles the man who wields it. It is a sword that heals."

It's often said that if you don't vote, you don't earn the right to complain. Voting is a form of activism—an easy way to make a difference. But I'll take that one step further: If you don't take the opportunity to work for a cause that's important to you, you haven't earned the right to complain about it. More important for Key #3 to *No Regrets Living*, if you *do* work for a cause that's important to you, you won't have regrets about not doing enough or trying hard enough.

The COVID-19 pandemic, and the societal inequities and deficiencies it exposed, generated widespread and diverse forms of activism. Among many other causes, advocates emerged, or re-emerged, for: universal healthcare; universal income; better disaster preparedness; improved childcare and eldercare; extended and expedited unemployment and small business support; debt relief; mortgage and rent relief; and increased funding for basic and medical research. The pandemic shined a spotlight on some of the most pressing challenges in society today. But how will we meet the next and most important challenge—continuing our activism and advocacy after the pandemic? If we fail in that challenge, the opportunity presented by this unprecedented crisis to advance along society's upward trajectory will have been lost.

KEY #4
APPRECIATE

THE FOURTH KEY to *No Regrets Living* asks that you take a few dedicated moments each day to reflect on what you are grateful for in your life. I guarantee you will surprise yourself at the length of your list.

GIVING THANKS ··································

My daily moments take the form of a reflective prayer, but yours should be anything you're comfortable with. The important part of these moments is that you take the time to recall the good things in your life. Although prayer for many people often involves requests, and I also make some of those, my prayer is more like meditation. It's a chance to pause in the midst of a day's chaos and choreography to focus on the positive. I say thanks for everything that happened during that day, that week, and all the times before. I say thanks for something that just happened a few minutes or hours before. It stuns me how much *new* in my life there is to be grateful for each day—and through those moments of reflection I'm able to slow down long enough to appreciate, quietly express that appreciation, and put life's disappointments and regrets into perspective. Regrets recall the negative, circumstances we wish could have been different, the "if onlys." But this daily reflection is one of gratitude for all that's right and good in life. Even on bad days, there are silver linings that comfort me when I recognize them. Without those brief pauses of gratitude, I find myself taking things for granted.

I give thanks for a healthy day and for the contentment and peace I experience in performing everyday tasks. Thanks for our parents and grandparents and great-grandparents who survived hardship and tragedy so that we could live in this remarkable country on this remarkable planet. Thanks for our children and grandchildren, the joys they bring and the challenges they teach us to meet. I give thanks for recovery from surgery or illness, even years after I or those I love have recovered. I give thanks for the ability to exercise, to see and hear, to smell and taste, to eat and drink, and even to excrete waste. I give thanks for waking up every morning (and lately a couple of times at night!). Gratitude for reaching my destinations safely and then returning home safely. Gratitude for my family reaching their destinations and then returning home safely. I say thanks for getting over colds and for healing cuts and bruises. Thanks for medicines and doctors who know how to use them. Thanks for allowing me to be one of those doctors and to have been allowed to help others over the years. Each day's gratitude is a little different based on events since the previous day. This is not traditional meditation during which the goal is to silence your thoughts, clear your mind, focus on breathing, and dismiss distractions. That's also a worthy daily exercise, but this meditation seeks quiet and laser-focused attention on the good.

I utter a short prayer of gratitude when I witness natural phenomena like beautiful sunrises and sunsets, rainbows, a full moon, an eclipse, a shooting star. I imagine the ancients' wonder at these phenomena, how they might have interpreted them as their gods being pleased or angry. When I'm in a beautiful outdoor setting, I often close my eyes for just a moment in gratitude for the natural wonder of our world.

You might be thinking, this sounds fine when life is good, but what about when we experience hardship? Ironically, minor adversities and even major tragedies can elicit gratitude as well. Recently a water main broke on our street and we were without water for several hours. I hadn't expressed gratitude for running water in a meditation or prayer for a very long time, but I did that day and for days afterward. While only a temporary inconvenience for me, I understood even more the desperation that devastating drought brings to many parts of the developing world, and then the request portion of my prayer during those days was for those people suffering for lack of water. Gratitude for the good things in our lives naturally elicits hope for those not as fortunate. Requests give me an action item to help cope with situations over which I have no real control. I keep a list in my wallet of people I know, or know about, who are in need of healing. I pull that list out at some point nearly every day and concentrate on the names with hope—and request—for their recovery. Putting names on the list gives me a role in their lives; I am with them, feeling their pain and suffering if only for a moment or two.

Not long after the water main break, a powerful snowstorm felled a neighborhood tree and left our block and two others without power for three days. Although the world has only known electricity for the short 140 years since Thomas Edison, so much in our lives is dependent on it. The outage brought a whole new appreciation of heat and electricity, of the internet and everything else we plug in. My daily reflections during the power outage included gratitude for Sara's dad, who lives a few blocks away where we could stay until power was restored. I was grateful for a warm home, something I took for granted too often in the past and, once again, I felt a deeper understanding of the suffering of those without electricity, a warm home, or a home at all. And that understanding serves as a call to action for me, additional motivation to give and to help.

Of course the water main break and the power outage I previously mentioned were nothing compared to the havoc in everyone's life caused by the COVID-19 pandemic. My appreciation for the everyday, mundane routines that were impossible during the outbreak was never greater, recalling for me the weeks following my heart surgery and the simplest tasks I could no longer do. Then, too, I craved normalcy and routine, but the postoperative immobility, pain, and painkillers were an ever-present reminder of why I had to refrain from my everyday activities. During the pandemic, thankfully I had no physical pain or immobility. But the restrictions again renewed my appreciation for our ability, during good times, to perform even the simplest errands and most menial chores, things I too often took for granted.

Each day during the pandemic, there was time for me to feel and express gratitude for all who were able to stay safe and healthy and maintain their livelihoods. And I gave thanks to all the heroes in our communities who made those things possible. There was also ample time, and ample cause, for making requests. Requests for healing of the pandemics' victims who were not as fortunate as me and my family to have escaped illness, and requests for comfort and condolence for those who lost loved ones. And there were some very novel requests, as well: more ventilators for those in need, more face masks and protective gear for healthcare workers, effective treatments, new vaccines, and, perhaps the most unique request I've ever made during my daily reflections—flattening of the curve!

A report in the *Wall Street Journal* titled, "The Science of Prayer," cited a study that found that more than half of all Americans prayed for the end of the COVID-19 pandemic. The report also described clinical research demonstrating both physical and emotional benefits of prayer. Among the findings, *spiritual* meditation was shown to have greater calming effects, relief of anxiety, and elevation of mood than *secular* meditation. Other studies found improved mental and physical health outcomes in people who pray to God as a partner rather than expressing anger to God or feeling punished by God. And praying for a spouse was found to improve marriages.[40]

A natural reaction to crisis is wanting to do something about it. Frozen in place by COVID-19 lockdowns and quarantines, prayer was for many, including me, a way to do something.

It may sound like I spend most of the day in prayer and meditation—I don't. My pauses for appreciation are usually quick, except when a special circumstance moves me for more intense concentration. In the rush of the day, my expression of gratitude is often as simple as a single word. I'll close my eyes for a moment and just whisper, "Thanks," as I get through a difficult or dangerous situation, see a beautiful sunset, finish a vigorous workout, or arrive home after a long commute. Or I whisper, "Please," when I'm confronted with a frightening or worrisome scenario, such as when someone dear to me is ill or injured (more in Key #7). There's time for more elaborate expressions of gratitude or for making requests later, but for now, a single word suffices, reminding me of the good and giving me hope during the not-so-good moments.

And here's the takeaway: During my daily review of gratitude for all that I have and all that I'm able to do, regrets about what I *don't* have or what I *wasn't* able to do diminish, and often even entirely disappear. That's why Key #4 for *No Regrets Living* is so important— it helps us live a life of wonder and contentment, a life in which we appreciate all that we have.

Envy

Envy is the flip side of appreciation, the dark side. Among the many gifts my mother gave me in my life, I believe the greatest was the lack of envy. I honestly don't think I've ever felt that emotion. I'm not blind, and of course I've admired the possessions others have, how others look, what others do. But I've never craved those things or felt resentment that others had what I didn't. I've never regretted not having more. If there's one legacy I could leave for my kids, it would be that gift their grandmother, my mom, gave to me. As a child of poor European immigrants, my mother was grateful for everything she had and worried that others would be *envious of her* for what she had. And she had very little. The few nice clothes in her closet were hand-me-downs from a dear aunt—and she hesitated to wear those clothes lest others be jealous. My mom always called herself "the luckiest girl in the world," and she felt that way—every minute of every day. I am blessed to have inherited that trait. I look at my life, my family, my home, and even our decades-old cars with 180,000 miles on them and feel like the luckiest guy in the world.

As an aside…To Sara's occasional chagrin, I inherited my mother's humble fashion sense as well. I had to go to a work-related black-tie event recently—I've never owned a tux, renting one when I've absolutely needed to, like for our kids' weddings. For this work event, I borrowed my youngest son's tux, which fit surprisingly well, and I was proud that I didn't need to spend the money to rent a tux for one evening. The pants were a little loose and I guess it's normal for tux pants to not have belt loops—so I did spend fourteen dollars on a pair of suspenders from Target, which I passed along to my son in case the pants ever get too loose for him.

Organized Religion

One traditional way to give thanks is through organized religious observance; all major religions incorporate gratitude in their prayer services. Although not necessary for *No Regrets Living*, I believe organized religion serves two potentially helpful purposes. First, religious observance can be a vehicle for self-discovery, providing defined times, places, and occasions for reflection. A discipline with which to facilitate prescribed moments of gratitude. Secondly, for some people and certain families, organized religion can be a tether to generations past. I certainly don't think one religion is any more "right" or "true" than any other. I like the Jewish rituals and traditions I grew up with because I know my parents and grandparents, and their parents and grandparents, observed them. For that reason, we raised our kids in the same tradition. Religious rituals also help me dissipate some of the regret I have for not knowing more about the generations that came before me—I do know they were religiously observant, and my observance of some of the same traditions gives me a connection I value.

Religious laws are trickier for me. Recalling my declaration of belief in both God and science, my belief in the Big Bang while also allowing for the possibility of God hearing my prayers, is it possible that the same God who does all of that cares whether I eat kosher food? Or whether I drive or walk to synagogue on Saturday? Or whether I go to synagogue at all? I don't really think God will punish me if I violate the Jewish laws of keeping kosher by eating a cheeseburger or lobster or pig products. But I don't eat cheeseburgers now because that's not how I grew up or what we did at home when our kids were young. Tradition, rather than Testament, guides my behavior regarding religious laws. I've tasted (and liked!) lobster and shrimp, but I usually avoid them. I accidentally had pork for the first time at a niece's wedding party (it tasted just like chicken!), but I've also intentionally tasted bacon and ham in the past. And, full disclosure, I used to binge McDonalds' cheeseburgers when I was a teenager and no one was looking (maybe my punishment is my high cholesterol . . .). Sabbath observance is central to Judaism and forbids driving from Friday sunset through Saturday sunset. But I think if Sabbath observance keeps families apart on a weekend when they could be together if only they could drive, they should drive. Family trumps observance of the Sabbath in my personal book of laws for *No Regrets Living*. Indeed, the religious Jewish laws were codified at a time when families lived within walking distance of one another and there were no cars. Today, without cars, many scattered families would rarely see each other. Although my observant mom never drove on the Sabbath, she always answered the phone on the Sabbath and initiated calls herself despite in every other way strictly following the laws that include prohibition of such behavior. She answered in case we called and called us when she was worried or missed us. For her, too, family trumped that particular Sabbath constraint and her compromise on that law helped me formulate my own level of observance.

But, having confessed to my lapses in observance, I think many religious laws are critically important, not because God will punish those who violate them but because they define moral and ethical behavior. Important not just for the survival of a particular culture but for the survival of society and humankind as a whole. In addition to introducing monotheism, Abrahamic law saved the world from the evils of other societies, pagan and organized religions alike. It codified humane treatment of animals and of our fellow humans. Yes, there are some arcane biblical laws that tell us to take an eye for an eye, for example, or to stone people for high crimes, but thankfully those are no longer practiced (some commentaries say they never really were). So I follow the big laws that make sense to me today, many of which also made sense in the past. For the sake of tradition and my family's cultural heritage, I observe some of the not-so-big laws as well. And with yet other laws and rituals, I make what I believe are reasonable compromises, as did my mother, albeit conscious that I am compromising for the sake of *No Regrets Living*. If not driving on the Sabbath means I would miss a weekend visit with my grandchildren, I'll drive. But I also respect those who don't drive; they are setting aside an entire day each week for quiet reflection and preserving a link to their heritage.

There is one aspect of orthodox religion—all orthodox religions —that I can't abide, and that's the treatment of women, an archaic remnant of a long ago and no longer relevant period of history. Orthodox Judaism prohibits women reading aloud from the Torah during services when men are present, or singing in front of men, or counting among the ten men needed for an official prayer minyan. Orthodox Catholicism bans women from the priesthood. Orthodox Islam conceals women inside burkas and prohibits them from driving. And those are just a few examples—women are second-class citizens in all of orthodoxy. I find it all reprehensible, and I can't believe the God who may have orchestrated the Big Bang nearly 14 billion years ago sees women as lesser than men. Each religion has its excuses for this antiquated sexist behavior, but none are acceptable to me. Those who say that religious laws are God-given, embedded in stone, inviolable and immutable, ignore the fact that in many, many other aspects of orthodox religious laws, deference has been given to modernity—but so far, not when it comes to women. My mother was never bothered by the role assigned to her by Orthodox Judaism; my daughter is very bothered by it, and I'm with her.

The COVID-19 pandemic made me aware of another aspect of organized religion I can't abide—the insistence by some on traditional observance regardless of the circumstances or the potential harm. In the face of social distancing directives across the country to slow the spread of the infection, most religious institutions adhered to government and health authorities' regulations and made accommodations for safe remote or virtual observance. But a number of congregations defied the orders and gathered in large numbers for prayer services. In my mind, those institutions (and they spanned all major religions) were no holier than the young people who flocked *en masse* to spring break beaches during the lockdown periods. The religion-above-all crowd and the college sun seekers put their own lives, and the lives of everyone they would subsequently come in contact with, at risk.

For those who observed the restrictions on large gatherings at the cost of not observing their communal religious rituals, there was reward in the sacrifice. Isolation in worship allowed for reconnecting with personal beliefs and personal relationships with God. Many who had habituated their prayers to the words in communal prayer books found their own words and their own voice. The quiet of isolation was, in its own way, spiritual. In a post-pandemic world, maintaining the individuality and personal connection of worship should be a goal, along with reconnecting with others in our houses of worship.

I've confessed to the liberties I personally take with religious law and ritual, and I've expressed my frustrations with certain aspects. But now I must admit an important caveat. Were every Jew to observe like I do, Judaism as a culture and the Jewish people would not have survived the past millennia and will not survive the future. The same is true for nonobservant or selectively observant members of any other faith. The continuity of religion and of culture depends on consistency and constancy. The classic parable about the old Jewish grandfather with the long, straggly, gray beard applies here. His many grandchildren were embarrassed by Zadie's appearance (you've read the term "*Zadie*" earlier—it's the Yiddish term of endearment for a grandfather, what I called my grandfather, and what my grandkids call me), and taunted by their friends about the "nest" under his chin and what might be living there. There was a particularly bad day of teasing at school, with classmates mimicking the old man's walk and stooped posture, gesturing as if they were stroking their beards down to their knees. Horrified that their beloved Zadie was seen that way, each grandchild independently came up with a plan. He or she would sneak into Zadie's room at night while he slept and snip off a small piece of the beard to make it just a little shorter, a little less weird looking. And so they did, one at a time, unbeknownst to one another until, by the morning, there was nothing left of Zadie's beard at all. As with Zadie's beard, if everyone snipped off the pieces of their religion and culture they find embarrassing or outdated, there would be nothing left. Since the beginning of organized religion, there has been a segment of each faith that has adhered strictly to laws and rituals, despite persecution (it is a disturbing irony that the most observant in every faith are often the most persecuted) and aggressive efforts at assimilating them from both internal and external forces. And it's that resistant and persistent segment that has assured the longevity that Judaism has experienced, as well as the successful survival of other religions.

If you practice one of the major religions, the decision between strict observance versus compromising for family or other reasons is a very personal choice. You should take the path you believe will lead to fewer regrets.

FAMILY

Family relationships are among life's greatest reasons for joy—and for regrets. Some family members make it easy to appreciate them, others not so much. Your role in your family is unique and special. The roles I play in my family, as I describe in the paragraphs to follow, are no more important or meaningful than the roles you

play in your family, but they are mine and, most of the time, I celebrate them. At other times, it's all I can do to tolerate family, but
tolerance of family is important, too. As you read a bit about my
family relationships, I hope you project your own into the narrative
and ask yourself how you might get greater joy from your family and
fewer regrets.

Child

My father's death nearly forty years ago, after thirteen months of
illness, had a profound impact on me, on my belief system, and on
my evolution in thinking about *No Regrets Living*. But the impact of
his death on my mom was even greater, leaving her a widow in her
early fifties. When her father, my grandfather (the aforementioned
Zadie), became a widower with my grandmother's death eight years
later, my mom was in her early sixties. That's when she became my
eighty-six-year-old grandfather's caregiver, chauffeur, and compan-
ion. I watched that relationship and learned from it. It wasn't easy
for either of them. My mom was too young to live the lifestyle of
an eighty-six-year-old, and my grandfather, stripped of his driving
privileges (by us), hated being dependent. Yet he was. They spent
so much time together and attended so many community events
together, those who didn't know them assumed they were a couple.
Healthy or not, that's how many European families handled aging.
My grandfather was physically and mentally strong enough to live
in his own apartment until he fell and broke his hip at age one hundred, but the apartment was across the hall from my mom's and he
spent most of his days in her place or joining her on her errands and
outings. He prepared his own breakfasts, but lunches and dinners
were across the hall at Mom's.

After my grandfather's death at 101, my mom remained independent for another ten years. We lived less than a mile from her and saw her often, but she drove, had social events with girlfriends, shopped on her own, kept her checkbook and credit card records, and was proud of all of it. Inevitably, though, time took its toll. As she entered her upper eighties, first her physical and then her mental faculties deteriorated, and as she declined, my responsibilities as a son dramatically increased. On her ninetieth birthday, as we gathered around her for cake and ice cream, she commented that she couldn't believe she was already eighty. We didn't correct her. Committed to fulfilling her wish to stay in her apartment of more than twenty years, Sara and I joked (without laughing) that we had put my mom in assisted living, but we were the assistants. From there it rapidly progressed to the even less funny joke that we had put Mom in a nursing home, but we were the nurses, again in her own apartment.

In an eerily parallel and almost simultaneous sequence of events, Sara's mom's Parkinson's disease accelerated, resulting in her physical and mental decline. Thankfully Sara's dad was well and able to provide much of my mother-in-law's care, but Sara still had a huge load with her mom—who lived less than a mile from us in the opposite direction from my mom. We were, truly, the sandwich generation, smack dab in the middle of our parents' homes and needs.

The choreography of coordinating our moms' care is a story known to many adult children caring for elderly parents. But it's an important part of *No Regrets Living* for those finding themselves in the caregiver role. When your parents are gone, what will you feel about your role in their declining years? Contentment or regrets?

I did the best I could for my dad when he fell ill many years ago also, but he had my mom as his primary caregiver and my sacrifice for him was mostly my time, worry, and prayers, combined with a lot of medical translation and liaising with his care team. For my mom, the needs were so much greater. Food, medicines, hygiene, transportation, caregivers, finances. I saw more of my mom in the bathroom than a son should have to see, but it was part of the job I assigned myself. Hours spent at her bedside at home and when she was admitted to the hospital or rehab facilities, looking at bed sores and inflamed joints, at bruises from the latest falls and struggling with her dentures, which some days fit and other days not so much. At the same time, a few blocks in the other direction from our home, Sara was doing the same for her mom, minus the dentures. Our stimulating dinner conversations revolved around weighty issues like when to go to Costco for more Depends and Ensure, who's driving to the next day's doctor appointments, and how to make our mothers' bathrooms safer from falls.

My mom and I had come full circle, now with me doing for her in old age as she had done for me as a young child. The most powerful epiphany of what her life, and mine, had become came when I was wheeling her home from synagogue services one Saturday morning and a man I recognized from the community, but didn't know well, came jogging after us. "Hi, I'm Dr. F, and I was watching you take care of your mom. I once took care of your grandfather in the hospital and saw how beautifully your mom took care of him. You are her reward for everything she did for her dad." I still choke up when I think of that exchange. Whenever I see that physician now that my mom has died, I am reminded of how grateful I am to him for noticing and for reminding me that what I was doing for my mom was part of a legacy of family love. I'm also grateful to him because my mom heard, really heard what he said about her care for her father. Like many elderly parents, she desperately wanted to not be a burden. She often resisted our trying to take her places, help her with housekeeping and cooking, and, most of all, help financially. But by Dr. F reminding her of how thoroughly committed she was to caring for her father, she was jolted into seeing herself in the cycle of life, now in need of help rather than being able to provide it for another. That was a reminder we tried to give her often, but it meant much more coming from someone on the outside who had seen her in action. Caring for our mothers became the hardest task Sara and I have ever had to perform, but, just as my mom's devotion to her elderly father left her with no regrets about not doing more for him during his life, we think Dr. F helped her understand that we wanted to feel the same. Now that both our moms have died, we are grateful that we do feel that way.

> The role reversal we experienced with our parents, needing to parent them in their old age, took an eye-opening turn for Sara and me during the COVID-19 pandemic. We observed, with a mixture of terror and gratitude, our kids beginning to think of us as being in need of being watched over much as we had watched over our parents. Our son and daughter-in-law were shut in at home with their three young kids, our grandkids. Preschool for their kids had been canceled and both our son and daughter-in-law were trying to work from home. Hoping to give them a little reprieve and quiet time, I texted to invite them to drop their kids at our house to play for a few hours. No response until that evening when all three of our kids and their spouses conference called us—and read us the riot act about taking care of ourselves to prevent getting infected. Sara and I, they pointed out, are both in high-risk groups and having our grandkids at our house would put us in potential danger. They promised to use technology to keep connected to our grandkids, and they did —with FaceTime and Zoom. (I try to keep up with

technology, but I hadn't even heard of Zoom before the pandemic!)

Their schooling us didn't stop there. We then got lectures about not leaving the house, about allowing our kids to shop for us. We negotiated going on outdoor walks, just the two of us, but they agreed only if we wore face masks and kept far away from others. They prefaced the instructions with, "It's a bit awkward telling an infectious diseases doctor how not to get infected, but after getting your text, we feel we have to. Now go wash your hands." After catching my breath, I told them they were better infectious diseases doctors than me and that was a perfect example of why a doctor shouldn't be his own doctor. And then I reminded our kids that just because we're letting them parent us this time, they shouldn't get used to it. Although the time will undoubtedly come, as it did for us with their grandparents, we're not ready for a complete role reversal quite yet.

Parent

The innate paranoia I would have anyway felt about my kids' health, had I chosen any other profession, was greatly exacerbated by my career as a pediatrician caring for the sickest patients in the hospital. By the time we had our youngest child, nearly every terribly ill patient I cared for was the same age as one of our kids—or an age at which I could easily project an image of our kids in the near future. With each fever or rash in our three kids, I imagined terrible diagnoses. There was the memorable case of our oldest child at age two years suddenly refusing to walk and crying whenever we tried to stand him up. Assuming the worst, I convinced his pediatrician to x-ray his feet (normal) and do blood tests (normal). The pediatrician noticed us struggling to get his shoes on after his exam, something I ascribed to pain in his feet. Nope. The shoes were too small, and the cure came not at the pharmacy but in the shoe store.

Next, I was one of the investigators in the largest pediatric trial of a potential new medicine for chickenpox, seeing hundreds of kids with the illness to confirm their diagnosis before randomizing their treatment to the new medicine or placebo. Despite that almost unparalleled experience, I misdiagnosed each of my own kids as having chickenpox when they had unrelated rashes. Meningitis, a severe and potentially lethal infection of the coverings of the brain, which I treated frequently as an infectious diseases physician, was one of my constant fears. More than once we rushed one of the kids to the emergency room with a high fever, me almost certain it was meningitis. One trip resulted in our son vomiting in the car and immediately feeling better and cooler; we turned around and came home. On another occasion I told Sara I thought our other son had a stiff neck (a potentially very serious sign of meningitis). In the back seat of the car on the way to the hospital, Sara took a package of gummy bears from her purse and held the gummies above our son's head, and then down toward his feet. He moved his neck just fine tracking the gummies, no sign of stiffness when a gummy bear was at stake, and again we turned the car around. It was episodes like those that finally convinced me to let Sara be in charge of all future medical decisions regarding our kids.

Although being a pediatrician made me a more neurotic father, being a father made me a much more conscientious and thoughtful pediatrician. I was able to treat the parents of my patients like compatriots, sharing a bunker in the battles of child-raising. Not only had I been through, with my own kids, many of the common problems parents brought their kids to me to evaluate, but their worries about their kids resonated deeply with me.

Parenthood also forced me to reassess my life goals and my career trajectory. By the time we had kids, my career as a clinician-scientist was taking off. My research on virus diseases was published widely and noticed. As my star rose in the very, very small firmament that is my specialty, the invitations for the honor of my presence increased: keynote speeches, advisory boards, prestigious panels, exotic meeting locations, all-expenses-paid trips with notes saying, "Please bring your wife if she can get away." With small kids at home, Sara was rarely able to get away. Success was intoxicating; it was nice to be recognized and admired by peers. I told myself my kids were still little and sleeping for most of the time I was out of town. Sara caught me up on the milestones I missed.

As the kids turned five, three, and almost one, they weren't sleeping as many hours as they did when they were younger, and they were starting to have experiences they would remember—in kindergarten and preschool, at playdates and Gymboree—without me. T-ball was starting in a month for our five-year-old, and our three-year-old's hair was just long enough for her first pigtails. The baby was walking —running really—to keep up with his brother and sister. I tried to keep up, too. To know their friends' and teachers' names, what they liked best on TV (how badly do I date myself if I tell you it was *Barney*?). But even when I was home and they were animatedly telling me about their day, my mind wasn't with them. Instead, I was thinking about the next colloquium I had to prepare, the next flight I had to catch, or the call I should make to a colleague to discuss the seminal lecture I would be giving in Scandinavia. It was during our middle child's third birthday party that I had my fateful Dorian Gray moment. I was filming my kids running around in party hats with ice cream cake on their cheeks. As I filmed my daughter opening her presents, I had a stark vision of my future, but I didn't look like me; I looked like Rick, Mike, and James.

Rick, Mike, and James were real people, colleagues I knew from my hotshot meetings, established megastars in their universes of influence. Million-Milers! There wasn't a major meeting in my field without one or more of the MMs on the dais. In the lounges after the meetings, they regaled us with travelogues; they had been everywhere and seen it all. For small talk, they compared frequent-flier mile accumulations and upgrades, and chirped about the extra legroom or flat-bed seats afforded them. Rick had trouble remembering if his second child was in tenth or eleventh grade but worried that his oldest, a college freshman, was probably drinking a little too much, as she did in high school when she got a DUI. Mike's three teenagers were estranged from him since he left them and their mother back east to move west for a big promotion. He was confident his kids would reconcile with him when they were old enough to understand adult responsibilities, and that they would grow to like his new wife. James's divorce came with a brutal custody battle. His wife made wild accusations about his extracurricular activities on the road, some of which I was witness to.

With a vivid and terrifying vision of becoming Rick, Mike, or James, and regretting terribly the time I had already missed with my kids, I stopped filming the birthday party and started really seeing it. I realized a few very important things: I liked hearing my kids tell me their adventures better than I liked hearing those of the MMs. I liked sleeping at home with Sara better than alone in a luxurious hotel room that I could only describe to her by phone. I liked hearing my baby giggle better than hearing polite applause from colleagues in a far-off ballroom. I wanted to be at my son's first T-ball game. Heck, I wanted to coach his team.

That was the day I grounded myself. Not all at once, of course. I still had commitments and obligations to fulfill. But I learned to say no, and I learned to be a lesser player. I was fortunate that my job didn't require the travel or the renown—those were merely accoutrements of my success. I could still earn a living and sleep at home, as long as my ego would survive a cut in prestige. I asked myself these questions: How much status and stature do I need? How much do I need to know my kids? How much do they need to know me? And, how much of their lives am I willing to miss during all those hours on the tarmac? The answers changed my life. Even though I lost my premier executive status with the airline and gave up the extra legroom, I gained something more precious—time with my kids that I'll always be grateful for, without the regrets that would have haunted me about their fleeting childhoods (thus begat my *No Regrets Parenting* book).[41]

And yes, I did end up coaching T-ball and continued coaching all the way up through my kids' high school teams.

Parenting during the COVID-19 pandemic changed dramatically. With tens of millions of kids forced out of school due to closures, parents had to find new and creative ways to provide at-home care, education, and entertainment. For those parents lucky enough to be able to work from home, juggling work time with play time was their biggest challenge. For many parents who had to leave home for work, identifying safe (in all the usual ways *and* safe from infection) care for their kids became an even more difficult challenge. Although kids themselves generally did not develop severe infection with the coronavirus, the fear that they would become infected and transmit the germ to their parents or grandparents was very real. Tens of thousands of online sites popped up almost overnight to help parents, those who were fortunate enough to have online access, amuse and edify their kids during the long hours at home.

The ingenuity of parents in coping with these stresses was further evident in the hundreds of millions of social media posts describing the chaos, confusion, creativity, and coping mechanisms the pandemic brought into their homes. Those social media memoirs and memes will serve as a legacy of humankind's—and especially parents'—ability to adapt to just about anything. As I wrote in the *No Regrets Parenting* book, time with young kids is priceless and finite, so despite the hassles and hardships of parenting during the pandemic, I doubt parents will ever regret the bonus time they had with their kids. However, the lasting impact of the pandemic on children remains to be seen, and the resulting challenges for parents have yet to be fully realized. In the months and years following the pandemic, parents will have to deal with the emotional and psychological repercussions on their toddlers and school-age kids of wearing masks and repeatedly hearing the fearful terms "coronavirus," "COVID," and "pandemic" as explanations for the denial of hugs and kisses from friends and loved ones. Parents will be confronted with the long-term effects on school-age kids and tweens of being deprived socialization in school, camps, and sports activities. And parents will also be tasked with helping their adolescents—already a demographic with good reasons for, and high incidence of, anxiety—recover from the pandemic's threats to their way of living and to their very lives.

Grandparent

Watching our son become a father was like nothing I had ever experienced in my life. As he and his wonderful wife held their newborn, I was overwhelmed with the power of fate (Key #5, to follow) and I stood there, in awe, rewinding my life to that point.

Of course, I felt great joy and wonderment at the births of our three kids, but the whirlwind of those hectic days blurred the big picture. So consumed were we with diapers and cribs and rashes and nursing and worrying about what's normal and what's not for a newborn (yes, I'm a pediatrician, but as I indicated earlier, that makes things even worse in the worry department), the history and circumstances that brought us to parenthood got a little lost in the commotion. Not so for becoming a grandparent. With the sanguinity and calm of being able to step back, watch our son experience with his son what we experienced with him, and leave the diapering to the new mother and father, I was able to reflect on the extraordinary sequence of events that produced this beautiful new life.

My father met my mother when he arrived from Europe after the war. As I mentioned previously, after liberation from the concentration camp, my dad contracted tuberculosis and was treated in a Czechoslovakian hospital. He had hoped to immigrate to Israel, but instead was sent to Denver. Mom was working with a resettlement organization helping the new immigrants find housing and work. Growing up in a home with immigrant parents, she spoke fluent Yiddish, the common language among most of the Jewish newcomers, making her the perfect translator. She always joked that because she was the first to greet many of the immigrants, she had her pick of the best-looking men. Without my dad's tuberculosis, my parents might never have met, but because they met, I came into this life. Sara's parents met in the cafeteria at Brooklyn College. They were each with a friend, and the friends knew each other so they all sat together. Sara's mom had a tuna sandwich and her dad hadn't had lunch, so her mom split her tuna sandwich with this stranger, the friend of a friend's friend, and a few years later Sara came into this life.

And then Sara and I met, in a most fateful way (story to follow), and we had our first child. And then a family immigrated to the United States from Denmark and enrolled their daughter in the school our son attended, and they met. How our daughter-in-law's parents met is yet another remarkable example of fate, Scandinavian style. And now we have a grandchild. And soon along came another, and another. Equally magnificent testimonies to serendipity and fate. Just like every family, everywhere has a history marked by serendipity and fate. My story of becoming a grandfather is no more remarkable or fateful than anyone else's. Great-grandparents have children who become grandparents who have children who become parents. Since the beginning of the human race, a universal truth of biology and genetics. But standing there, emotionally unpacking our family's history, stunned me in a way I hadn't imagined even with the birth of our own kids. How many thousands— no millions, tens of millions—of inflection points, flaps of butterfly wings, along the way through our family's history might have gone a different direction and this child, this most unique and cherished little baby, would not be here, in his parents' arms as he was that day of his birth.

Becoming a grandfather, I watched that little baby open his eyes and see the world for the first time, a world of which he was the product and the future, the result of hundreds of generations of fateful events without which he wouldn't exist and about which he'll know little. And I took a few moments to ponder what his existence will mean for the future of our family, of our world? How he might be part of a greater plan beyond our ability to imagine. What will happen downstream when he flaps his wings someday?

The hundreds of thousands of people around the world who died during the COVID-19 pandemic each represented not only a lost life but a lost *line of lives*. The little baby our son and daughter-in-law held in their arms is the descendent of four grandparents, eight great-grandparents, and sixteen great-great-grandparents. Some of those great-grandparents and great-great-grandparents survived the Holocaust or pogroms in Russia. All sixteen great-great-grandparents, when they were children or teenagers, survived the influenza pandemic of 1918. But what if they hadn't? What if that deadly pandemic a century ago, so much deadlier than COVID-19, had taken the life of even one of those sixteen great-great grandparents? This precious new life we were blessed to witness would not have come into existence. So many precious *future* new lives were lost to COVID-19.

The irony of the epic history that precedes the birth of every baby is that until now, most of those babies knew little of whence they came. The fortunate ones, raised in a close family structure, know their parents and often their grandparents. But great-grandparents? Or great-great-grandparents? Back in the "old country," wherever that was for each family, generations of family were born, grew up, and died within walking distance of one another. Children not only knew their grandparents but knew where their grandparents were born—which street, which house, which bedroom. I knew my great-grandmother on my mother's side because she followed two of her children to Denver from Europe in her older age. I never knew her husband, my great-grandfather, and certainly not her parents. But whereas actually knowing them when they lived two hundred years ago would have been impossible, I could have known about them. Had I asked. Had my mother or grandmother told me. Why don't we share those histories with our kids? Too busy? Too distracted by the choreography of each day and each year? Too focused on today's worries and on future generations to learn more about the past? In some lucky families there is an archivist or unofficial historian who makes it his or her mission to delve into the past, into lineage and heritage beyond the immediate past generation or two.

In this way, the advances in technology and science have given us an unprecedented opportunity. Genome testing is now available to the masses, as is ancestry tracing. Simple online resources can provide remarkable insights into our families and their origins. Once it was the self-assigned task of the one or two family members who had the time and motivation to dig deeply, to take verbal family histories, to visit the library for rare books on small towns and shtetls, or even to visit the "old country" to stalk town records or cemeteries. But now a few hours invested online can uncover generations of family connections. Family members are discovering unknown cousins across the globe, and those cousins often know slices of family history unknown to others.

Of course, I am not only a grandparent but also a grandchild. Both of my grandparents and both great-grandparents on my father's side were killed in the Holocaust. On my mom's side, my grandmother was one of seven children who dispersed to three different continents to escape Europe. The products of those children were nine first cousins and twenty-four second cousins. Five of those first cousins and all of the second cousins are alive. The children of my great-grandmother remained close throughout their lives, long before the days of email and cell phones. They wrote letters on bygone blue international postal aerograms, thin foldable sheets of paper with prepaid postage, the letter and envelope one and the same. They sent these aerograms across the world to each other weekly and traveled across continents as often as they could afford for family events. The nine first cousins also stayed in touch, although not as regularly or with as much commitment as their parents, and by the time we have reached the second cousins, my generation, distance, the distractions of daily lives, and family rifts have resulted in much thinner and more frayed communications. Sara and I recently attended family celebrations for two different second cousins' kids (i.e., my second cousins once removed, who are third cousins to each other) and realized how much has been lost. I brought pictures of grandparents' and great-grandparents' vintage so my cousins and I could try to piece together their histories as we each recalled them. There were more holes than threads, family members whose names we couldn't recall and whose stories we never knew. The third cousins' celebrations we attended were three thousand miles apart and those third cousins didn't know each other and didn't attend each other's celebrations.

And what will my kids and grandkids know of their family tree beyond the living grandparents and great-grandparents they've known? How will they appreciate the struggles and sacrifices of their ancestors, which underlie the comfort and comparative ease of their existences? The seven children of my great-grandmother, who grew up in the same shtetl in Poland, escaped to lead productive and meaningful lives on three continents, staying in touch throughout their lives. But the legacy of their family is fading and soon will be lost entirely. I regret that.

No Regrets Living says it doesn't have to be that way. Like my great-grandparents, Sara's great-grandparents on her mother's side had seven children, although one died young. The remaining six stayed close throughout their lives (three of them, Yudi, Yishi, and Yank,

appeared previously in this book—as elk!). Their descendants—
many scores of children, grandchildren, great-grandchildren, and
now great-great-grandchildren—remain close through the frequent
family celebrations that come with so many relatives, and by holding family reunions every few years. Those reunions are the pinnacle of extended family life for Sara and her cousins. As a result,
third, fourth, and fifth cousins know one another. The best part of
the reunions is the sharing of stories and yellowed photographs, the
passing on of an oral history from generation to generation. Yes,
the younger generations often roll their eyes when a story is told for
the hundredth time, but they remember the story and some of the
names of the family members in the generations that preceded them.
Written and online versions of their family tree and the stories are in
various stages of preparation, as well.

> The pandemic created a new opportunity for Sara's family to stay close—
> at the same hour every Sunday, as many family members as are available
> gather for a Zoom call. They see each other's faces, hear each other's stories,
> and pass those stories along to their kids (who are usually too busy to join
> on the call!). Many families used Zoom or other online networking venues to
> stay in touch and celebrate big events. The pandemic helped us realize the
> technology is available to connect with distant family so much more easily
> than by plane, and so much more satisfyingly than by multiple individual
> phone calls (which most of us never take the time to make). I believe those
> online connections will remain long beyond the pandemic; Sara's family has
> already planned to make their Sunday mini-reunions a permanent tradition.

As a grandparent now, I would like our grandkids and, someday,
their kids and even their grandkids to know about Sara and me. Not
every detail of our lives, certainly, but the kind of people we are, the

values we hold, and the efforts we made for them before they were even born. I would like them to know how much we loved them, how invested we were in their futures and in their happiness. How worried we were for the world into which they were born and how hopeful we were that they would somehow contribute to healing that world. As a start, I hope our kids give their kids this little book you're reading. And maybe this book will encourage you to record your own family legacy for the generations that follow, or perhaps to search online and connect with your more distant family. So you won't regret not knowing your story and telling your story, and your descendants won't regret not hearing it.

The COVID-19 pandemic changed the lives of untold numbers of grandparents. In some cases, as with us, grandparents and grandchildren were relegated to virtual hugs over FaceTime, Skype, or Zoom. Those were the lucky grandparents who had the wherewithal and the technology to stay in touch with their grandkids and the health to hear and see their family. Other grandparents, who lived close enough to their grandchildren, saw them through the windows of their home or assisted living facility. The sadness we saw, in-person or during news coverage, on the faces of grandparents in hospitals, nursing homes, veterans' homes, or hospice, separated from their grandchildren and surrounded by strangers in masks and gowns, are tragic images I'll never forget.

At the other end of the spectrum, in many cases grandparents who were able put themselves at risk to provide day care for grandchildren whose preschools or schools had closed and whose parents had no choice but to go to work outside the home. In many ways, those families' adaptations brought them closer to the "old country" model where several generations of family lived together and looked after one another.

Spouse

After more than thirty-five years together, Sara and I have a sym-
biosis that is deeper and richer than any other relationship in my life.
There were bumps along the road, as there are in any relationship.
We had to work through difficult periods in our marriage, but our
commitment to each other never faltered. We knew we had to make
it work. We wanted to make it work.

An important part of appreciating family for *No Regrets Living*,
especially for spouses and life partners, is a willingness to honestly
acknowledge each other's strengths and weaknesses. That was easy
for Sara and me because our skill sets are so different. The result
has been a very effective division of labor, and we made sure our
kids knew which of us to come to for any particular issue. An example: shortly after our youngest son and his wife moved into their
new home, the boiler blew. Our son called Sara. The right choice.
Sara does all our home and car repairs because growing up she held
the flashlight for her dad, and because I consider power tools to
be weapons of mass destruction. For Mother's Day one year, the
kids chipped in to buy Sara a fancy ratchet set; on another occasion,
they bought her a rototiller. I get gift certificates to bookstores. Sara
always jokes that my job was to earn the money, hers to spend it.
That's really not true, though—she earns money, too, and I've done
my share of spending. For the reasons I previously described, Sara
was in charge of taking the kids to doctor appointments, but as
adults, they call me for medical advice (and then they double-check
with Sara). She also handles computer and other highly technical
problems (like turning on the TV) because I don't know the difference between a modem and a router, or how to reboot either, and
the autocorrect on my iPhone makes me look like an idiot when

I text. When the kids were young, I handled homework questions and test panics because Sara still suffers from her own residual test panic. Sara does most of the cooking because otherwise we have to eat my burrito pies (recipe available upon request); I handle cleanup. Sara balances the checkbook, but I'm the bad guy keeping us on a budget. I taught the kids sports, but Sara taught them to have fun. I taught them spelling and math rules; she taught them strategies for Scrabble and Settlers of Catan.

But it's how Sara and I met that most influences my thinking about appreciating family, and about accepting fate (Key #5, to follow). Because without the sequence of events that brought us together, none of what we built as husband and wife would have happened.

As I noted earlier, my dad died young, at age fifty-eight, from pancreatic cancer, and I returned to Denver to be near and support my newly widowed mom. A year and a half after my dad died, and despite a freezing snowstorm, I took my mom to a community program, encouraging her to start socializing again. There, a colleague from work spotted us sitting in better seats than hers and moved down to join us. My colleague was with a friend of hers, who in turn came to the program with an employee of his. Sara, his employee, had recently been transferred to Denver from Oklahoma where she worked as a geophysicist in the oil industry. Complaining to her boss that it was hard to meet people (men) in a new town, he convinced her to brave the snow and join him at this event. Sara and I sat next to each other that night, had our first date three nights later, and now have three adult kids and grandchildren.

I still grieve for my dad and for the many, many joyous events he missed, for the daughter-in-law and grandchildren and great-grandchildren he never knew, and for the wonderful milestones in their lives that he missed. I grieve knowing the suffering he endured in the Holocaust and how hard he worked on his fruit truck to support us, and I grieve for the apparent lack of reward later in his life. Although he never met Sara, I really hope that somehow, somewhere, my dad knows it was his illness and death that brought Sara and me together.

During the pandemic, isolated from our kids and grandkids, sharing a tiny safe circle with Sara made the sacrifices required by the pandemic more bearable. That's the importance of each ONE person in our lives, a singular thread and lifeline. Growing up in the home of a Holocaust survivor, I was always conscious of what the loss of my dad's family meant to him personally, and to us. A visit to the United States Holocaust Memorial Museum in Washington, DC, with its archives of victims' family pictures and memories, is a jarring reminder of how massive numbers of lost lives can mask the impact of every single lost life. Similarly, the incessant news reports of the tragic, massive loss of lives during the pandemic threatened to blur the impact of each individual lost life. Although the global and national numbers of pandemic fatalities are staggering, for me, the most important statistic is ONE. Each one life lost is irreplaceable and comes with a story of immense sorrow for the survivors in that victim's family and community.

Uncle George

For memories of lost family to be fond ones, without regrets, our relationships with our family during life must be carefully nurtured. That's how butterflies, blue jays, dragonflies, and the like can become meaningful signs in one's life. But it doesn't always work out as we would like. My favorite local news interview was of a family in a Denver suburb. The reporter sat with a husband who was a family physician, his wife, and their two daughters. The family was typical in every way but one—the physician's brother had just left for another of his solo trips to Afghanistan to hunt Osama bin Laden. With nothing but a backpack, the girls' uncle went from cave to cave in the mountainous region of Tora Bora, guided by a Sherpa he hired locally and from whom he borrowed an AK-47 each year. Oh, yes, he did this each year. If that wasn't unique enough, the uncle required dialysis three times a week for kidney failure. For a month each year, he went off the therapy for the hunting trip and was forced to return when the toxins in his body built up sufficiently to make him physically ill. So, the reporter interviewing the family asked the girls what they thought of all this. One of the daughters answered quickly and brilliantly. "You know," she said, "every family has an Uncle George."

And she was right. It's hard for me to think of a family where there isn't someone who makes being his or her relative a challenge or even painful. In the best of situations, an Uncle George understands his quirks and the effect they have on his family and consciously tries to fit in. In the worst of situations, Uncle George can divide and even destroy a family. *No Regrets Living* asks that you do everything you can to make a difficult family relationship work. As I wrote at the outset of this section, often family must not only be appreciated but tolerated as well. Give more, even when you feel you've already given enough. Be the peacemaker, the listener, the compromiser, the apologizer, and even the groveler if necessary. And when you've done all that, if the relationship with Uncle or Aunt George still can't be repaired, you won't have regrets about not trying hard enough.

KEY #5
ACCEPT

IN APPROACHING a mathematical or scientific problem, or trying to prove a theory, often certain assumptions must be made without proof. These are also referred to as *givens*. Many situations in life require assumptions even if they can't absolutely be proven. For example, in formulating the Theory of Relativity, Einstein made the assumption that light travels at constant speed in a vacuum. The famous science fiction writer, Isaac Asimov, wrote this about assumptions:

"…it is incorrect to speak of an assumption as either true or false, since there is no way of proving it to be either (If there were, it would no longer be an assumption). It is better to consider assumptions as either useful or useless, depending on whether deductions made from them corresponded to reality…"[42]

There are three assumptions that can't absolutely be proven, but I believe to be very *useful*, even essential, to accept for *No Regrets Living*: Fate; Reward and Punishment; and Time.

FATE

Songwriters Jay Livingston and Ray Evans may have described fate best, but without Doris Day's memorable rendition, this legendary song may never have become an Academy Award winner, a megahit, and my mother's favorite song: "Que será, será" which translates from Spanish to , "What will be, will be."

My parenting repertoire has been all about teaching and encouraging my kids, supporting them in everything they hope to accomplish, celebrating their milestones and achievements with them, and comforting them when things don't go as they had hoped. The latter is always the toughest. For the minor disappointments— lost baseball games or tennis matches, bad test grades, or the science fair project that didn't win—a simple dinner of Indian food or burritos (depending on which of the kids we were trying to console) or a walk in the park with an ice cream cone (that worked for all the kids) usually did the trick. There will always be other games and matches, you'll do better on the next test, not everyone can win every time; somedays you eat the bear and other days the bear eats you. But for the big disappointments in our kids' lives and, for that matter, for the big disappointments in our lives, I have always invoked fate as the explanation: Que será, será, what will be will be. No room for regrets about how things turned out because that's how they were supposed to turn out. Our family has experienced so many examples of what seems to be a bad outcome turning out to be a blessing in disguise, having a silver lining, or at least not being as bad as feared. And when the worst *is* realized, when bad really *is* bad, I surrender to fate. Acceptance of fate, that certain things are meant to happen, is my escape from feeling I should be able to control everything.

I also credit fate for the good things in my life, and I like to believe they were also meant to happen—for reasons I may not understand but am grateful for. Our kids know the story, backward and forward, of how Sara and I met because we remind them of it whenever they have the big disappointments that can't be cured with burritos or an ice cream cone. Without my dad's death, I wouldn't have moved back to Denver when I did, around the same time Sara was transferred to Denver for work. Our kids also know the stories of how their grand-parents met, my mom and dad at the resettlement center and Sara's mom and dad in the cafeteria over a tuna sandwich. We reminded them of those stories when they didn't get into their first-choice col-lege, broke up with someone they cared about, didn't get called back for a second job interview, or got scooped on the house they were hoping to buy. The clichés, "Things happen for a reason," and "It just wasn't meant to be," are even more cliché in our home because I use them all the time. Of course, the grief over my dad's death at such a young age and all that he missed remains a powerful force in my life, but it's softened by the events that followed directly as a result, most important, my meeting Sara and creating our wonderful family. No, I don't think my dad died so Sara and I could meet. But in the grand scheme of things, and, as I've said, I believe there is a grand scheme (much of which we'll never understand), infinite inflection points precede every momentous event in our lives, and, without each of those inflections, we wouldn't be who we are or where we are. Acceptance of fate is a reality check on the power we think we have. So, I accept that what will be, will be. Que será, será.

This is going to sound even hokier, but I also believe fate has backup plans. Our kids have now lived enough to have experienced their own examples of fate and things happening for a reason. Both our boys met their future wives while still in grade school—the fortuitous decisions about which school we and the girls' parents sent all of our kids to were critical to the paths of the boys' future lives. I believe that had we or our future daughters-in-laws' parents sent kids to different schools, there was a backup plan in place for our boys to still meet their future wives. I can't prove it. But I *can* prove the backup plan for my daughter meeting her future husband. That chain of events began when I entered medical school, fifteen years before our daughter was born. My closest friend in medical school, Harvey, has remained one of my closest friends forty years after graduation. Although we live two thousand miles apart, we have kept in touch and shared in our families' major events. One of those major events was Harvey's son's wedding. Sara and I traveled east to attend the ceremony and had a lovely visit with Harvey and his family. The best man at the wedding, whom we didn't meet or really even notice at the wedding (we had no way of knowing how important he would become in our lives someday!), lived and worked in DC He and Harvey's son had grown up together and attended the same grade school and, like Harvey and me, had remained close throughout their lives. So close that this grade school friend was Harvey's son's best man.

Our daughter was in graduate school in DC at the time, and it dawned on Harvey that his son's best man and our daughter, both single and living in DC, might enjoy meeting each other. Of course we had to get our daughter's permission for the set-up (a couple of my previous interventions were busts), but they met, fell in love, and were married about two years later. So what's this about a backup plan? When our daughter was moving to DC for graduate school, Sara flew out to help her find an apartment. Of course, there are hundreds and hundreds of apartment buildings in DC, and they had only a week to nail something down. They found a sweet apartment in a nice building a short commute from her school and left a deposit to hold it. Relieved that they had found a place, they were walking back toward their hotel when they ran into a cousin. (As I noted earlier, Sara has a very large family and running into a cousin almost anywhere in the world isn't a rare event.) It turned out this cousin lived in the area and told Sara and our daughter that, although a nice and safe part of DC, it was the wrong demographic for our daughter—"too many strollers and young families, not enough single young professionals." So our daughter and Sara continued looking and found a place in a somewhat edgier part of town where a lot of fellow millennials were moving. They retrieved the deposit from the first place and confirmed a reservation at the second place. End of story, right? But when our daughter met her future husband a year later through my decades-old medical school connection, she discovered that he lived in the first building where she had put a deposit! What are the chances? Coincidence, you say? Not in my worldview.

In my view of fate and its backup plans, had Harvey, my close friend from medical school and I not been admitted to the same medical school, or had one of us decided to go elsewhere, and had we never met…our daughter and her future husband would have ultimately met anyway, perhaps in the gym or elevator or common area of his apartment building where she would have also rented an apartment and not withdrawn her deposit. It was only because plan A for their meeting worked that plan B wasn't necessary and our daughter chose another apartment building. That's really how my brain works in putting life's events together, and it leads me to *No Regrets Living*—we can't regret what seem like missed opportunities because if something was meant to be, it will be, and if it wasn't meant to be, it won't. Things happen for a reason, and if there's any doubt about how they will happen, there's a backup plan in place. I dare you to prove me wrong.

The COVID-19 pandemic was, for many, an act of fate like no other. For months, everyone's carefully and casually made plans were postponed or canceled. Weddings, graduations, travel, reunions, birthday and other family celebrations, and worship services. Funerals and memorial services were restricted to close family only (separated by safe social distancing) or conducted virtually. Tragic stories emerged of families who hadn't been allowed at the bedside of dying loved ones, only to not be allowed at their funerals, either. Work deadlines became meaningless as did, for many, work itself. Meetings went virtual, as did almost everything else that could be handled online. Even the deadline for filing income taxes was delayed. A friend complained that the worst purchase he ever made was a 2020 desk calendar.

How else to explain the disruptions, disorder, and turmoil other than as fate, out of our hands and beyond our control? The most poignant epiphany for me was how willing almost everyone was to accept the inevitability of the pandemic's far-reaching effects. Of course we can't have meetings or gatherings. Of course we have to distance ourselves from others. Of course there will be shortages of everything from food to cleaning products, disinfectants, hand sanitizers, and toilet paper. Of course plans for college enrollment, career changes, vacations, and almost everything else in our lives will have to wait. We had no choice in the matter, no control. It was just bad luck, bad timing... or maybe it was fate.

But as the lockdowns and closures dragged on for months, and as unemployment soared, the stresses of the pandemic on families and businesses eroded patience. Acceptance had its limits, and many decided to take back control of their situations rather than leaving them to the hands of fate, or to the dicta of government. It was how individuals chose to express themselves during the pandemic that illustrated the importance of kindness for a free and tolerant society, and the harm that lack of kindness can cause.

REWARD AND PUNISHMENT

Believing our actions are subject to reward or punishment can help us achieve *No Regrets Living* by giving us powerful motivation for doing the right thing. But *are* we *actually* rewarded or punished for our actions? Yes. In at least one way I'm certain of.

I think of reward and punishment in three broad categories: those that we feel almost immediately as a result of our actions; those that may come down from above, i.e., from God; and, finally, rewards and punishments that may follow in a mysterious afterlife. I am not prepared to make the case that God rewards us for our actions— that's a matter of personal belief. Nor am I able to attest to an afterlife, also a matter of personal belief. So I will focus on the type of rewards and punishments that I'm certain do exist: those which we feel inside almost immediately after our actions. It's safe to say that at one time or another in our lives we have all felt a sense of fulfillment and contentment from performing a good deed. It's also safe to say we have all felt guilt and regret, at times, after doing something we knew to be wrong. That inner emotional feedback loop, causing us to feel contentment or regret, provides us with immediate reward or punishment for our actions, and the memory of those emotions helps guide our future actions. Contentment always feels better than regret.

What follows are suggestions for achieving more emotional rewards than punishments in your life, for having fewer regrets, and for achieving contentment. I know these may seem obvious, but I hope the examples I give will inspire you as they have me.

Honesty

Zadie, my grandfather, always paid his bills in cash; he never had a checking account or credit card. When he went to the supermarket, he safety-pinned his "billfold" into the "bosom pocket" of his coat and took it out when it was time to pay. After getting change, he pinned the billfold back and left the store. On one shopping trip, the billfold contained much more cash than he needed for groceries because he had just come from the bank where he withdrew an entire month's worth of cash, $600, to pay his monthly bills: heat, electricity, phone, insurance. When he arrived home, the billfold with all the cash was gone and an open safety pin dangled from his pocket. He was devastated—an entire month's worth of cash, gone. He cried and cried: money was scarce, and, for a small-village European immigrant living in a big American city where even normal daily life often felt overwhelming, this loss elevated his sense of insecurity and paranoia. And then, two days later, the call came. From a man who found Zadie's billfold in the parking lot, reported it to the grocery store manager, whom my grandfather had been calling nearly hourly. The store manager gave the finder Zadie's phone number and the Good Samaritan returned the billfold with every dollar still inside.

My grandfather was now crying tears of joy, so grateful to this kind stranger that he offered him anything: a reward, a home-cooked meal for his family, a gift for his children. The man declined everything—he said it was just the right thing to do, and it made him feel good to have made someone else so happy. The Good Samaritan said he was getting up in years and more than ever tried to do the right thing. Zadie asked how old he was, and, when he heard, my grandfather replied "I'm old enough to be your father! And your father would be very proud of you, and so am I." That Good Samaritan is my poster child for *No Regrets Living*. How fulfilled (rewarded!) he must have felt the night he returned the money to my grandfather—contentment worth far more than $600.

Not long ago I was walking out of a supermarket and found two twenty-dollar bills lying on the sidewalk. I picked them up, and then stood in that spot for ten minutes waiting for someone to come running back from the parking lot, or from inside the store, to find their lost cash. No one came. Of course, I immediately thought back to my grandfather's experience with far more cash, but this was the same general idea in the same general venue. I left a note at the manager's desk with my phone number in the event anyone called to ask about their missing money. I left another note with the security guard standing in front of the store and asked him to pass it along to the next shift. I never heard from anyone about the money, so we donated it to charity, in Zadie's memory.

Of course there's another meaning for the word honesty—truthfulness. Truthfulness in our relationships with others is almost always a virtue. We taught our kids that we were less upset about their doing something wrong than about their lying about it afterward, and that telling us the truth (confessing!) could mitigate most punishments we might otherwise impose. But there are certain situations where white lies can be good things, too. As my grandparents got older, my mom would shield them from bad news, and then Sara and I did the same for our parents as they aged. Several years ago I wrote a piece for the *New York Times* called "Fudging the Facts, for Peace of Mind" in which I confessed to the liberties we have taken with the truth to protect people we love from unnecessary worry.[43]

My grandfather, Zadie, he of the lost billfold, had a tragic childhood. He survived the pogroms in Russia where he saw the Cossacks rape and murder his mother and sister. His survival came at a tremendous price as he suffered unimaginable emotional trauma and later post-traumatic stress disorder (PTSD, see Appendix C for a little more about Zadie). Understandably, he constantly (pathologically, one could say) worried about the safety of his family in America. As an example, when I was a third-year medical student in New York City, he called from Denver very early one morning, waking me and my roommates. He had been listening to his transistor radio on one of his many sleepless nights of worry and had heard that a Staten Island ferry boat had crashed, injuring numerous passengers. There were more than 7 million people in NYC at that time, and I lived in Manhattan, not Staten Island. But Zadie called at 4 AM to make sure I wasn't one of those injured. He would caution us against taking any sort of risks, like driving in the mountains or on an undivided highway. A two-lane, undivided road takes us to our favorite spot in the mountains with a climb up on the mountain side and a steep descent on the cliff side. We never mentioned those drives to Zadie; rather, we told him we were driving to Colorado Springs, a drive he knew well to be flat and on a divided highway. Zadie urged our boys, his grandsons, to become doctors so if war broke out they would be behind the lines; and they promised they would. He made our daughter promise to never drive alone after dark, and she promised she wouldn't. Zadie died when our kids were in their teens, never knowing that the boys didn't become doctors and that our daughter does sometimes venture out at night. An ongoing legacy of using occasional white lies to protect those we love.

Of course, even though our kids are all adults now, we still worry about them. And we've noticed they are starting to worry more about us. We're grateful they tell us about their activities and their lives, but we're beginning to wonder…

Peace

Although surely of paramount importance, I'm not talking about peace among nations now, but rather peace in our relationships with others, to prevent the regrets we feel when relationships go bad. The rewards of peaceful relationships among family, friends, coworkers, and others are very real, as are the punishments for failing to restore peace when relationships become strained.

The seven children of my great-grandmother who I described earlier were, indeed, close for most of their lives, communicating lovingly and frequently across three continents. But then there was a breach. Two of the brothers, business partners, had a falling out that they never repaired, and now, two generations later, the children and grandchildren of those brothers, first and second cousins to one another, have no contact. I cringe when I think about how devastated the matriarch of that family, my great-great-grandmother who escaped Europe just in time, would be to know about a schism that never healed among her children. A schism that was then inherited by her grandchildren and great-grandchildren who today don't know each other, wouldn't recognize one another on the street in the city they all live in, and probably have no idea why.

Ironically, some of today's greatest challenges to harmony among loved ones sitting at the dinner table or coworkers in the lunchroom arise because of differences of opinion on national or international issues. Disputes about politics and policies, over which most of us have little control other than by voting, have threatened to divide families and friends the way they have divided the country. It's not worth it. When there are strong, simmering feelings on different sides of an issue, and those feelings threaten to erupt, invoke an "issues-free zone." Talk about the weather or the kids or sports (unless of course there are Red Sox and Yankees fans in the same space). We have many family members and friends who recognize and respect our perspectives on things, and whose perspectives we recognize and respect; to keep that mutual respect, we keep our mouths shut on certain subjects, and so do they. If the subject creeps into the conversation, perhaps because of the latest breaking news, we make like the three wise monkeys (who see, hear, and speak no evil).

It's within everyone's ability, and should be everyone's responsibility, to ease tense relationships and restore peace. Reap the rewards of peaceful relationships by holding your tongue rather than having the last word. Agree more than disagree. Compromise, boost others' self-esteem, praise liberally. Respect boundaries. Recognize that the needs of others can be as important as, or even more important than, your own needs. Be the first to apologize after a fight, and the first to forgive. Pride should have no place in important relationships. Be comfortable saying you're sorry, even if you *know* it's not your fault. Don't wait for the other person to make the first gesture; you should start the dialogue toward reconciliation. And often the only dialogue necessary will be the two simple words, "I'm sorry." Life's too short to not apologize, forgive, forget, and move on. Breaches in important relationships easily spread beyond the parties immediately involved and may last for generations. Finally, as I mentioned earlier when discussing "Uncle George," certain relationships can't be fixed regardless of the efforts you make. In those situations, you may have to give up, but with the knowledge that you tried your best and needn't regret not doing more.

The coronavirus pandemic tested our abilities to bring peace to our

relationships with others. On the one hand, many reached out to people they had lost touch with over the years to check on their well-being and to catch up. Friends, families, colleagues, and worshippers found one another by email, phone, FaceTime, or Zoom. Neighbors reconnected with neighbors and greeted strangers who walked by. On the other hand, animosities flared between and among others: those wearing masks and those not; those fearing loosening of public health restrictions and those demanding them; those pleading for schools to reopen and those pleading for them to stay closed; those pleased with their governments' responses to the pandemic and those angry about them; Democrats and Republicans (shocking, I know!); those advocating for mail-in election ballots and those opposed; older citizens and millennials; lenders and borrowers; landlords and tenants; small business owners and police enforcing social distancing rules; store owners and customers who refused to wear masks; and on and on. Confined to home, many families reported increases in domestic violence.

On the whole, under the stress of the pandemic and its impositions in

our lives, the effects of the pandemic on peace in our interpersonal relationships have been mixed. But on a global scale, the opportunity for finding
common ground and solidarity was clearly missed. An international crisis, a
war against a germ that knew no borders and affected all the world's peoples
should have fostered improved relations and cooperation among nations and
instilled a sense of global solidarity. Instead the pandemic only exacerbated
preexisting international tensions with finger-pointing and accusations,
conspiracy theories and retributions. Nationalism prevailed at a moment in
history when globalism was more necessary than ever. Peace is hard to come
by, in our homes, in our communities, and in our world. Regrettable.

Fairness and Justice

There's no greater test of one's fairness than parenting more than
one child. Our sons always accused us of having a favorite child—
their sister. It was more teasing than accusation, and in their heart-
of-hearts, I don't think they believed it, but they made a strong case,
particularly after she got the bigger bedroom—the one with the
bathroom. All the explanations we offered about a girl needing her
own bathroom in a house full of brothers didn't carry water (bad
metaphor, sorry). The bathroom decision simply proved their point.
Our daughter, for her part, called the boys princes and accused us
of enabling their sense of entitlement—to the favorite chair at the
dinner table or to our full attention at their sports events, which we
dragged her to whenever a playdate wasn't available. Sara and I have
no regrets about the bathroom decision, the dinner chair, or the
sporting events—we always did our best to be fair, and continue to
now that they're adults, married, and leading professional lives. I'm

hoping that, looking back, they understand some of the decisions we made that looked like we were playing favorites. One of our sons now has kids of his own, two boys and a girl. Heh, heh, heh . . .

Acting fairly, as if there is reward and punishment, goes far beyond resolving childhood skirmishes and sibling rivalry. Fairness requires equal justice for all. For a society boasting that all people are created equal, and holding up the Constitution to prove it, inequities abound. Success in life has always depended on the country, neighborhood, and home a person is born into. Those of us who had the good fortune to be born in the right place at the right time have resources and opportunities others don't. The have-nots in the world often lack food, adequate shelter, access to healthcare, access to the internet, and, most of all, they lack opportunity. In the words of Reverend Martin Luther King Jr., "Injustice anywhere is a threat to justice everywhere. We are caught in an inescapable network of mutuality, tied in a single garment of destiny. Whatever affects one directly, affects all indirectly." We are all harmed when any of us is harmed, and each of us fortunate enough to have enough has a responsibility to seek fairness and justice for those least able to succeed and thrive. There are many ways we can do that through charity, volunteering, activism, and advocacy (see Giving section, to follow). Perhaps the first most important thing we can do for those in greatest need is to recognize their need. It's too easy to avoid the unpleasant realities faced by so many—we simply turn the page in the newspaper, change the channel on the TV, click the next story online, and drive by the man holding the sign on the street corner. When we force ourselves to confront the unfairness and injustice in the world, we are more likely to want to do something about it.

The COVID-19 pandemic didn't wait for us to confront the inequities in society—it thrust them upon us with each day's soaring hospitalization and death totals. The disproportionate severity of the disease among minority communities, immigrants, the homeless, and the elderly is a stark reminder of our need to do much better, to correct the injustices underlying the pandemic's selective severity. Not surprisingly, inadequate access to health care proved to be a major determinant of outcome from the infection—those presenting to clinics and hospitals late in the course of their illness typically fared the worst. We must do better during a crisis, to be sure, but much better *between* crises to prevent each subsequent challenge from resulting in the tragic consequences we see with COVID-19.

The pandemic's devastation is much broader than clinical and health outcomes alone. The downstream effects of our response to the pandemic— the closure of schools and lockdown of businesses and entire cities, as necessary as they may have been, came with their own severe and disproportionate effects on our most vulnerable populations. School breakfast and lunch programs, which in New York City alone benefit more than 70 percent of public-school children, were crippled. Kids in low income families fell further behind in school than their more fortunate classmates who had internet access for homeschooling, or a parent who could afford to stay home and teach them. Unemployment soared to levels not seen since the Great Depression of 1929, with low-wage, gig, and minority workers suffering the most while many higher income workers were able to maintain their jobs and salaries working from home. The unprecedented levels of unemployment insurance claims overwhelmed outdated and inadequate online state insurance systems, delaying payments for the millions of eligible workers who had internet access and could apply, while further highlighting the inequality of internet access for many low-income families. Unemployment also led to abrupt loss of health insurance for millions insured through their work, increases in evictions and homelessness due to inability to pay rent, and defaults on a panoply of loans—mortgage, auto, credit card, and student loans, among others. Numerous studies showed that the economic devastation of the pandemic affected women disproportionately, with job losses and by requiring them to stay at home with kids out of school.

Residents of nursing homes, veterans' homes, and assisted living centers had the highest rates of infection and death, resulting in widespread bans on visitation by even immediate family. Countless heartbreaking stories of loved ones losing their parent or grandparent without a chance to say a final goodbye reminded us the aged community has long lacked adequate safety nets. The pandemic also disrupted the oversight of at-risk children, the foster care system, and adoption. So many injustices need fixing.

How we respond as a society to the inequities and unfairness exposed by the pandemic will say more about us as a nation and as individuals than how we responded to the pandemic itself. COVID-19 has given us a chance to hit the fairness reset button and reap the reward we'll feel for doing the right thing.

Kindness

When our oldest child was a toddler, he had a habit I feared would become a problem as he got older. There is a history of obsessive-compulsive disorder (OCD) in my family and I worried that his habit was a forerunner of it. I called the most prominent pediatric behavioral specialist in the country, a man whose books made him a household name both within the pediatric community and among parents in the real world. I reached him quickly by phone—announcing that I was a physician usually got me through the gatekeepers and directly to any colleague I was trying to reach. In this case, I knew of the famous man, but he didn't know me. He picked up and said, "This is Dr. X, how can I help you?" I briefly explained my concerns about my toddler and asked if I should be worried. I'll never forget the words he said or the tone he said them with: "Dr. Rotbart, if I gave phone advice to every physician-parent who called me, without seeing the child for a proper evaluation, I would never get anything done. I suggest you find a pediatrician locally who can help you with this. Have a nice day." It's hard to adequately describe the hurt this famous pediatrician caused me.

Several hours later, recovered from the first experience, I called another famous person in the field of developmental pediatrics, a well-known psychologist, and the author of as many books as the famous pediatrician. As with the famous pediatrician, this was a complete "cold call." Dr. Louise Bates Ames also picked up the phone quickly and asked how she could be of help. I didn't know Dr. Bates Ames and she didn't know me. I repeated the same question I had asked the famous pediatrician. Dr. Bates Ames then spent nearly an hour on the phone with me, asking questions and getting details, and then reassuring, comforting, and explaining the fluctuating stages of childhood development that often revealed concerning, yet perfectly normal, phases of a child's growth. Our son's behaviors were common and not worrisome. They would disappear, she predicted, within six months or less. If that period passed and I was still concerned, or if I had questions before that, she insisted that I call her again to revisit the issue. In the meantime, she suggested the best course of action was to neither call attention to the behavior nor ask our son to stop. She advised we ignore the behavior as it wasn't causing our son or anyone else any harm. Ignoring, rather than focusing on, behaviors like this was a much more effective strategy to speed their resolution. We did exactly as she said, and so did our son, whose worrisome habit was gone within a couple months. Dr. Bates

Ames passed away eight years later. I grieved when I read the news because I know how many parents' lives she touched with her gentle and patient wisdom. Hers was a kindness to a stranger that I have tried to repay throughout my career whenever concerned colleagues, whether I knew them or not, called me about their own children. I hope I've done as good a job for others as Dr. Bates Ames did for my family, now more than thirty years ago, but I am certain I've never treated anyone the way that famous pediatrician treated me. I don't know if that famous pediatrician was capable of feeling regret, but I doubt he ever felt the rich rewards Dr. Bates Ames surely felt for the kindnesses she showed during her career. She is another poster child in my life for *No Regrets Living*, an important role model for my career, and one of those to whose memory I've dedicated this book.

We are dependent on others, and others are dependent on us. Zadie was right—as he warned us, cars drive too fast on both sides of the undivided road up to our favorite spot in the mountains (which, as I mentioned, we avoided telling him about). We are so dependent on others on the road. We can be as careful as possible, yet catastrophe is only one drunk or distracted driver headed in the opposite direction. And it's not only on two-lane, undivided mountain roads. Every day there are stories of drivers speeding through a red light across an intersection and "T-boning" an innocent car that was rightfully in the intersection. And even of drivers crossing a *divided* highway barrier and crashing head-on into cars driving where they were supposed to be. Just such a story almost killed a close friend's child and did cause the deaths of four others involved in the crash. The driver of the malfeasant car was high on methamphetamines, proven by tests of his blood during his autopsy (more about this in the story of Toni in Key #7).

As Tennessee Williams famously wrote in *Cat on a Hot Tin Roof*, we are all dependent on the kindness of strangers.

It's not limited to the road. Whenever we interact, in person, on the phone, or online, we rely on others' decency. Whether bullying and harassment occur on the playground, in the workplace, or on social media, they are dangerous and can cause permanent harm. The anonymity of online bullying makes it too easy and too common, a symptom of our digital age. Social media, like the internet as a whole, has much to offer society while also posing great risks. Zadie would have asked, had he known what the internet was, whether the digital highway is divided. It's not.

What distinguishes a civil society from a dystopic one? The number of kind strangers.

Our interdependence, the crucial need for strangers showing kindness to strangers, became more evident than ever during the COVID-19 pandemic. Each of us relying—perhaps even for our lives—on others around us keeping their distance, self-isolating when ill, wearing masks, washing hands. We depended on the kindness of strangers at grocery stores, post offices, gas stations, and when simply passing on the street. In turn, we were called upon to protect others in the same ways. For those who became infected, healthcare workers, as always, were the heroes, putting themselves at risk while staffing the most concentrated areas of the pandemic to provide lifesaving care and kindness to those most affected.

Kind heroes emerged outside the clinics, hospitals, and nursing homes as well. Of course, first responders—police, firefighters, ambulance crews —were again called upon to go above and beyond, and not just on lifesaving missions. First responders across the country brightened birthdays for shut-in kids and senior citizens with drive-by greetings using their sirens and loudspeakers. Regular duty and reserve military personnel were called into action to deliver food, supplies, and medical equipment. Teachers innovated ways to reach their students at home, sometimes even one at a time, making sure kids remained attached to their learning and classrooms. Parents' creativity and stamina were tested as they multitasked and juggled, holding their households together, often while also working from home and homeschooling their kids. Workers across many disciplines courageously continued to provide for us during the crisis—in grocery stores, essential factories, on farms, and on public transportation. Workers in utilities, banks, labs, courthouses, pharmacies, and charitable organizations came to work despite personal risk. And neighbors showed kindness to neighbors.

Without those kindnesses to one another, the pandemic would have lingered even longer with untold additional pain, suffering, and death. A simple search of "acts of kindness during the pandemic," in quotes so as to get the entire phrase in the search results, yields tens of thousands of Google hits. Kindness is contagious, even more contagious than the coronavirus.

Finally, the pandemic and its aftermath give parents an opportunity to teach their kids the real meaning of being a hero—it's not just about the highest scorer in a basketball game or the leading home-run hitter or the newest TV heartthrob. Those celebrities are important for kids, and fun, but *hero* should be reserved for true heroes.

Paul Cary was a true hero. Mr. Cary was a sixty-six-year-old paramedic in Colorado who volunteered, despite his age putting him in a high-risk category, to go to New York during the height of the pandemic to help. There, he provided medical transports for COVID-19 patients all across the city until he became infected, requiring hospitalization and a ventilator. Tragically, he died of his infection shortly thereafter. Moving tributes poured in and poignant memorial ceremonies were held in both Colorado and New York. His family's statement announcing his death read, in part: "He risked his own health and safety to protect others and left this world a better place. We are at peace knowing that Paul did what he loved and what he believed in, right up until the very end." I have dedicated this book to Mr. Cary's memory as well.[44]

Giving

I'm not breaking new ground to say that acts of righteousness, charitable acts, and volunteering, should be vital—perhaps the *most* vital—part of a person's life. The rewards of giving charity and volunteering are great, and they are the only investments I know where the return is *always* greater than the outlay. I learned about charity from my mother, at least the check-writing variety. We grew up poor, but my mom was committed to giving. She gave to just about everyone who mailed her a solicitation, and each gift bred more solicitations since donor lists are shared, a disturbing truth about charitable organizations. My mother wrote $5 checks to well-known charities and to obscure ones no one, including her, had ever heard of. Her checkbook looked like a Who's Who of worthy and questionably worthy causes. Not the wisest strategy, of course, and not one I'd recommend. But in a year when mom had $500 left over from the Social Security income she depended on, she'd donate the full $500, $5 at a time.

There is a much more thoughtful and purposeful approach to charitable giving, and for that we can look all the way back to twelfth century Spain and one of the most revered scholars and philosophers in history: Moses ben Maimon, also known as Maimonides.

Maimonides's work has the distinction of not only resonating for nearly one thousand years but resonating within both Hebrew and Islamic cultures. Born in Spain, he and his family were forced into exile, first to Morocco, where he wrote his seminal biblical commentary, called the Mishneh, and then to Egypt where he became the head of the Jewish community there. A true polymath before the term was invented, Maimonides was also a rabbi, physician, and astronomer. Among the most widely cited and relied upon tractates of his Mishneh is the Eight Levels of Charity, a road map for giving that I believe remains, until today, the truest metric for giving.

In reverse order, from lowest (Level 8) to highest (Level 1), Maimonides's Levels of Charity, along with my sidebars, are

8) Giving unwillingly

There's an old joke about a man choking on a piece of steak in a restaurant. All efforts by patrons and staff members, including the muscular maître d', to apply the Heimlich maneuver failed. As the victim turned blue and was near collapse, a little old lady stood up from the corner of the restaurant, calmly walked over, and with two hands firmly squeezed the man's testicles, at which point he coughed up the steak and breathed normally. "How in the world did you know how to do that?" the burly maître d' asked the little old lady. "Easy," she replied, "I'm a fund-raiser for a big nonprofit." If donors have to be squeezed to "cough it up," their donations are less worthy.

7) Giving willingly but not giving enough or as much as you could

Each person has his or her own capacity for giving, determined by a multitude of factors known best only to the donor, and should not be subject to the judgments of others. It's how close donors get to their full giving capacity that is the most telling measure of their generosity.

6) Giving enough but only after being asked (solicited)

The $5 checks my mother wrote to the first one hundred organizations soliciting her helped her feel better than had she thrown away the mail solicitations of *possibly* deserving charities. Not what Maimonides advised as the best strategy, but he didn't know my mother.

5) Giving enough before being asked

This is tough to accomplish since we are asked so frequently and are so aggressively solicited by so many worthy causes. One way to do this is to focus locally—you know the organizations in your community that do the best job with the least fanfare and lowest overhead. Approach them before they approach you and ask how you can donate, or volunteer. Money is just one way of giving. Time is another important way. Your unpaid time given for the benefit of others, even before you are asked to help out. Almost all institutions and organizations need volunteers. There is no school in your community (or for that matter anywhere), public or private, that doesn't need, and wouldn't welcome your time. Ditto places of worship. Do you love animals? The humane society needs you. Love the outdoors? Your state or national park needs you. Are you good in the kitchen? Homeless shelters and food banks need you. Love sports? Coach kids in city leagues or Boys and Girls Clubs. And wherever you volunteer, if you have kids, bring them along. Show them that others matter to you and that the world outside your kids' comfortable homes isn't always as comfortable.

4) Giving where you are known to be the giver, but the recipient is unknown to you or to others

Don't be ashamed if you want your generosity to be noticed. Giving to an organization that gives to others whom you don't know, and that recognizes you on their donor list or with a plaque bearing your name, doesn't negate the worthiness of your donation. When others see your name, it may inspire them to keep up with you, and give as well.

An uplifting form of generosity in this category, where the giver is known but the recipients are not, emerged during the COVID-19 pandemic. Cultural giving. Artists, musicians, comedians, and writers all gave freely of their trade to provide comfort and inspiration on television and online platforms. From megastars to everyday YouTubers, programs and posts appeared by the tens of thousands to entertain, encourage, cheer, and tickle those in isolation, quarantine, or sheltering at home. Creative cultural giving flourished during the pandemic, bringing hope.

3) Giving anonymously to a known recipient

Knowing who's receiving your donation can be a powerful motivation to give, and the direct knowledge of who is benefiting by your generosity makes you a recipient as well, a recipient of the rewards for having done good for a real person, someone you can picture. Respond to the heartrending stories of misfortune seen on the nightly local news or in GoFundMe campaigns, the poor in your community who are barely getting by, the homeless on the streets, the victims of fires and floods. For this high level of charity, keep the faces of those in need in the forefront of your mind, but keep your face in the shadows. Your secret generosity will make you feel especially righteous—and you are.

2) Giving anonymously to an unknown recipient

This very high level of giving, where you aren't known to the recipients and they aren't known to you, can be through an intermediary individual or organization that is reliable and committed to distributing your donation honestly and with the lowest overhead costs. There are online sources of valuable information on organizational overhead and allocation for many of the organizations you might choose to support. Here's one such resource: www.charitynavigator.org.

Next time you peruse a list of donors to a charity of your choice, notice how few are denoted as *Anonymous*, and ask yourself if you wouldn't feel even better about your donation if your name wasn't mentioned, if you kept it just between you and your heart.

Finally, the very highest form of giving:

1) Giving in a way that alleviates the recipient of current or future dependence on others—such as giving (or helping find) the person a job, or giving a loan or grant

Maimonides phrases this as "holding him up before he falls." In other words, this is preventive or proactive charity: protecting a person who currently relies on others for his existence from slipping deeper into dependency on others; or noticing someone beginning to slip into dependency on others and acting to prevent that from happening. Maimonides's levels of charity hold giving a job, loan, or grant higher even than giving an outright, anonymous, and generous donation. The modern-day meme version is "Give a man a fish, and you feed him for a day. Teach a man to fish, and you feed him for a lifetime."

During the pandemic, unemployment in the United States reached the highest levels since the Great Depression. Despite the government's efforts to provide payroll protection to small businesses, millions of employees lost their jobs, many permanently, as businesses collapsed. Many of those employees received, in the short term, enhanced unemployment benefits from the government, but it is clear that the economic recovery from the pandemic depended upon those businesses that survived acting on Maimonides's highest form of giving—hiring and rehiring workers who were rendered dependent by the unprecedented turmoil in the labor market. Include in that highest form of giving during the pandemic those banks that withheld on foreclosures and those landlords who forgave late or unpaid rent.

Into this category, the highest level of charity that can help someone avoid dependency on others, I include another way of giving, one that is easy, painless, and absolutely free—giving praise. When a salesperson in a store, the barista at the coffee shop, or the postal worker behind the counter at the post office is efficient and courteous, I'm often moved to be effusive in my appreciation, even asking for their supervisor's name to send a grateful evaluation. I rarely if ever ask for a supervisor's name after poor service; I don't want to be the one to ruin a person's life by reporting a bad performance. Hopefully it was just a bad day for him and atypical, but if not, it will catch up with him soon enough. But by acknowledging excellent performance, I hope I can boost someone's work life, help him keep his job or even get a promotion. I will often tell the boss that if I was running a small business, this is a person I would hire.

These are four actual, verbatim email responses I've recently received from four different employers I've written to about one of their employees:

Mr. Rotbart, Thank you very much for taking the time to share this outstanding compliment for [ ]. He is a very valued member of the team and your experience reinforces how highly we think of him. We will certainly recognize him for the great experience he has delivered. I really like the concept of your hall of fame! May I also say how refreshing it is to receive such a glowing compliment. Though we do receive these for our team members, it seems rarer these days.

Dear Harley, Thank you so much for reaching out. We truly appreciate your wonderful comments on the performance of [ ]! I want to make sure that he receives this recognition and I have forwarded your kind compliment to his manager. Few people take the time to let a company know when they are impressed by an associate. We are lucky to have customers, such as you, that take time out of their day to write a note of appreciation.

Mr. Rotbart, We are very appreciative of your kind words and the time you took to provide this incredible feedback for our team. Though I am partial, I think we have an excellent team as well, though I wouldn't be able to confirm that without wonderful clients like you and your family... We are very appreciative of your business and we know that it goes further than business—it becomes personal and we enjoy that.

Harley and Sara, These notes are the best part of my day. I thank you for taking the time to write to us. [ ] is a valued and excellent member of our [ ] family and I am not surprised to read about your experience; this is what

[ ] does so often. I am so glad [ ] and [ ] were here for you and gave you the peace of mind that is so important during these times. Thank you for your faith in [ ], the trust in our team, and your courtesy in writing this note. We will continue to be here for you and those you love and continue our tradition of putting our clients first. Thank you again.

Praise took on new sounds during the pandemic. Millions who were stuck at home came out each evening, from the balconies of their high-rise apartments or the yards in their neighborhood, to pay tribute to the frontline workers who risked their lives for all of us. Applauding, banging pots, shouting, and howling filled the air for two minutes of gratitude each day during the height of the pandemic. Some institutions blared "God Bless America" from loudspeakers. Those two minutes became the highlight of the day for many—not just the frontline workers who heard it on their way into or home from work, but also for those who heard each other paying tribute, uniting neighborhoods and entire cities. Lawn signs expressing gratitude appeared everywhere; tips given to takeout restaurant and delivery workers doubled and tripled in amount. Gift card sales for stores closed during the lockdown soared, bringing welcome short-term income to businesses in hopes they would last long enough for customers to use the cards. And the online universe erupted with all manner of posts of gratitude—songs, poems, videos—giving praise to our heroes.

Courtesy

A simple wave of the hand can set the day's tone for you and for whomever you're waving at. So can a simple word of thanks. Recall the Butterfly Effect (Key #2). Neither a hand wave nor a "thanks" is too strenuous, and you forget about them almost instantly. So why is it that so many people fail to make that simple wave or utter the simple words of gratitude when shown a courtesy? On the highway, for example when you allow another driver to change lanes or merge in front of you, or in the crosswalk when you stop your car to allow a pedestrian to cross, or when you hold a door for someone, or give them change at the cashier's desk? When did we become so entitled that we don't have to acknowledge and return a courtesy? Why do we think we're *owed* that courtesy rather than granted it voluntarily?

I coached my kids in sports for many years. Sports are a great venue for teaching common courtesy. When my daughter's tennis opponent hit a winning shot, I taught my daughter to say, "Nice shot," and even use her tennis racket for silent applause. I've seen that happen maybe three times in professional tennis. When our sons were pitching in their Little League and high school baseball games, occasionally an errant pitch would hit a batter. I taught the boys to jog out to the batter as he was taking his free pass to first base…and apologize. I've seen that gesture maybe…*never* in professional baseball; typically, the pitcher turns away from the batter and looks in the other direction (unless the batter charges the mound in anger!). Why does the machismo of professional sports not allow for common courtesy? What does that lack of courtesy teach our young athletes about sportsmanship and, for that matter, about courtesy on the highway or in the crosswalk? I also taught my players after a game to run up and say, "Nice game," to the coach of the opposing team and to say thanks to their own coach (with an admitted ulterior motive since I was one of their coaches). While our team may not have had a reputation as a baseball powerhouse, we were respected for the courtesy we showed during and after the game.

Courtesy is contagious. The more we show, the more we are

rewarded with courtesy in return. And when we don't get it in return, at least we know we've taken the high road and pushed the world's needle slightly in the right direction. That, too, is reward.

Comfort and Condolence

The most difficult times in our relationships with others may also be the most important—when people who are important to us are seriously ill or in mourning. Hospital and hospice visits, funerals and condolence calls. The thought of going to any of them can be upsetting; I know it is for me. Yet it's rare that I don't feel better—rewarded—for having gone. The life stories of the deceased told at funerals remind me of something my grandmother used to say: everyone's life story is a book waiting to be written. When eulogies and remembrances are shared during times of grief, we always learn things about the departed that we never knew when they were alive. Achievements and disappointments. Hurdles overcome, kindnesses shown, impacts made. Visiting ill friends or family in the hospital can be even more upsetting and painful, especially when the illness is serious and the outcome in doubt. What to say, how to act, how long to stay? I've often thought that this is the most difficult role for clergy, visiting the seriously ill; in many ways, even more difficult than officiating at a funeral. At a funeral, clergy can memorialize the happy times of a person's life, bring comforting words to grieving loved ones. The uncertainties of serious illness make those visits more awkward and uncomfortable. Yet, at times like those, we all must bring out our "inner clergy." We need to remember that showing love is easy when everything is rosy, but for someone going through a major life challenge, in grief or in illness, love and concern are all the more important and the more meaningful.

Tragically, COVID-19 gave almost everyone more opportunity than we ever would have wanted to feel the rewards of providing comfort and condolence. Unable to enter hospitals, nursing homes, or hospice centers because of visitation restrictions brought on by the pandemic, our need to "virtually hug" was intense and the efforts we made to fill that need were valiant. Whether by phone, mail, social media, or Zoom, we reached out as best we could.

I attended several Zoom funerals during the pandemic. They were all painful for me, one particularly so. The bereaved widow watched, through the Zoom camera mounted at the cemetery, as her husband was laid to rest. Because of her own risk factors, she couldn't attend the burial in person; her son and grandchildren stood in for her while the rest of us joined with her digitally. I've been to many sad funerals over the years, but watching our friend's face as her beloved husband of fifty years was buried without her at his graveside was heartbreaking in a whole new way. A COVID-19 way. Yet even during that saddest of experiences, it was clear that the widow's ability to see loving friends and family on the computer screen her kids had set up for her brought her comfort—and those of us in the little Zoom boxes reaped the rewards of seeing that happen.

Timeliness and Connectedness

The window for appropriately expressing love during someone's most difficult challenges is often narrow. Waiting too long to make a condolence call, a hospital visit, a phone call, or even sending a card or email depreciates the value of your effort. As I'm writing this, I'm thinking of a dear friend from many years ago who lost her husband in a tragic accident. I called her at the time but waited a little longer than I should have because…well, I don't really have an excuse other than what I wrote earlier—it's a really hard call to make. My friend could not have been more gracious and appreciative, waving off my apologies for the delay. But I felt badly, and even if it wouldn't have made a difference to her, I know I would have felt better about myself had my call been timelier. An emotional reward rather than the emotional punishment I had experienced for waiting too long. And now, as I'm writing this, I realize I've done it again—I haven't spoken to the same friend since that call over a year ago, and I'm feeling more emotional punishment. I'm going to pause writing and call right now.

Update: Although this writing project wasn't meant to be real-time narrative, I do want to say I just called my friend. It was a bit awkward at first, but we spoke for almost forty-five minutes, and I feel so much better than I did when I was just thinking about calling. Doing the right thing at the right time makes a difference.

Timeliness depends on connectedness. Recently we heard about the passing of a dear friend, the mother of boys who grew up with our boys, went to school with them, shared their sports activities, had sleepovers at their home and ours. Cheryl's boys were meaningful friends to our kids, as were Cheryl and her husband to us. We knew of Cheryl's cancer diagnosis several years ago, but our last contact with her was reassuring: she was back at work, feeling better, recovered. And then, life got in the way and Cheryl and her husband fell off our radar and we lost track—until the notice for the funeral came out. Our devastation on hearing of Cheryl's passing was magnified by our regret and guilt for having lost our connection with her, not even realizing she had recently taken a turn for the worse. More emotional punishment. It's hard to keep up with everyone as lives evolve and priorities change. But Sara and I are particularly bad at it (example: we have never sent holiday cards with those family updates tucked inside, even to friends who send greetings and updates to us; we're just *so* busy, we tell ourselves). We heard about Cheryl's passing from David, another friend with whom we are in close touch and see frequently. He is wonderful at keeping up with people, sending birthday and anniversary greetings, maintaining contact with long-ago and not-so-long-ago friends. We could learn a lot from David; he defines the virtues of timeliness and connectedness. The sadness at Cheryl's funeral reminded us of how much we cared about her and how long it had been since we'd spoken to her. Later, at her home for a condolence call, we reconnected with her boys and her husband, a wonderful, tearful reunion and, once again, an opportunity to apologize for the time lost. Since then, we've stayed in touch with her husband and sons. Perhaps we're educable after all. Maybe we'll even send holiday cards next year.

One of the sweetest and most impactful outcomes of the pandemic was the outreach it created among family and friends whose busy lives had separated them from one another. People reconnected with long-lost contacts, checking on their health and safety, offering help when possible, but mostly just sharing time and concern, usually virtually. Organizations assigned volunteers to make calls to the most vulnerable members of their groups, and individuals developed their own call lists. As senior members of our circles, Sara and I received many calls and emails during the pandemic and, in turn, made many calls. I again called my friend who lost her husband all those years ago and had a much less awkward visit than the last time. I also asked her for contact information for mutual friends I hadn't been in touch with for too long. I took outdoor walks with Cheryl's husband (wearing a mask and at a safe social distance). But the number of calls and notes and care baskets Sara's ninety-two-year old father (who lives near us and was part of our safe circle during the pandemic) received and gave exceeded ours at least tenfold. The pandemic gave people much more time, and reason, for connecting with others. Time that otherwise is lost to the chaos and choreography of our lives. But the pandemic should also be an important lesson to make every effort to never again fall as far out of touch with the people we care about.

And what of the *actual* touch of people we care about? What's to become of our physical connectedness? Symbolic of the distances the pandemic placed between us, we stepped aside from others on sidewalks and trails so as not to be within the safe social distance restrictions. It felt like *antisocial* distancing. Masks prevented seeing friendly smiles among strangers passing on those sidewalks and trails, and in the grocery store or at the gas station. When we can physically hug again, we should, often, and we should remember how much we missed giving and receiving empathy, sympathy, and love physically and in person. We need to again greet one another with handshakes (yes, I'm an infectious diseases doctor and yes, I approve of returning to handshakes after the pandemic has passed. I also recommend hand washing because, not only is the novel coronavirus transmitted by hand-to-hand contact, so are the commonest of common colds that keep us from going to the office and school!). Of course, for long-distance connections with friends and family, video is wonderful. It brings grandchildren into the homes of grandparents hundreds or thousands of miles away. But for those personal interactions that *can* be done with actual face time rather than FaceTime, they should be.

Intimate, fact-to-face connectedness is critical beyond our interpersonal relationships as well. How can we even consider replacing in-person visits to our healthcare providers with telemedicine (unless the patient can't get to the clinic or hospital she needs)? Not only is the care of patients potentially compromised on a TV screen, but the well-being of the providers is impaired—physicians and therapists reported significantly heightened stress and fatigue during the pandemic because of the challenges of providing online rather than in-person care. Quality healthcare requires the full picture of a patient, which is best achieved with the patient in front of the caregiver, but it also requires the touch and warmth of a caregiver-patient relationship.

The pandemic taught us that the work many of us do for a living can be done remotely. The benefits of video conferencing for some types of work are real and tangible; colleagues can collaborate across the country or across the world without debilitating plane trips. But what video conferencing lacks are the hugely important intangibles: we miss context, nonverbal cues, body language, and eye contact. We miss physical connectedness, the pleasure of hearing and seeing those around us. Education, from preschool through college and graduate school, is also best provided in person, in the classroom, where teachers are closely connected with their students rather than online where socialization with classmates and eye contact with teachers are lost. Attention spans of younger kids are short, and without the in-person teacher and classmates, learning online for school age kids is inadequate.

Our ability to share real three-dimensional space with real three-dimensional people is what connects us to one another and makes us human. It is true that being around people, touching, kissing, hugging, eating in a restaurant, sitting in a baseball stadium or concert hall, will always put us at risk for germs, some of which may be dangerous. Because of the severity of COVID-19, we gave up those quintessential human connections during the pandemic. We must reclaim them.

It's sadly true that some of the concessions to safety we made after the 9/11 terrorist attacks continue today, but those were largely sacrifices of convenience, giving up some of the ease and joy of travel, for example. The precautions that remain after 9/11 haven't interfered with our connections to others. Similarly, after the Tylenol cyanide poisonings in Chicago in 1982, when seven people died, product safety measures have necessarily continued until today, but without interrupting our connectedness to others. However, if the concessions of human kinship we made for safety during the COVID-19 pandemic persist for years, we will have lost much more than precious lives due to the infection.

Divine Rewards and Heaven

As I wrote earlier, rewards and punishments from God are strictly a matter of personal belief. Many attribute their good fortune in life to their good deeds—rewards given from on high, and motivation for doing right. Others point to the many, many exceptions—good people whose lives are committed to good deeds but, as with the story of Job in the Bible or my father's family in Auschwitz, seem to be punished more than rewarded. For those who don't believe in divine intervention, bad events in good people's lives are proof of randomness and chance, of natural laws that cannot be altered by prayer or belief. Rabbi Harold Kushner, in his seminal book, *When Bad Things Happen to Good People,* wrote:

"God does not cause our misfortunes. Some are caused by bad luck, some are caused by bad people, and some are simply an inevitable consequence of our being human and being mortal, living in a world of inflexible natural laws."[45]

For believers in a divinity, interpretation of those seemingly misplaced bad events merely prove that we will never understand God's ways, much as the two-dimensional beings of Planar in "The Miraculous Event" short story (Appendix A) could not understand a sphere. For those believers, God is present, but beyond human capacity to comprehend. Rabbi Lord Jonathan Sacks, the late Chief Rabbi of the United Kingdom, retells the story of a rabbinic sage who lost his wife and all eleven of his children in Auschwitz. The sage, Rabbi Yekusiel Yehudah Halberstam, was asked how could he not want to know from God why those tragedies occurred to his family. He responded that if he asked God that question, he would surely be summoned to heaven to hear the answer, but he would rather be on Earth with questions than in heaven with the answers. On Earth, the sage committed the rest of his life to improving the lives of others, including the founding of schools, an orphanage, old age home, and a small hospital which grew into a major medical center.[46]

In the spirit of Rabbi Halberstam's actions after surviving the Holocaust, many theologians, including Rabbis Kushner and Sacks, answer the question of why bad things happen to good people by changing the question. They teach that we should instead be asking when bad things happen to good people, what should they do about it? How should they respond? Viktor Frankl, an Austrian psychiatrist and also an Auschwitz survivor, in his book *Man's Search for Meaning*, writes:

> "You cannot control what happens to you in life, but you can always control what you will feel and do about what happens to you."

More about Frankl's work in Key #6 to follow.

And what of heaven, an afterlife where reward and punishment might be doled out in ways we cannot possibly foresee or understand during this life? Earlier I mentioned that I hope somehow, somewhere, my dad knows that it was because of him that Sara and I met—his illness bringing me home to Denver, where Sara had just been transferred. Where might that somewhere be, the place where my dad might know that his death led me to move back to Denver, meet my wife, and have a cherished family? Where might he be now to know that we named our eldest child after him and our youngest after the brother he lost in Poland? Is there an afterlife? Is there really a heaven?

When Zadie, my grandfather, lay dying at 101 years of age, he was unconscious during his final hours. Weak and not moving for days, we spent many hours at his hospital bedside talking to him but without getting a response. Sara was visiting him shortly before he died, and the hospital chaplain was sitting with her in my grandfather's room. Suddenly, after days of not moving or speaking, he opened his eyes widely, looked up at the ceiling, and lifted his arms skyward. "All the people, look at all the people," he said over and over. And then, after a bit, he closed his eyes, lowered his arms, and didn't speak or have any meaningful movements again. Sara was stunned and didn't know what to make of what she had just seen. The chaplain, who also saw this happen, told her he's seen similar events many times among terminal patients. Seemingly seeing something others in the room don't see, something "otherworldly," for lack of a better description.

As I've mentioned, I collect medical miracles, and I solicited essays from esteemed physician colleagues about their experiences with patients they cared for whose stories were unforgettable and, often, unexplainable. The result was the book, *Miracles We Have Seen*, several stories from which I retold in the section on medical coincidences in Key #2. Other stories in that book tell of patients who "saw beyond" their hospital rooms, written by the physicians who witnessed the events. And the lay literature is filled with descriptions of near-death experiences where patients describe seeing a tunnel with bright lights or other phenomena they couldn't explain, including experiencing interactions with deceased family members or religious figures. Lack of oxygen? Brain decay in the final moments of life? A chemical discharge causing dreams or hallucinations? We can't really design a scientific experiment to explore those biologic possibilities. Or, is it possible that rather than a biochemical imbalance, patients are really seeing heaven?

Of course, I don't know the answer to that. But this is a book about living life with no regrets, so I'll confess that in addition to trying to act in a way that leaves me feeling as if I've done the right thing in the moment, because that feeling itself is the reward, I also think about doing good as a way of hedging my bets in the event there is something else out there, something that follows this life, with reward and punishment.

As I've noted repeatedly, and in concert with Key #1 for *No Regrets Living*, I do believe there is more to our lives than we perceive and experience in our day-to-day existence. Perhaps the "more" can be attained simply by reaching a greater level of consciousness during our lives, e.g., through meditation or hypnosis or prayer or long-distance running. Or, perhaps the more is an afterlife that awaits all of us, a place to which our soul transcends, a place where my dad might know that because of him, I met Sara. Maybe there's even a "before life." There's an interesting book by Yechiel Michel Tucazinsky called, *The Bridge of Life: Life as a Bridge between Past and Future.*[47] His argument is that our fetal life is a state of profound naiveté about what lies outside the womb. At birth, we are introduced into a world unimaginable to us as a fetus. Similarly, he suggests, our life after death is unimaginable to us now in this life but will be as profound and astounding to us as this worldly life is to a newborn. I like that way of seeing "after death."

Even if those long tunnels and bright lights, or "all the people" my grandfather saw, were simply biochemical changes of dying and not peeks into the next phase, acting *as if* there might be a next phase can help us live this life with appreciation and good behavior. In that way, we experience the rewards of our immediate good deeds, feel contentment, have fewer regrets, and perhaps even have less fear of death.

TIME

I believe the concept of linear time, progressing from the past to the present to the future, is a construct by humans to explain our existence. Much as the two-dimensional inhabitants of Planar interpreted the passing of a sphere through their planet as a dot and then a circle and then a dot again, *changing with time*, we interpret our birth, aging, and death as the effect of time on who we are. For me, some of our existence is better explained by a nonlinear concept of time. Key #1 for *No Regrets Living*, the belief in something greater than ourselves, helps us accept an alternative to linear time, a dimension, perhaps, in which the future is known simultaneously with the past and present. It's all known, at once and always, perhaps like a circle (yes, another human construct), without a distinct beginning or end, a continuum.

I wrote earlier about the three types of reward and punishment. The first, the immediate and tangible sense of fulfillment or regret after our actions; the second, reward or punishment from on high, from God, for our good or bad deeds; and, the third being reward or punishment in an afterlife. Let's revisit for a moment the second of those categories of reward and punishment through the lens of a non-linear time frame. Perhaps good occurrences early in our life might be advance reward for our deserving behavior later in life, or misfortune in our young lives a punishment for bad deeds we will commit later. While in our linear perception of time, *early* and *later* are sequential; a nonlinear continuum of time views all of life in the same time frame—good deeds may be rewarded and bad may be punished, but not necessarily in logical (human logic) order. As I said, I leave the conclusion about whether there is reward and punishment from on high during our lives to your personal belief. For me, although a provocative concept, nonlinear time still doesn't help explain the horrific tragedies that befall true innocents. How can sending a baby or young child to the gas chamber possibly be explained by any concept of time? Or a child's terminal illness or fatal accident? For those unthinkable, yet too real occurrences, I again revert to Key #1 for *No Regrets Living*, belief in something greater than what we can understand, and to Key #3, my hope that we will someday be able to heal the world of those tragedies.

In addition to considering the possibility of nonlinear time, controlling two aspects of how we spend time—anticipation and replay—can help us achieve *No Regrets Living*. There are good events and bad events that we know of in advance and anticipate. On the one hand, anticipation of good events is felt by some to enhance the event itself—the weeks, days, and hours leading up to something we are excited about can be as exciting as the event itself. On the other hand, the dread we feel anticipating upcoming unpleasant events can make the time leading to those events as unpleasant as the event itself. To live a no regrets life, we should realize that anticipation of happy events speeds up time while anticipation of unhappy events slows down time—but both waste time. Much of *today* is lost eagerly awaiting, or dreading, *tomorrow*. It's cliché to say we should spend more time in the moment. I took the training in traditional meditation, practiced it (when I had the ten minutes to spare!), and have preached it. But even after a successful meditation to stay in the moment, the moment ends, and tomorrow's agenda or next week's agenda pops into your head and speeds the rest of the day. We can become so focused on how much time is left before tomorrow's event that today is gone before we know it. By the end of each day, you may find yourself wondering how you spent it and what you missed as your mind raced ahead. Vacations are wonderful, meant to slow things down and allow for enjoying the moments. But even then, it can take days to unwind at the start of time off, and then inevitably we begin thinking about how much time is left, anticipating our return to the grind.

Anticipating, predicting, modeling, and in every other way looking toward the end of the COVID-19 pandemic became a national pastime, and I succumbed as well. Drawn in by my infectious diseases perspective and "insider's knowledge," I binged on each day's news and numbers, joining with colleagues in the debates and discussions about best practices and historic precedents. Disease experts, statisticians, politicians, business owners, laid-off workers, and just about everyone else indulged in rampant anticipation of a return to "normal," yearning to again be immersed in the everyday, mundane routines we have become so accustomed to. *Addicted* to. I yearned, as well. Time felt muddied during the pandemic (a popular meme on social media suggested "Blursday" to describe any day of the week during the pandemic), weekdays felt like weekends, and our anticipation of an end to the isolation and restrictions reached pandemic levels.

And then there was the COVID-19 "two-week incubation period countdown" form of anticipation. After a possible exposure, perhaps someone coughing near us in the grocery store or friends from out of town paying an unexpected visit, we began looking forward to the two-week mark after such an event at which time we could feel safe that we hadn't caught the infection. Anticipating the future in two-week intervals is exhausting.

Although anxiety over when and how life as we knew it will resume has been a part of my pandemic experience, during the peak of the lockdown I regularly tried to snap out of my sense of deprivation and appreciate the lull and the quietude. I found myself more able to live in the moments (the very long moments!) of the quarantines and isolation, take comfort in the inevitability of the events, and accept the circumstances. I found myself more productive than during normal times and realized the obvious—the routines I craved were more distracting from, and disruptive of, my most creative efforts. I wrote more consistently and, I hope, more cogently during the peak pandemic days than before. I also appreciated the little niceties of life I had been too busy for before the outbreak: downtime for reading, a gentle walk outside; quiet moments for a cup of coffee or glass of wine with Sara; hearing the howling of our neighbors (and joining them in howling) at 8 PM every evening in tribute to our frontline workers; seeing neighborhood kids playing with their parents in their yards.

When we finally enter more normal times, we should create our own shelter-in-place order during which we slow down, take deep breaths, contemplate, and appreciate the moment, if only for a brief interlude each very busy day. I suggest that we find a bit of pandemic in our daily pandemonium, pausing to appreciate how wonderful our mundane routines are, seek escape from them when we feel the need, and then emerge and reconnect. And we shouldn't waste those pandemic pauses in our routines by anticipating tomorrow and next week.

Much as anticipation wastes the moment and undermines *No Regrets Living*, so does our tendency to replay, spending time today thinking about what we did or should have done yesterday. If we are truly to live a no regrets life, what's past is past and wasting time rewinding it and wishing we could undo it or do it all over again is an indulgence we can't afford with the limited time we have to do all we hope to in life. Those are regrets, which we don't have time for. I taught my kids that once they finished taking a test in school, they shouldn't look up the answers to see if they got them right. When it's done, it's done. The same is true for major decisions we make in our life—the decision has been made, the results will happen whether we worry about it or not, time to move on. What's done is done. Replays breed regret and distract us from the moment we should be focused on—that's time poorly spent.

Time, be it linear or circular, quantifiable or intangible, is finite for each of us. Our lives have term limits, and we shouldn't waste time awaiting what's to come or rewinding what has passed. There is one technique that has helped me appreciate the present. I "channel." Because my dad died so young and never met Sara, our kids, or our grandkids, at special moments in our family life, I pause and channel him into the scene: I try to see what's happening around me with enough concentration and focus for him to see it through me. Now that my mom has died, I include her in the channeling. Channeling slows down the moment for me, forces me to really notice *now*. The price I pay is that sometimes the people in the room think I've zoned out or am stoned (recall I live in Colorado), or both.

KEY #6
SEEK

NO REGRETS LIVING asks us to be in search of four worthy goals: purpose, self-forgiveness, community, and simplicity.

PURPOSE

Viktor Frankl was a controversial Austrian psychiatrist whose book, *From Death-Camp to Existentialism (Man's Search for Meaning)*,[48] became the foundation of an entirely new theory and practice of psychology called logotherapy. Briefly, logotherapy holds that finding purpose in life is the key to healing, thriving, and, even, under extreme circumstances, to surviving. For background, Frankl was a Holocaust survivor, like my father. He was very briefly interned in the Auschwitz death camp, arriving about a year after my father did and leaving for another internment days later. Frankl is a controversial figure for reasons that are beyond the scope of this discussion.

What is relevant, I believe, is Frankl's doctrine that there is no single purpose in life, no one "meaning" that applies to all people in all situations. Rather, finding one's meaning in life is a very personal quest, continuously subject to modification and reassessment. What the actual ultimate purpose one finds for his or her life is not nearly as important as simply having purpose at all. That is, without purpose, life is futile and frustrating, leading to psychological torment. Frankl took this even further, asserting that those with purpose in their lives were more likely to survive the horrors of the Holocaust than those who didn't. Once again, very controversial, bordering on blaming the victims for their own deaths. Yet the message outside the context of gas chambers is worthy of our consideration—purpose gives us reason to live and strength to overcome difficulties. In the context of *No Regrets Living*, seeking and finding purpose leads to fewer regrets about what we haven't achieved—yet! Because we're on the path toward a known destination.

In the late 1960s, my formative teen years, the Beatles famously traveled to India to find their purpose under the guidance of

Maharishi Mahesh Yogi, the founder of the Transcendental Meditation movement. As a result, the Beatles reportedly gave up drugs and entered the most prolific songwriting period of their careers. The image of John, Paul, George, and Ringo climbing a mountain, entering an ashram, and discovering the true meaning of life is a romantic one but unrealistic for most of us. Our "mountain" probably will be closer to home, perhaps *in* our home, yet the discovery of purpose can be just as impactful. Numerous clinical studies have associated having a sense of purpose in life with an improved aging experience, overall longevity, and even higher chances of surviving cancer.[49]

We are close friends with two families who lost children to suicide. The tsunami of sadness and despair caused by depression overwhelmed any purpose those troubled kids may have found in their young lives, rendering their lives meaningless in their eyes. Of course, this sounds simplistic and obvious: helping troubled and potentially suicidal youth discover or rediscover purpose and meaning in their lives can literally save their lives. The challenge is to recognize the disease in time to intervene. As much as I would like to believe the medical establishment, including my fellow pediatricians, can provide crucial screening for these young people, I am doubtful—adolescents and young adults visit their physicians infrequently and when they do are often stoic in describing their mental status. For families fortunate enough to recognize their children's struggles and be able to afford proactive mental health therapy for them, therapists can make a huge difference in helping kids see purpose in their lives. But for the vast majority of society, the hope for meaningful and timely intervention lies with families and schools. Greater efforts at educating parents and teachers, and teens themselves, regarding the worrisome signs of depression and the available resources for help are essential. However, awareness is only part of the solution—as a society, we must derive methods to combat some of the root causes of depression, such as bullying, racism and other bigotries, gender identity crises, social media pressures, and domestic abuse. Thankfully, most kids facing those hurdles don't commit suicide, but addressing root causes in suicide-prone kids will improve the lives of all kids. There can be no greater regret in life than feeling more could have been done to save a child's life.

Projections during the pandemic indicated that suicide rates would increase in the wake of COVID-19's devastating health and economic effects.[50] While it will take time to determine if those statistics bear out, prior economic collapses have clearly been proven to increase suicide rates.[51] The conclusion, as it pertains to *No Regrets Living*, is that too many people link their purpose in life, or perhaps their ability to achieve that purpose, to their financial status. A worthy outcome from the pandemic would be for us to learn how to recognize and help troubled individuals see beyond immediate stresses to a time when their lives will be better and their purpose renewed.

For those of us fortunate enough to face only the more manageable challenges of daily life, the lesson of finding purpose also holds. It's easier to deal with everyday ups and downs when the big picture is in focus, when we know where we're going, even if we're not always certain how we're getting there.

As I am writing this section, I'm sitting on the porch watching starlings in flight, circling, diving, cavorting. Are humans the only species in need of finding meaning in life on their own? I suspect those little birds know their purpose instinctively—it's probably to procreate, build a nest, provide for their young, teach their babies to fly on their own. Broadly speaking, those are purposes prescribed by nature for most species. Biology and the natural laws I spoke of earlier have innately provided purpose for nonhuman creatures. Animals live by instinct—when to hunt, when to eat, when to breed, when to nurture, even when to die. Humans alone have been tasked with going beyond instinct to find our unique purpose in life.

Finding purpose in our lives can lead us back to more instinctual behavior, to find our "inner starling," behavior reflexively focused on achieving our purpose and leaving us feeling more content at the end of each day because we have strived toward our purpose. And perhaps even giving us more days to live. The section on Activism in Key #3 and the section on Giving in Key #5 have suggestions for seeking and finding purpose in our lives.

> One of the most important silver linings of the pandemic was the opportunity it gave many of us to reassess our purpose in life. Not only were we confronted by a potentially deadly disease, we were forced to stay at home with plenty of time to reflect on our lives. We thought about our mortality and our loved ones' mortality. We thought about what we normally did each day and whether or not that was meaningful use of our time. We noticed how much of what we thought we needed may not be as necessary as we thought, and we also noticed how important other things we previously took for granted actually were. We imagined how we might do better during the next crisis in our lives. We wondered how we might help others through the pandemic, what skills we had that could be valuable to those not as fortunate as us. We considered how our post-pandemic lives might be made more meaningful, more contributory, more...purposeful. The pandemic forced us to reassess our purpose in life; our challenge is to keep that focus, seek that purpose, as we emerge.

SELF-FORGIVENESS

After liberation from the concentration camp, my father became part of a kibbutz in Europe, a group of young survivors like himself who helped smuggle other Holocaust survivors to Israel. An underground railroad. Still under British control, emigration to Israel was tightly regulated and effectively off limits to Jewish victims of the Nazis—that's the story line of Leon Uris's famous book, *Exodus,* and the subsequent Paul Newman movie of the same name. One of the immigrants Dad helped reach Israel ultimately came to Denver where she tracked down Dad to thank him for, as she said, saving her from Europe and allowing her to live for many years in Israel. As I wrote earlier, while working with this underground railroad, Dad contracted tuberculosis (TB) and when it came time for him to immigrate to Israel, he was hospitalized in a Czech "consumption" (TB) facility and couldn't go. Because Dad's fellow "kibbutzniks" all did ultimately leave for Israel and helped defend and build the country, he always felt unworthy of even visiting Israel. His guilt at not being there when the country needed him was overwhelming, kept him from fulfilling a lifetime wish of seeing "the Promised Land," and left him with a lifetime of regret. Although unable to forgive himself for not getting to Israel after the war, Dad did find contentment in his life in America, as I wrote several years ago for the *New York Times.*[52]

Among the other traits I inherited from my father was his propensity for guilt. Several years ago, Sara's sister and brother-in-law invited us to take a trip to Africa with them for a safari experience. Sara joined them; I couldn't. During three decades in medicine, I had many opportunities to travel abroad to volunteer in underserved parts of the world where a pediatrician's skills could be life altering, even lifesaving, for those in greatest need. I didn't have the courage to do it, and I've had trouble forgiving myself ever since. I cared for some of the sickest children in the United States—kids with devastating infections complicating devastating underlying diseases. And that work was very fulfilling for me, even during the many sad moments when our best efforts failed. At least I was in the fight. But my insecurity with my general pediatric skills, skills that I hadn't practiced since residency training and would be required in international clinic environments, prevented me from traveling to those clinics and trying.

In retrospect, that was unfounded insecurity. Even though my day-to-day practice of pediatrics was limited to the sickest kids requiring the most intensive care, I'm now certain enough of my basic pediatric knowledge would have resurfaced as patients in Haiti or the Dominican Republic or Africa would have required. Instead, I stayed home, worked diligently on tough cases, but slept in my own bed at night and didn't push myself beyond my comfort zone.

And I have felt guilty ever since. Guilt that spoke to me with these words, *When you had the chance to be in Africa to make a difference, you didn't go. Now you want to visit as a tourist, an elitist, a voyeur? To enjoy the beauty of the land and ignore the poverty and disease you did nothing to change?* I didn't feel like I had earned a vacation adventure in Africa. Like father, like son. I regretted what I hadn't done, the opportunities I missed to make a small dent in parts of the world that need so much. Guilt and regrets are closely related.

When guilt affects our decisions, it's time to reexamine the source and substance of the guilt in hopes of self-forgiveness. In both my father's case and in mine, there are enough redeeming actions and exculpatory reasons to have allowed us to forgive ourselves and move on. That's the second surest path toward losing guilt: finding worthwhile and meaningful actions, either already accomplished or waiting to be accomplished, to compensate for the shortcomings you feel. The surest path, however, if still possible, is doing the right thing in arrears. Rather than look back at what you feel you should have done or shouldn't have done—the action or inaction that is causing the guilt—do the right thing now, albeit belatedly.

Here's an admittedly simplistic example. Sara and I were driving home from a medical appointment and stopped on the way to get takeout sandwiches. Standing on a street corner at a traffic light about five miles from our house was a homeless man holding a sign, ANYTHING WILL HELP, GOD BLESS. I opened the car window, ready to give him my sandwich, but then the light changed to green, cars behind me got impatient and honked, so I kept driving. When I got home, I felt terrible about driving past the man, so I turned around and drove back with the sandwich. By the time I got there, he was no longer on the corner. I parked my car and walked around the block hoping to find him, but I didn't. My guilt remained, but in arrears I tried to do the right thing, helping me to forgive myself a bit. Next time I'll try to do the right thing in the first place.

You may be wondering why I don't go to Africa (or Haiti, or the Dominican Republic, or Puerto Rico) now, making amends in arrears for my lack of courage when I was younger. A good question. Now, even more removed from the day-to-day practice of pediatrics, and older enough that health issues have crept in, it remains a difficult decision for me, but I'm working on it.

Self-forgiveness has become critically important for many during the COVID-19 pandemic who fear they may have transmitted the infection to others. I'm an infectious diseases doctor, so trust me when I say this: Everyone who became ill or died from COVID-19 caught it from someone else. Everyone. In the best-case scenario, the person who transmitted the infection was unknown to the victim and the transmitter didn't know he or she was contagious. In a worse-case scenario, the transmitter was known to the victim. And in the absolute worst-case scenario of all, the transmitter was not only known but was discovered to have transmitted to multiple people and had his or her identity revealed.

There is an unhealthy curiosity during widespread infections to identify "Patient 0," the index case who started it all. The Typhoid Mary. We most famously saw it during the HIV-AIDS epidemic. During the COVID-19 pandemic, several Patient 0s were identified by zealous disease detectives, and then inadequately shielded by a breathless media and voyeuristic public. There was the thirty-five-year old man in Washington State who had just returned from Wuhan where he was visiting family and became widely identified as the presumed Patient 0 in the United States. And then the fifty-five-year old attorney in New Rochelle, New York, with no known exposure, yet far too much press coverage, who was the first in a county-wide outbreak. Italy's Patient 0 was a German tourist, but Italy's "Patient 1," a thirty-eight-year old man named Mattia, became infamous as a "super spreader" who infected many people, including his elderly father (who died of the infection) and his pregnant wife. Far too much information for the world to know about this poor man.

But now we know, with the improvement and greater availability of testing, there were likely cases circulating in this country and elsewhere before the Patient 0s and Patient 1s were infected—the earlier cases simply weren't recognized as such because the pandemic itself hadn't yet been recognized. The first recorded death in the United States due to the coronavirus was initially thought to have been in Washington State on February 29, 2020, but since then we've learned that numerous previously unexplained deaths in California and elsewhere have proven to have been due to COVID-19. Patient 0s aren't always the first, again proving the risks of identifying and labeling. Even more relevant to us than the purported Patient 0s and Patient 1s who should feel no guilt are the thousands of other people who also unknowingly infected family, friends, or strangers, perhaps with tragic results. As a virologist with decades of experience from which to pontificate about virus transmission, let me tell any of you who feel you might have infected another or others, and especially let me tell the Patient 0s and Patient 1s of Washington, New Rochelle, California, Italy, or in your community—the pandemic is not your fault, nor are the infections others may have caught from you. You didn't do it purposely and you had no idea you were infected. Germs always move from person to person, despite our best efforts at prevention. It's what germs do, and have done, since the beginning of time. Now it's time to forgive yourself and move on.

For those who may have been unknowingly infected and contagious but knowingly disregarded public health measures of social distancing, quarantine, and masks during times of peak disease spread, I can offer no similar absolution. You didn't have the right to put others at risk by your own risky behavior. And then there are the even less forgivable stories of COVID-19 parties: gatherings of young people intent on transmitting to, or catching the virus from, the other partyers. Such parties have their roots in the days of measles parties and chickenpox parties where parents, hoping to infect their kids "naturally," flocked to the homes of other kids sick with those infections. All such parties ignore the fact that each of these diseases including, of course, COVID-19, while usually benign in otherwise healthy individuals, can have severe and even fatal complications in low-risk as well as in high-risk individuals. Infections are not reason to party.

Dialectical Behavioral Therapy is a methodology psychologists use to treat some of their most challenging and difficult patients, especially those with self-harming or suicidal thoughts. DBT helps patients accept who they are, recognizing the issues and behaviors that trouble them while also guiding patients to change those behaviors and resolve those issues. The therapy teaches patients to wholly accept themselves and their troubling behaviors while simultaneously working to change them. For those of us fortunate enough to have less severe challenges to overcome, seeking self-forgiveness asks us to use a similar approach: recognize and accept what's causing our regrets or guilt, and find emotional and practical ways to move forward.

I suggest that a meaningful strategy for moving forward is simple substitution—replacing the regrets you're feeling with a well-deserved sense of pride in the positive accomplishments in your life. Much as I wish my father had been able to focus on all the good he had achieved in his life to help him alleviate his guilt about not joining his comrades, and much as I am working on myself to do the same about not helping in troubled lands. The biggest risk to *No Regrets Living*, to a life of contentment, is being so fixated on our shortcomings that we overlook, forget, or dismiss our strengths.

COMMUNITY

Sara and I are part of an Orthodox Jewish community centered on a small synagogue in our neighborhood. As I confessed earlier, we are not Orthodox in our observance or, as evidenced by much of what I've written on these pages, even in our belief system. Our belonging to this community came about unexpectedly, the result of my religiously observant mother needing a synagogue she could walk to on the Sabbath. When she could no longer walk there on her own, Sara and I began accompanying her and soon Sara's mom joined us as well. But the community has since become an important part of our lives. It's a very young community with dozens of strollers blocking the entrance and older kids playing on scooters in the empty parking lot (this group doesn't drive on the Sabbath!). Sara and I are among the senior congregants, and our mothers were the *senior* senior members—and as such, they were treated as royalty of sorts whenever they came to services. The rabbi and fellow congregants would greet them on their arrival and say goodbye before they left for home, ask about their health, and tell them how happy they were to have them as part of the congregation. We got to know most of the members of this community quickly and felt welcomed by them. Although most of our new friends were more observant than us, we never felt judged.

But the power of community became even more evident to us when our mothers passed away, exactly seven weeks apart from each other. The traditional Shiva (Jewish period of mourning) periods following their deaths were filled by visits from many dozens of people from the various communities of which our moms had been a part during their lives, but especially from the synagogue. This also highlighted for us the difference between friends and community. Of course, friends came by for condolence visits. But the majority of well-wishers in those sad days—the people paying respects, bringing food, sending cards, and making donations to our moms' favorite charities—were not friends in the conventional way of describing friends. They were not people we or our moms socialized with. Rather, they were kind and thoughtful people who knew our mothers from their communities and wanted to express their condolences and fondness for our moms. They spoke to us about how much they enjoyed just seeing our mothers at services—or at the swimming pool, in the supermarket, at book club, or in the lobby of the apartment building or community center. In close and welcoming communities, the loss of a community member affects everyone. My grandfather used to say, when asked about a particular event he attended, "I saw everyone I wanted to see and everyone I didn't want to see." True that being part of a community may involve sometimes awkward socializing and forced pleasantries. But the support we received from our mothers' communities and our communities was very important for our healing, cementing our connections to "those we want to see" and forming new friendships with "those we didn't want to see."

Belonging to a community, or communities, is important for *No Regrets Living.* The more isolated we feel, the more of life's joys and pleasures we miss because so many of those experiences come from friendships and companionship. As we look back at our lives, we will regret those missed experiences and the contentment they would have brought. Of course, quiet time alone can also bring contentment, as I wrote in Key #4. But when those quiet and private moments end, it's time to seek out your community. Isolation is bad for health, physical and mental. Innumerable studies have shown that social isolation increases illness rates and shortens life. In fact, isolation has been proven to be as strong a risk factor for increased illness and early death as obesity, smoking, lack of exercise, and high blood pressure.[53] And, isolation can even contribute to and exacerbate those other risk factors as well as depression and suicide.

If you already belong to one or more communities, nurture those relationships; if you're not now a part of a community, find a group of people who share a common interest and join them in their activities. You'll be surprised at how welcoming strangers can be, and then they won't be strangers any longer. Social media networking and being part of an online community, while having its own potential benefits, is not the same as regularly seeing your community in person. Purdue University President, Mitch Daniels, said, in his 2020 commencement address to graduates: "For most of human history, personal contact was hard to avoid. Suddenly, our digital age can mean it requires extra effort."

COVID-19 removed any doubts anyone might have had about the importance of community and challenged us to develop novel ways to find and maintain community. Forced to shelter in place, maintain social distance, and limit group activities, the pandemic suddenly threatened us with damaging isolation. So we sought new ways to connect. Zoom was accessed by hundreds of millions of users each day[54] and became the most widely used free app in the country.[55] Other video networking options also soared—Skype, FaceTime, Microsoft Teams—all allowing friends to connect and check on one another's well-being. Millions of individuals shared internet memes and created YouTube videos about their lives—some of which "went viral" (to use a newly complicated phrase) and cheered up even faraway strangers. Numbers of WhatsApp, Facebook, Instagram, and TikTok users and followers exploded, nearly overwhelming the capacities of those platforms. And as if we needed more proof of the value of companionship, the pandemic saw pet adoption skyrocket and animal shelters empty.

When possible, we found ways to leave our screens and phones and join three-dimensional, in-the-flesh communities. Those of us fortunate enough to live outside crowded urban centers walked parks and empty streets with friends, separated by safe distances, shouting greetings and news about our lives through our masks. We stood outside the homes of our elderly and infirmed neighbors and friends and gestured through their closed windows. We left care packages on doorsteps and sang from our balconies. We invited friends and family to sit in our backyard, safely separated from us and without sharing food or drink (Sara commented that this was the easiest entertaining we ever did!). We proved that community plays a central part in our lives. And we gained new empathy for those who live alone during normal times, recognizing the need for us to reach out to them more often, whether there's a pandemic going on or not. So many of the most vulnerable members of our society live in poor and crowded conditions without access to either safe outdoor spaces or to the internet. For them, finding companionship of any kind during the pandemic was next to impossible—and dangerous—predisposing them not only to the risks of infection but also to all the hazards of isolation and loneliness. We have to do better.

The pandemic also removed us from wide swaths of our extended communities—people and places we would normally interact with in person, now, relegated to digital images and voices, or falling out of touch entirely. Our doctors practiced telemedicine; our schools and universities gave online-only classes; our colleagues held virtual meetings; our houses of worship offered Zoom services; our friends shared their morning coffee and afternoon happy hours with one another online; our movie nights out became Netflix nights in (Netflix even provided a platform for syncing movies with friends so they could talk during the show and not get shushed by the people sitting behind them—because there were no people sitting behind them!); our groceries and other essentials were ordered online and delivered by parades of vans and trucks; eating out in restaurants was replaced by ordering in; sales of cars and houses were conducted with digital signatures; life cycle events where guests would normally have arrived in their cars or flown in from across the country were replaced by creative similes of the events, all subject to the limitations of bandwidth and buffering.

These were understandable accommodations to an unprecedented hinge event in our lives (*hinge event* refers to a major occurrence that alters the course of history). Those accommodations, however, were devastating to our economy, which again put our most vulnerable individuals and communities at a risk as great as, or greater than, the virus itself. Community is essential not only for individuals' health but also for a healthy society and a healthy economy.

But here's the scary part: There are many who have interpreted our replacement of face-to-face human interactions as a *good* thing, an advance that we should carry forward in the post-pandemic world even though we can again do in person what the pandemic forced us to find alternatives for. There are those who believe that the time we save by not commuting to the office, to class, to worship services is time we could better use doing other things—presumably also digitally! Why spend money on tuition and dormitories when you can earn a college degree in your mom's basement? Why drive across town to sit in a conference room in an overpriced office building with colleagues when you can conference at home in a *Hollywood Squares* (vintage TV game show) or *Brady Bunch* (vintage TV sitcom) digital box in your pajama bottoms? Who needs the waiting lines at restaurants and movie theaters when the food and entertainment are only a couple of keyboard clicks away?

Advocates of not going back to the way it was before the pandemic argue that there were many more benefits than just money and convenience. With tele-everything, pollution decreased, rush hour traffic jams disappeared, the number of car crashes decreased, gas prices and airline fares decreased, and wildlife flourished. I agree, those downstream benefits were, indeed, realized and were unexpected silver linings of the pandemic. But rather than conclude from those silver linings that we should continue to stay in our homes and connect virtually with the rest of the world, I believe we should conclude that the pandemic restrictions proved human impact on the environment around us has indeed been substantial and damaging, and we must find ways to reduce that negative impact without retreating into personal silos. But as I wrote earlier about the importance of connectedness, we should also conclude that we need the community and companionship we find in meeting rooms, restaurants, bars, theaters, and coffee shops, and that a robust economy and the workers it supports depend on those venues as well. We should conclude that there is pleasure in squeezing cantaloupe, trying on clothes, choosing eyeglass frames we can try on from an entire wall of choices, playing with gadgets, and matching makeup color to our skin tone, all of which we can only do in brick-and-mortar retail stores where employees are paid a living wage and can support their families because of our patronage.

The solution to maintaining the unexpected and welcome silver linings of the pandemic's restrictions is *not* to stay in our silos but rather to find ways to restore human communities, in person, while still minimizing our footprint on the environment and maximizing our support of the economy. A worthy challenge for the prepared minds I wrote about earlier.

I agree with those who say the pandemic merely sped along societal changes that were already happening, taking preexisting trends and turning them into inevitabilities almost overnight. Yes, telemedicine was emerging, brick-and-mortar retail stores were falling victim to behemoth online marketplaces, universities were increasing online classroom options, robots were taking over human factories, a cashless economy was unfolding, driverless delivery cars and Ubers were in advanced development, bank tellers were being replaced by digital deposit options, video streaming networks threatened the viability of movie theaters; and meal delivery services threatened restaurant occupancy—all well before the pandemic. Meeting fellow single people online has been around for a long time, but the pandemic took the next step with actual *dates* going virtual. A seemingly relentless march away from human contact and human community to a cyber community of pixels and kilobytes. And yes, the pandemic turned that relentless march into a stampede. A British study, which I sincerely hope will be proven wrong someday, found that average adults will spend thirty-four years of their lives in front of a digital screen,[56] and that was *before* the pandemic.

So now we are left with two options for how to proceed: Should we allow the disruption caused by the pandemic to increase our virtual lives even more? Do we further surrender our humanness and deem the droid community inevitable? Or has the pandemic given us a preview of the future that jolts us into realizing the precious individuality and human communities we will be losing, and frightened us enough to not let that happen? I vote for the latter—let's shake hands on it!

SIMPLICITY

Too often, what we seek in life is more, better, faster, and fancier. We aggressively strive to advance in our careers and in our personal lives. Climbing our achievement ladders. And as we climb, we seek more elaborate lifestyles, which in turn require more elaborate and expensive devices and toys. We feel detached and anxious away from our smart phones and computers, so we use our car dashboards to stay online while driving the latest model, digitally-designed automotive marvels. We require ever-more extravagant equipment for our physical exercise, our morning coffee, the utensils in our kitchen, the computers on our lap or on our ergonomic desk, and the TV screens in our home theaters. Our mirrorless cameras are mounted on our lightweight drones; our investment apps monitor the changes in our bitcoin portfolio; and our manicured pets wear collars with digital tracking and camera features. None of this comes cheap, forcing us, not only to choose between our wants and our needs, but also between our wants and *others'* needs—where does charity fit into a life of seeking more, better, faster, and fancier? And not only do we seek loftier lives and the accoutrements that come with them for ourselves, we seek the same for our kids, pushing them into competitive schools, sports, and social groups. Of course we do it for *their sake*—what parent doesn't want the best for his kids, but their success also reflects well on us, giving us another ladder to climb. Recent scandals surrounding college admissions attest to just how far down the rabbit hole seeking our kids' (and our) success might take us.

For *No Regrets Living,* rather than seeking the more elaborate and more sophisticated, I ask you to discover a lower rung on your ladder, to seek simplicity. It's not easy to put on the brakes (see my story of Rick, Mike, and James in the Parent section of Key #4). We feel compelled to keep up with the upward mobility of others, with what's parked in their driveways, in their gated communities. We don't want to fall behind society's technological advances, lest we lose advantage in the race for…the race for what, exactly? It's natural to want the latest and greatest—to *need* the latest and greatest—to feel satisfied and accomplished. But the contentment that comes with slowing down and needing less can be even more profound and truly liberating.

There are times when we are reminded of that in powerful ways. Six years ago, I was riding my bike on a nearby trail and developed terrible heartburn. It had also happened a couple weeks earlier while I was on a brisk walk. I, the wise physician, self-diagnosed "exercise-induced reflux." To confirm my insightfulness, I called my friend Harvey (he of the fateful introduction of my daughter and future son-in-law), who is a gastroenterologist (specialist in gastrointestinal diseases) in Pennsylvania and asked him what antacid he recommends for the diagnosis I gave myself (just another example of why a doctor who is his own doctor has a fool for a doctor). Harvey asked me to describe my symptoms, and then said, in no uncertain terms, "Get the heck to a cardiologist, NOW!" (he didn't actually say "heck" or any other word that starts with a letter other than F). I did what he said and had quadruple bypass open-heart surgery the following week.

Following my surgery, all I wanted was quiet and restful time to recover. To read and to meditate. To sit outside with my leg elevated to help heal the sites where the replacement veins for my heart were taken. And the healing was slow. My first walk around the block, arm in arm with Sara for support, was breathtaking, literally and figuratively, for the gratitude and relief it brought me. On that walk I realized I would ultimately heal, would be able to return to my daily routines and my work, and I would have more days with those I loved. But I also realized what many recovering from illness or injury realize, that life is finite and precious, and each minute wasted is time lost forever (more about making the most of every moment in Key #7). There were so many needs I had before surgery that I no longer needed in recovery. Sure, the smart phone and computer returned to my life in the weeks that followed, but my other needs became easier to meet and my appreciation for sitting outside and taking walks has stayed with me. The long scar on my chest and the smaller one on my leg remind me, every day, of what's really important and what's really worth worrying about. Since the surgery, my connections with people are more personal than digital, my home is more comfortable than classy, and my little 1994 Honda Accord still gets me where I need to go—most days, except when it's very hot or very cold outside.

Much as serious illness forced me and forces many others to simplify our lives and appreciate our most fundamental needs, COVID-19 forced the entire world to simplify—suddenly and dramatically. As if a light switch turned off much of our daily activities, routines, and indulgences. The pandemic took us back nearly two generations, to a simpler time before the advent of so many of the luxuries and efficiencies we had come to expect—and need. And as painful as that regression was for so many, with lost lives and lost livelihoods, the pandemic brought new meaning to *stop and smell the roses*. The pandemic taught us, forced us, really, to embrace less consumption and more conscientiousness.

Unable to go to gyms and health clubs, we spent more time outside breathing the fresher than usual air and appreciating parks, walking trails, and open spaces. Without restaurants, we sought new recipes and cooked more of our own meals. Theaters were closed, so we invented new forms of home entertainment. We played board games and football and Frisbee with our kids. We nurtured old hobbies and developed new ones. We cherished the companionship of our small safe circles. We greeted neighbors (from a safe distance) whom we hadn't had the time to speak with in a long time. Worship without organized prayer services became less structured and more personal. Chalk hopscotch squares appeared on our sidewalks and home-made zip lines and hammocks connected trees in the neighborhood. Drive-ways became outdoor playrooms. If we were fortunate enough to be able to work from home, we left our cars in the garage, our work clothes in the closet, and logged on in our sweatpants. Without organized sports and after-school activities, kids (and adults) rediscovered their bikes and scooters and took them for rides on newly empty streets. Televised sports ceased to exist, leaving fewer potatoes on our couches and long-languishing honey-do's completed. We gave each other haircuts and discovered our true hair color. Our pets got shaggy, too, but they didn't seem to notice. Our credit card bills shrank with all the money we saved on coffee kiosks, restaurants, gas, health clubs, styling salons, and manicures.

Sadly, of course, although the pandemic reminded us of what a simpler life can be, it also came with millions of lost jobs for those who worked to provide us with our usual indulgences. My hope for all of us is the economic recovery will fully restore livelihoods without erasing our memory of what a simpler existence could be like someday, beyond the shadow of a pandemic.

KEY #7
GROW

AS WE AGE AND our experiences accumulate, we have the opportunity to evolve in our worldview. As I've written in the previous Keys, school, career, marriage, children, grandchildren, and surgery all changed me, as your experiences over the years have undoubtedly changed you. Our ultimate challenge in reaching a life of contentment is to grow. Growth requires moving on from the past, including from any regrets you might have, forgiving yourself if necessary (Key #6), and recognizing all the good you've done in your life and all you have to be proud of.

Take a step back and take the time to recognize your growth and evolution so far, marvel at how different, how much more mature and wise, your perspectives are now than they were when you were younger. The changes speak to your willingness to learn and to develop the prepared mind I wrote about earlier.

Looking back, I think I have always believed in something greater than me (Key #1), even as a child and young adult, but I don't think I ever knew why as clearly as I do now. Life experiences prepared me to accept—and even embrace—all that I *don't* understand. As a physician mentoring medical students and trainees, I taught that sometimes, when you're stumped, the most powerful and reassuring words doctors can utter to their most ill patients can be, "I'm not sure, but I'll do my best to find out." How can that be reassuring to patients looking to their doctor for answers? Because it tells them their doctor is human, honest, and not willing to bluff her way through this most difficult and worrisome time in patients' lives. I told my students that when they then come back to their patients and tell them what they looked up or learned from consulting other experts, their patients will know they're in good, caring hands. Admittedly, there were times when I returned to my patient's bedside without the answer because there was none. That was harder for me and my patient to accept, but an opportunity for both of us to work together, with what we knew and didn't know, to come to the best decisions.

I've come to believe this advice holds true in all our lives. As I wrote in Key #1, one of the reasons to believe in something greater than ourselves is it allows us to accept certain events, circumstances, and contradictions as being beyond our understanding and control. But now, for Key #7, we will commit ourselves to seek answers *within* ourselves. That's how we grow.

MILE MARKERS

Recall that Key #4 for *No Regrets Living* asks that, as a path to contentment, we regularly give thanks for the good in our lives. I wrote that although my daily moments of reflection take the form of prayer, that certainly isn't necessary or even preferable for many people—prayer is only one way of appreciating all that we have to be grateful for. But, because prayer is *my* way, the evolution of my prayers over time has been a useful proxy for me to track my own growth. Since becoming an adult, I have used my moments of prayer as a way of recognizing that everything we think of in our lives as being normal or ordinary is actually miraculous, extraordinary, and impossible to fully understand. Beyond appreciating and giving thanks for the normal and the ordinary as a starting point for my prayers, there have been profound changes in my prayers over the years. I share these few mile markers in my growth in the hope you'll reflect back and identify your own mile markers, the signs along the way that demonstrate and celebrate your personal growth. And then you can look forward to the road ahead for the growth still to come.

Gitel

I was in middle school when my great-grandmother, Gitel, was dying. It came as a shock to me because not long before she took a turn for the worse, we were in her nursing home room taking family pictures with her, and she seemed fine. I knew my great-grandmother well (I previously mentioned her and her seven children who all emigrated from Europe to three different continents just in time, before World War II). I would visit her after school several times a week, walking the few blocks from school to the nursing home where my mom would pick me up to go home. I can still smell the nursing home. So when my mother called from the hospital to say my great-grandmother was very ill, I was stunned. I took my younger brother into our shared bedroom, opened a prayer book, and we recited a traditional prayer I had learned in Hebrew school. My prayer that day was that of a child, an exercise in reflexive belief—a loved one was in trouble, pick the most obvious prayer, and say it fervently. When my great-grandmother died later that day, I wondered why God hadn't answered my prayers for her recovery even though I said every word in the prayer book. How had I failed?

Gitel, from author's personal collection

Anatomy Lab

Jump ahead ten years and I'm now a first year medical student. Anatomy class took us into a dissection lab where human cadavers became our first true teachers in the wonder of the human body.

This was not a blissful experience, another smell I'll never forget. The lab was drenched in the fumes of formaldehyde and there was death everywhere—literally. The cadavers were either individuals who had willed their bodies to science for the betterment of medicine and mankind or, more typically, homeless, often unidentified people who were sent to the medical school by the city morgue. Today's medical students pay tribute to those individuals with a ceremony of gratitude and remembrance for lives lost and bodies donated; that level of sensitivity had not yet emerged in my era. Rather, disrespect and pranks were more common means of coping with the stress, the smell, and the optics of anatomy lab. It didn't help that our lab proctor, a professor whose social skills explained why he was overseeing a room full of cadavers rather than a clinic filled with patients, chain-smoked while showing us the important landmarks in the body. More than once as Dr. G stood over our cadaver, a cigarette dangling from his mouth while his hands pushed aside organs to show us what lay underneath, ashes from his cigarette dropped into the body cavity of the cadaver. We silently, and sometimes not so silently, gasped, gagged, and occasionally dry heaved, but Dr. G was undeterred in his search for this gland or that duct.

There were a few students in each first year class who couldn't bear anatomy lab any longer and chose to leave school rather than spend another moment in medical school's hurt locker. Most students saw anatomy lab as a necessary hurdle, perhaps even a trial of fortitude, thrown into their path on the way to an MD degree. Anatomy lab was no more aesthetically pleasant for me than for my classmates, but on most days the profound appreciation for what we were seeing during our dissections overcame my apprehension and nausea. This was what all those nights in college spent in the electron microscopy lab or memorizing biochemical structures had led to. Now I had my first clues as to why all those tiny cell structures exist in our bodies and why those arcane chemical formulas mattered. The inside of the human body is beyond dazzling. It's, well…miraculous!

In today's era of robotics, engineering a machine that can walk, talk, vacuum our floors, and even think a bit is doable. But the human body is more than a walking, talking, vacuuming, creation. The human body is an unimaginably intricate labyrinth of interconnected components providing feedback and regulating each other; responding to commands from a nervous system that is far more complex than the most powerful computers we have developed; nourishing every one of the trillions of microscopic cells that comprise our bodies; and disposing of waste in such a proficient way as to prevent contamination of the rest of the body. Anatomy lab helped everything start to make sense for me. It also left me in awe of what could *not* be dissected or revealed in a laboratory. That which makes the body more than a mechanical marvel. The "us" within us: the thoughts, inspiration, understanding, compassion, conscience, moral compass, and, what some might call, our *soul*. Those cadavers were once living and breathing human beings whose extraordinary anatomy belied the even more extraordinary elements that made them human. It was for the souls of those cadavers that I prayed, even though I wasn't sure what that meant. And I'm still not.

That was also the period in my life when I began giving thanks, in earnest, for all that works inside us, especially when I began my clinical rotations in the third year of medical school. One example: Our team saw a clinic patient who had a Bell's palsy, facial muscle paralysis usually caused by a viral infection. The symptoms typically resolve over a matter of a few weeks, as they did in our patient. But in the meantime, our patient couldn't close her left eye—the eyelid muscles on that side were paralyzed. The production of tears in her left eye was also impaired, another Bell's palsy symptom. The combination of a paralyzed eyelid and decreased tear production resulted in her having a very uncomfortable dry eye for several weeks, requiring frequent eyedrops during the day and eye ointment at night. How often have you appreciated the "miracle" of your eyelids? The ability to blink when an object gets too close, keep out dust, close for sleep, and even wink at our friends all depend on our eyelid muscles, about which I had never really given much thought. Until caring for that patient, and ever since.

I'm not the only one who sees the intricacies of the human body and the delicate balance required for our health as reasons for gratitude. Two quotes, from the *Miracles We Have Seen* book I've mentioned previously, from colleagues who didn't have a specific miraculous patient experience to tell but felt the power of more subtle miracles:

> *Doing what we do as doctors, and seeing all that can go wrong, I've come to appreciate that every healthy day is a miracle.*
>
> —Nathan Rabinovitch, MD, professor of pediatrics at
> the University of Colorado School of Medicine

> *The longer I live, the more convinced I am that every breath, every heartbeat (and yes, even every bowel movement) is itself a miracle. We spend so much of our professional lives as doctors dealing with what is wrong in our patients (and ourselves), that I fear we have become inured to appreciating all that goes right.*
>
> —Allan Gibofsky, professor of medicine at
> Weill Cornell Medicine

Medical students taking anatomy during the COVID-19 pandemic were relegated to virtual labs where the "dissections" they undertook were on a computer monitor. No smell, no professor's cigarette ashes, no pranks or disrespect. I have been mentoring a first-year medical student who began the school year online because of the pandemic. True, in-person anatomy lab is no joy ride, but my mentee describes trying to learn anatomy online as ineffective, frustrating, and lacking the awe I told him I had experienced with the hands-on learning in a traditional medical school anatomy curriculum. My mentee has told me that his medical school is now discussing taking anatomy lab online permanently. I hope that doesn't happen. The young women and men who, like me, might be deeply moved by the intricacy and elegance of the human body in an actual anatomy lab will likely lose out on that emotional impact by seeing images on the same screen they may later in the day use for email.

The Ambulance and the Elevator

It's now five years later and I'm in my pediatric residency training. Second year residents took ambulance transport call, serving as the head of a three-person team sent to bring kids who were too sick to be cared for locally to the mother ship, Children's Hospital of Philadelphia. Along with a pediatric nurse and our driver, I was called to a large hospital northwest of Philadelphia late one night to pick up a baby in their nursery who was hemorrhaging. The story was of a full-term baby born with Rh disease (aka hemolytic disease of the newborn), meaning one component of his blood type (the Rh factor) wasn't compatible with his mother's. His mother's immune system formed antibodies that were destroying the baby's red blood cells, causing him to be severely anemic. The treatment for this condition is transfusion of compatible blood to the baby. Transfusions were begun in that nursery, but then a strange complication developed—the baby began bleeding from his nose, mouth, and rectum, and even from old IV and blood test puncture sites. The baby was losing blood as fast as the doctors were pouring it in by transfusion. That is not part of Rh disease—something else was going on.

Our ambulance sped upstate from Philly, full flashing lights and siren; the normal one-hour drive took us only twenty-five minutes. Then I saw the scariest thing I had ever seen as a young doctor—nursing staff in the parking lot of the hospital desperately waving our ambulance in. "Thank God you're here doctor—this baby is dying." Oh my goodness. I'm thinking that if this baby's life depends on me, barely out of medical school for a year, we're all in big, big trouble. I closed my eyes for just a moment, and whispered a single word prayer, "Please." The ambulance nurse and I raced into the intensive care unit where the baby's doctors and nurses were huddled over the warming bed, pushing blood through a large syringe into a tiny IV in the baby's arm. As advertised, there was blood oozing out of the baby from every orifice and needle hole, a leaking human pincushion. The arm IV site the doctors were using was leaking even as the blood was being pushed in through the same vein. First things first, we needed better access to the baby's blood stream—the IV in the arm didn't allow nearly enough blood to go in fast enough. I asked for a bedside surgical kit and cut down the baby's belly button stump to expose the large blood vessels in the residual umbilical cord, something I had done several times during my neonatal intensive care unit rotations during the first year of residency. More bleeding, but at least now there were two big veins into which we could slip larger IV tubes and give more blood faster.

Then I asked about the blood supply and couldn't believe the answer. The blood bank had run out of the baby's blood type, but there was a "universal donor" on staff, a nurse with type O-negative blood that can be given to anyone without the worry of incompatibility. Over the past several hours, the staff had been drawing blood from the nurse and injecting it directly into the baby—a heroic maneuver that under other circumstances might have saved the baby's life. But when blood comes from a blood bank, it's carefully anticoagulated, or "thinned," to prevent it from clotting in the bag and tubing. I asked the doctors to tell me how they were accomplishing that with the nurse's blood since delivery of blood through the small IV site in the arm was very slow. How did they prevent the blood from clotting in the tubing before it was given? They used heparin, a standard anticoagulant (blood thinner), which they added to the syringes before drawing blood from the nurse. How much heparin are you using and how do you know how much to use? They showed me, and clearly they had badly miscalculated the heparin dose; there was almost as much heparin in the syringe as there was blood. Enough of the anticoagulant, in fact, to anticoagulate the entire baby, prevent clotting anywhere in his body, and cause him to bleed from everywhere in his body. The potentially lifesaving transfusions were killing the baby!

Trying to stay calm, I called my supervising attending physician back at Children's Hospital and, out of earshot from the nursery staff, told him what I thought was happening. What should I do? The antidote to heparin is a drug called protamine, he told me. At which point I remembered that lecture from medical school. Of course! How much? He looked up the dose for me, the nursery's pharmacy rushed the protamine to the baby's bedside, and we began infusing it through the belly button line I had inserted. Within minutes the bleeding stopped. Clotted blood began appearing in the baby's nostrils and at the puncture sites. But there was still no safe blood to be had and this baby had lost a lot. Again, my attending physician had the answer: order fresh frozen plasma from the blood bank to stabilize the baby's blood pressure and "haul your butts back to Children's" where the blood would be waiting (fresh frozen plasma is the liquid portion of blood that contains no cells and is therefore compatible with everyone; it is in ample supply in all blood banks for the treatment of shock due to low blood pressure). And we did just that.

I sweated completely through my scrubs that night, and my hands didn't stop shaking until the baby was safely in our ICU at Children's. At which point, I closed my eyes for a moment and whispered another single word prayer, "Thanks." For the baby, the baby's parents, and for me. Along with our nurse and our ambulance driver, I had saved my first life, and that's when I knew I would be okay as a doctor. I was grateful for the path that had taken me to medical school, to residency, and, that night, to a hospital northwest of Philadelphia.

Not long after that, I saved my second life—a fifteen year-old boy with cystic fibrosis (CF), a terrible genetic disease that results in stiff and poorly functioning lungs. Well, actually it was Mark's nurse, Kate, who saved his life by noticing that the sounds she heard from his left lung weren't normal. I was the resident on call that night at Children's Hospital of Philadelphia, and Kate called me to listen to Mark's lungs. I wasn't convinced—his lungs never sounded normal due to his underlying CF, but because he was also having more difficulty breathing and complaining of chest pain, I agreed with Kate that we should take him for an X-ray to be sure. As she and I were escorting Mark back from the third floor radiology suite to the adolescent unit on the sixth floor of the hospital, Mark developed much more severe respiratory distress. The X-ray had shown a twenty-five percent collapse of his left lung, which in a patient without underlying lung disease might not be an emergency; but in kids with CF, dependent on every air sac in their lungs to breathe, that degree of collapse was critical and life-threatening.

When a lung collapses, air that had been in the lung accumulates in the chest cavity outside the lung, compressing the lung further and preventing it from re-expanding. Mark's suddenly-worsening condition justified the urgency of our subsequent actions—he was turning blue, in much worse chest pain, sweating profusely, and struggling for every breath. He cried out that he was suffocating. The X-ray technician had called security, and a guard was holding the elevator open for us as Kate and I ran, pushing Mark's gurney ahead of us. In the elevator, he became even more short of breath and more blue; I was afraid we would have to do CPR in the elevator, where I again whispered to myself my one word prayer, "Please." We rushed him to the treatment room on the adolescent unit where I asked for a large bore needle as Kate was scrubbing his chest wall with iodine. I knew from medical school that in an emergency, when a patient was in critical condition because of a collapsed lung, chest wall puncture was the required treatment. I had never done a chest puncture, and never even seen one done. With the senior resident pointing to the spot for me to insert the needle so as to avoid major arteries and veins, and after another silent "Please," I pushed the needle through Mark's chest wall—and he immediately gasped a sigh of relief. His breathing became less desperate and his color returned to baseline. I withdrew multiple fifty cc syringes full of air through the needle hole. A surgeon arrived shortly afterward and inserted a plastic chest tube into the hole I had made for a more permanent release of the still-accumulating air between Mark's chest wall and his now re-expanding lung.

The late author Peggy Anderson wrote a beautiful chapter about this episode in her book, *Children's Hospital.*[57] In it, she of course disguises Mark's identity, as well as his nurse's and mine. (For the book, she renamed me "Darryl Barth," so now you know my literary alias ☺.) Based on interviews with Mark and the rest of us shortly after the episode, here's how Anderson described the moments following the lung puncture:

> All told, Darryl Barth extracted 600 cc of air from the inside of Mark's chest. With every moment that passed, the boy grew more comfortable, more animated, more talkative. Barth had never seen a change as dramatic.
>
> "I feel so much better!" Mark kept saying. He wiped his face with tissues held out to him by Kate. 'I can't believe how much better I feel! I was so scared! It's such a scary feeling not to be able breathe!" Though still inhaling with effort, he was ebullient with relief. He looked at Barth. "You saved my life!"
>
> "Kate saved your life. She's the one who picked up that your lungs didn't sound right."
>
> The boy turned to the nurse. "*You* saved my life!"
>
> "Luck of the Irish!" Kate was able to reply. Her heart had only just left her throat.[58]

Looking back, and re-reading Anderson's book, I realize that, although still sweaty and shaky, I wasn't nearly as rattled after saving my second life. But my one word prayer afterward, "Thanks," was just as heartfelt. The next morning after rounds, as I was leaving the hospital for the day after my eventful night on call, I paused in the hospital's chapel for a few longer moments of gratitude.

As I look back now, with time to reflect on those dramatic experiences, as well as on my much more mundane life experiences, I'm amazed at what human beings are capable of. Where does the capacity of the human mind and body come from to perform even everyday tasks, to say nothing of emergency responses? How is it that a thought in our brain is instantly acted upon with precise movements of our body? Bring me a bedside surgical kit! Hand me a large bore needle! How did we evolve to become the physicians, engineers, architects, coal miners, bus drivers, psychologists, social workers, computer technicians, data analysts, public relations experts, actors, linguists, attorneys, and construction workers that we are? Did those capabilities just happen accidentally? A random combination of chemicals and elements following the laws of nature and resulting in beings who can design skyscrapers, put men on the moon, explore the depths of the ocean, and insert a large bore needle into the chest of a dying child?

Dad

Just over a year later, my dad was diagnosed with pancreatic cancer. He told me that when his eyes turned yellow he went to his doctor who ran tests. The saddest thing I remember about that conversation with my dad was his telling me that his doctor told him had Dad been a drinker, this would have been less worrisome—drinkers' eyes turn yellow but their liver disease isn't as bad as what my dad had. Doctors say stupid things, sometimes. I was now in my final year of residency training in Philadelphia. I knew his chances of survival were

5 percent or less and the average length of survival after diagnosis was twelve months. With the help of my gracious and compassionate fellow residents, I rearranged my call schedule to be in Denver when I needed to. There, I watched, close up, his daily struggle with recovery from the extensive surgery he required to remove the tumor. Postoperatively, his intestines were blocked for months, requiring intravenous nutrition, and he grew more and more despondent with his inability to eat and drink. I prayed every day, many times a day, between the time of his diagnosis and his death. My prayers during his illness were short and concise: please let him be among the 5 percent who survive, and please ease his suffering; help him open up his digestive tract so he can eat and drink again; help him gain weight; help him feel stronger and more hopeful. But, in contrast to the prayers for my great-grandmother fifteen years earlier, and the momentary prayers at my young patients' bedsides, my prayers for my dad were realistic and personal, not reflexive. I spoke to God in my own voice rather than through traditional prayer (although I did some of that, too, to cover all my bases). Dad's final eight or nine months were painless—his digestive tract did open up, he was able to eat and drink normally, return to work, and feel stronger and more hopeful—just as I had prayed for.

Then the call came from the flea market where he set up his fruit stand on weekends—Dad had collapsed, was unconscious, and an ambulance was on the way. I sped to the flea market and arrived shortly after the ambulance, in time to start an IV line that the EMTs had trouble with and help with their CPR. All to no avail. His death was from a heart attack, likely induced by the cancer, but without suffering.

By then, with an adult perspective (and that of a physician, to boot), my belief system had matured. I didn't know if God had answered my prayers but thought that my father's improved final months might be evidence of that, and for those months I was grateful. I also believed his death was evidence of the inevitably of natural laws—in this case the laws governing pancreatic cancer. It was a terrible disease (and still is) and prayers for a miraculous cure were unlikely to be successful. That didn't prevent me from trying, but it stopped me from believing there was more I could have done. I was able to accept the reality that there are many things in life that are out of our control.

Jonathan

Three years later, in the summer of 1985, now in the final year of my infectious diseases fellowship in Colorado, I was called to see Jonathan, a two-year-old former premature baby who couldn't shake his pneumonia. What started out looking like a routine case of a benign winter viral pneumonia, a common infection in young children that typically lasts a week or two, instead lingered well into the spring. Whenever his doctors tried to wean Jonathan from the oxygen he was treated with, he developed breathing distress, his lips turned blue, and the oxygen levels in his blood dropped. When I was asked to evaluate Jonathan for the cause of this persistent lung disease, my first thought was his doctors had called the wrong specialist. Infections don't often cause chronic lung disease in children and I predicted my involvement with Jonathan's case would be short lived. I was wrong.

My colleagues and I agreed on a panel of tests to perform to rule out infection as the cause of Jonathan's illness. During that next week, we tested Jonathan for all of the germs we thought might be possible. All the tests were negative. Our only remaining option for finding a cause and being able to get Jonathan off oxygen and back to a healthy toddler's life was a lung biopsy.

Four days later, the biopsy results came back. The diagnosis was one I had never heard of, nor had anyone else on our infectious diseases team. Lymphocytic interstitial pneumonia, or LIP. For context, the first cases of AIDS in gay men had been reported in the early 1980s in New York and San Francisco. In December 1982, the first suspected case of AIDS acquired by blood transfusion occurred in California. On March 4, 1983, the United States Public Health Service (USPHS) issued a warning that individuals in high-risk groups should not donate blood.

Jonathan was born on March 19, 1983, two weeks after the USPHS warnings about high-risk blood donors, and two years prior to the development of a blood test for the presence of HIV, the virus that causes AIDS. As a tiny premature baby, he required numerous transfusions of blood given by donors to the blood bank prior to the warnings. We consulted with physicians caring for adult AIDS patients in San Francisco—LIP, the finding on Jonathan's lung biopsy, was a classic finding in AIDS.

This was devastating news. We and Jonathan's mother and the rest of the reading world all knew AIDS was a fatal diagnosis. There were no known survivors of the disease at that point. There would be no approved treatment for AIDS in children until 1990. Jonathan was the first child with AIDS in Colorado, and one of the very first in the United States. For a newborn infected with AIDS in 1983, first diagnosed with the disease in 1985, and then untreated for years until the first medicine became available, based on everything we knew then and even everything we know now, there was a 0 percent chance of survival. As for my dad a few years earlier, my prayers for Jonathan were for a painless period of life and a gentle death. They were more than answered.

Today, Jonathan is thirty-seven years old, alive and well, living in Utah where he runs a restaurant with his brother. Jonathan's fourteen-year-old son is uninfected, as is his ex-wife (the mother of his son). Jonathan is still HIV-positive and still takes medicines—now highly effective medicines—every day. And therein lies the awe and wonder of medicine, and life, and one of the bases for my deep-rooted respect for all we don't know and all we'll never know. I spoke with Jonathan by phone recently and told him how grateful I was to have been part of his life story and witness to his "miracle." His story also appears in the *Miracles We Have Seen* book.

Me

Since being diagnosed with severe coronary artery disease ("hardening of the arteries") at age forty-seven, I followed strict diet and exercise programs in hopes of halting or even reversing the disease. I lost forty pounds, dramatically improved my exercise tolerance, and was quite proud of myself. Maybe I really could beat this thing, not need intervention, and not die of a heart attack. And then, as I described in Key #6, fifteen years later, I had my first chest pains during exercise. When I was hospitalized in preparation for bypass surgery, I seriously prayed for *myself* for the first time. Yes, I had said thousands of prayers of gratitude over the years, gratitude for all the good in my life, in my family's lives, and in my patients' lives. But as I was being prepped for surgery and then wheeled down the hall for kisses from Sara on the way to the operating room, I prayed for

myself. I was just older than my father when he died before knowing his grandchildren. I wanted to know grandchildren someday. I
needed to be around for my elderly mom whose needs were rapidly
increasing. And I loved my life and wasn't ready to find out what
came after.

The surgery went smoothly, the recovery not so much. As is the
practice these days, I spent only a few hours in intensive care where
I saw Sara and my kids, and then to a regular hospital room, groggy
but relieved. Until the next day when they had me up and walking,
during which I collapsed; as I was losing consciousness, I heard the
nurses call a code blue. When I woke up, I was back in my hospital
bed, surrounded by the resuscitation team, ready to shock, pump,
and breathe for me should I need them. Thankfully, I didn't. The
cause of the collapse wasn't cardiac, probably fluid or electrolyte
(mineral) imbalance, but my presurgery prayers morphed into
post-surgery prayers for recovery. Recovery was slow and painful.
Ironically the chest wounds and pain resolved without fanfare over a
couple weeks, but the leg wound (where they took the replacement
blood vessels to sew onto my heart) took many weeks to heal, and
then only after draining a huge clot. But that, too, finally resolved.
And now, more than six years later, the prayers I utter for myself have
returned to ones of gratitude for all the good in my life, including my
recovery from surgery.

Toni

Three years ago, a dear friend's daughter was involved in the horrific car accident I mentioned earlier: a methamphetamine-addicted
driver crossed the highway and struck the vehicle Toni was in, head-
on and at high speed, killing four of the five people in the two cars.

Immediately behind Toni's car that early morning, on a remote stretch of highway with little traffic in either direction, was a car driven by a paramedic who, upon seeing the tragedy unfolding in front of him, pulled over and ran to the wreckage of Toni's car. Seeing Toni still breathing, he called for emergency help while talking to Toni the entire time, telling her she'd be okay, help was on the way, be strong, hang in there. Talk to me, he kept repeating, talk to me. The first responders needed the Jaws of Life equipment to cut Toni from the car; they then transported her to the nearest emergency room, and then on to the university hospital's ICU. Toni's parents, our friends, are good and righteous people who have spent their lives in service to others, and to God. Toni is also a wonderful person—a loyal friend, a youth leader of several major charity efforts, and a frequent volunteer for worthy causes. Such a good person that she had been awarded her high school's annual award for most exemplary community service. How was any of this possible? Would this be yet another example of bad things happening to good people or would this become a miraculous survival story, a divine reward for lives well lived? Either outcome would be unexplainable in my mind.

I had already come to believe that so many of our experiences during life are impossible to understand; I saw the paramedic's presence at that critical juncture as further evidence. Without his call for help and the immediate support he provided, it's doubtful Toni would have survived, and her death would have been a tortured one, alone on the side of a highway. During the many weeks and months of Toni's very difficult recovery, involving a dozen or more therapeutic and reconstructive surgeries, Toni was on that little card I keep in my wallet listing those in need of healing, and she was in my prayers. Every day. Prayers for Toni's survival and recovery. But once again, my prayers had evolved and now bordered on confrontational: I beseeched God to do what was right, to breathe life back into Toni, and to guide her doctors' hands as they rebuilt her. Toni and her family deserved no less than a full recovery—do what's right, God! Me asking God to do right? Me *telling* God to do what's right? Yes. By then, for no reason other than personal growth over the years, I had developed that kind of relationship with God, and I was comfortable invoking it. Toni survived and recovered. She has physical and emotional scars bearing testimony to her struggle, but she's here to tell the story and is moving on with her career.

It would be easy to say that Toni's survival confirmed for me that God heard me and the hundreds of others praying for her. Too easy because so many questions will always remain unanswered. Was it divine intervention or just a coincidence that the paramedic was right where he was needed at the moment of the accident, there to expedite emergency responses and transport? For that matter, are coincidences themselves signs of a divine presence, or of fate, as I alluded to in Key #2? How could Toni have survived the accident when no one else did? Where was God for the four who died? Three of those who died were in the errant car, the one driven by the man on methamphetamines, so the easy answer would be they "deserved" to die. But the fourth fatality, a young friend of Toni's, was in Toni's car, the same car happened upon by the paramedic, and was as innocent as Toni. And finally, why did Toni have to be in the accident in the first place? What did she do to deserve that?

Mom

Last year, when my mom lay dying following a series of strokes, my prayers were strictly for her comfort; recovery was too much to ask for, was medically impossible, and she did not even have the 5 percent chance my dad had. Again, very personal, entirely improvised, and nearly constant prayers said silently, even as I was working with her hospice nurse, helping my mom sip water, and changing her bedsheets. But despite my prayers (and my pushing the morphine provided by the hospice team), my mom's final twenty-four hours were not comfortable; she struggled and suffered. We couldn't seem to make her comfortable. But I didn't blame God for that, nor did I wonder why my prayers hadn't been answered. No confrontation there. Rather, my prayers immediately before and then following her death were prayers of gratitude for the long life she had and the many joyous moments during those years. My daily ritual of remembering all there is to be grateful for served me well in those difficult final days and hours of my mom's life. Even then, when she was struggling, there was joy—our son and daughter-in-law, knowing Mom was dying, called from their home in New York to tell her, and only her, that they were expecting another child. I think Mom understood what they said—she smiled, the crooked smile of a stroke victim, but it was definitely a smile. They wouldn't tell the rest of the family for weeks. The baby, a girl, was born seven months after mom died and is named for her and for Sara's mom who died seven weeks before my mom (and before our kids knew they were expecting).

By the time my mom died, my belief system had evolved to where it is today: acknowledging that I won't always understand life's events, and only sometimes will I be conscious of my prayers possibly being answered. Other times I simply accept, as I did with my inability to make my mother comfortable in those last hours, that there's much I can't control, and I'm okay with that. And even when it does seem that my prayers are answered, I recognize that it may be my imagination or wishful thinking; I may be the only one hearing my prayers—I'll never know for sure, at least in this life. I've also come to accept that natural laws are almost always followed and can explain much of what we think of as normal and ordinary. We can choose to see natural laws as miracles in and of themselves, but asking for miracles outside those laws is likely to be futile. Mom's death also taught me that gratitude for all we have can overcome grief at what we've lost.

COVID-19

The pandemic once again pushed my belief system and marked yet another milestone in my spiritual growth. As the number of cases across the United States and the world skyrocketed, and as an infectious diseases doctor and virologist, I became obsessed with tracking the pandemic. I followed the growth of cases and fatalities in every country and every state of our country. And that obsession changed my daily reflections—forever. Although always deep in my sub-consciousness, the realization that we are truly one global people sharing one global home exploded into my awareness and into my prayers. This virus crossed all man-made borders.

I rewrote the little card I carry in my wallet, the one with the names of people in need of healing for whom I say a little prayer each day, and inserted the entire population of the world atop the list. The pandemic made it clear that we all need healing, every one of us, whether we were infected with the virus, infected with fear of the virus, or infected with apathy about the virus. I asked God for strength, healing, comfort, wisdom, and guidance. Strength for me, my loved ones, and all those across the globe who were healthy to resist the infection and help protect others from becoming infected. Strength for the frontline fighters, those in the mouth of the beast trying to save lives. I asked for healing for the millions of victims infected with the virus, fighting

to overcome it. And comfort for the hundreds of thousands of families grieving the loss of loved ones. I prayed for wisdom for our leaders, for medical
experts and scientists to make the right decisions, to establish sage policy,
to provide the needed beds, equipment, and tests, and to develop the crucial
medicines and vaccines. And I prayed for guidance about what I might be
able to contribute to the fight against the virus.

My prayers during the pandemic have been longer and more detailed,
louder and more desperate than any I have uttered before. And my prayers of
gratitude are even more heartfelt than before. Although unimaginably painful and tragic, the world is getting through it, as we did prior pandemics.
Effective medicines and protective vaccines were developed in record time
thanks to the lessons of those past tragedies and the blessing of our prepared minds. It could have been even worse, and because of this pandemic,
the next crisis won't be as severe or the toll as great. Our trajectory as a
people and as a planet remains upward, albeit with many hurdles and hiccups along the way. Surely reason for gratitude.

TAKE RISKS

There are risks everywhere. Our day-to-day decisions and actions,
from the momentous to the mundane, pose risks. Relationships pose
risks. Medicines and surgery pose risks. Childbirth is risky, as is childhood. Cars and airplanes pose risks; so do trains and buses. Snow and
rain are sometimes risky, as is too much sun. The job you take can
be a risky decision that may not work out right; ditto the school you
send your kids to. The house or apartment you rent or buy, and the
car you lease or buy, may turn out badly. Life experience is the best
preventive against taking unnecessary risks, but even the most weath-
ered among us make mistakes. It's one thing to be risk averse, another

to be so terrified of hurt or failure that you build a safety cocoon around you and rarely emerge, missing all the joy that comes with the good decisions we make and the actions we take that work out well.

Forty years ago in New York City, I was in medical school and walked past a street performer who was shuffling three playing cards on a makeshift table. One of those cards was the queen of hearts. The game was to put $10 on the table at the spot where you saw the queen land, at which point if you guessed right, the shuffler would hand you your $10 back and reward you with a fresh $10 bill. It was easy—I watched as three people before me immediately spotted the queen and made a quick $10. Of course, those three players were part of the scam. When I put down my $10 at the spot where it was absolutely clear the queen had landed, the queen was in one of the other spots and my $10 was in the shuffler's pocket. As I wrote earlier, my roots were humble, to say the least. I measured the cost of everything in terms of how many apples my dad would have to sell on his fruit truck to cover the cost of whatever I thought of buying. To say nothing of how many apples my medical school tuition cost. Losing $10 was heartbreaking for me, and I never forgot it. I've told my kids about it repeatedly as they've explored online gaming, fantasy sports leagues, and even the stock market and other traditional investments. How will you feel if you lose? How much are you willing to lose? How will you deal with the regrets of having placed the bet? Assume you'll lose it all before putting down your $10 on the queen. That doesn't mean one shouldn't invest or even gamble—just be prepared to lose—and have the resources to survive the loss. There are no sure bets, and the house usually wins.

On the flip side, fear of risk can be crippling and can lead to its own regrets. My European immigrant father watched as other newcomers to America invested their few dollars in apartment buildings, nursing homes, restaurants, and convenience stores. He was offered several investment opportunities over the years, but my highly risk-averse grandfather, Dad's father-in-law (Zadie, of the famous bosom pocket billfold incident), scared my father about the risk of losing his meager fruits-and-vegetables income on a bad investment with a wife and kids to feed at home. To his regret, my dad walked away from numerous investments that he mentioned to my grandfather. I don't know how those investments would have done—one was a chicken farm, so there's that.

And then there's the saga of my grandmother's shingles. Her son, my uncle, wanted to invest in US silver dimes. Actual dimes. He'd buy them at face value, ten cents each, and store them in a safe deposit box until the day the value of silver went up and/or the supply of silver dimes decreased, and their value increased. Ten dimes for a dollar, US cash for US cash. My grandmother, having never shed her shtetl mentality, which was so endearing in other contexts, was so upset about the risk she thought her son was taking that she developed shingles. As an infectious diseases doctor, I attest that severe stress can, indeed, reactivate latent chicken pox and result in the painful skin eruption known as shingles. So, this was real. Investment aversion was so powerful among my European immigrant grandparents that an absolute-zero-risk investment in dimes caused shingles. The denouement? My uncle didn't buy the dimes lest his mother become even more ill. As I said, fear of risk can be crippling.

Financial planners work with clients to determine their risk tolerance. My grandparents, having lived through horrors we should never know, had zero risk tolerance. But taking calculated risks can enhance our lives, and that is true for far more than just financial investments. Where do great writers, artists, playwrights, inventors, and scientists get their inspiration? We all have inspirational moments in our lives, moments from which we have an opportunity to grow as people. But the difference between those who achieve greatness from their inspiration and the rest of us is the ability to act on the inspiration. That ability depends on many factors, the most important of which are *time* and the *courage* to take risks. Most of us don't have the time to follow up on a great idea. We have jobs, financial obligations, kids, family responsibilities. We're usually exhausted by the time those daily hurdles are met, and by then we've forgotten or given up on the inspirational moment we had. It's happened to me innumerable times. In my early days as a laboratory researcher, pursuing an idea for a unique experiment would have required risking the funding I had been given for a more conventional approach; sometimes I took that risk, other times I didn't. I always wondered what would have become of the unique ideas I didn't follow through on—until I read that someone else had tried it and succeeded (although failures aren't often published, so there were probably some of those I also avoided). Thankfully, the more conventional (and funded) experiments I opted for also resulted in what I hope were meaningful advances for the field, but still I wonder what might have been, what direction my career might have taken. More recently, ideas I've had for writing projects get to the outline or early draft stage and then are shelved by the realities of daily life, only for me to later see a nearly identical book written by someone else. I'm determined to finish this one before that happens again.

Sara has conceived half a dozen brilliant product inventions that ended up being scooped by others with similar brilliant ideas (albeit not nearly as cool as Sara's), and more time and/or resources to spend developing them. In the original draft of this book, I listed several of Sara's best ideas that hadn't yet been usurped, but she asked me to leave out the specifics in hopes that she may still bring them to fruition. I really hope she does—they would make lots of lives easier. (Only half in jest, consider this an open and flagrant call for investors: Sara is willing to consider proposals for large infusions of cash, à la Shark Tank, and will gladly share her invention ideas with angel investors and venture capitalists if they're reading this.) Our adult kids have also had fabulous ideas for products and books but then got enmeshed in jobs or graduate school. I even had a business brainstorm that would have required extensive knowledge of baseball as well as financial savvy. I do know baseball…

Unless you're independently wealthy, moving beyond inspiration to action also requires courage. The courage to walk away from secure paths and perhaps even from making responsible choices. Courage to take risks. Acting on inspiration requires an element of irresponsibleness to avoid the regrets you feel when you see your idea with someone else's name on it. And irresponsibleness is a very slippery slope—you must know when to cut your losses and retreat to reality. We know people who didn't know how to do that and, instead, dug deeper and deeper holes, chasing dreams that came from inspiration and would have been game changing had they worked out. But with one failed dream after another, we saw an addiction creep in, not unlike a gambling addiction, believing the next brilliant idea would come to the rescue. When things go bad, they can go very bad and then even the quality of inspirations declines, further reducing the chances of success. The cost to those sliding down that slippery slope, and to all the people they take with them, can be substantial.

So, how should we balance the benefits of courageously acting on, and growing from, an inspiration or opportunity with the risks of endangering our security and our family's security? There are potential regrets along either path. The answer lies in the strength of the safety net you create for yourself, which in turn depends on the answers to these five questions:

1. What's your exit strategy if the plan doesn't work?
2. Can you reclaim your previous stable situation?
3. How many people are put at risk besides you?
4. Can someone provide temporary support for you and your family in the worst-case scenario?
5. Finally, and most important for purposes of *No Regrets Living*, which will lead to greater regret: taking the chance and failing or opting for safety and security and not taking the chance at all?

If the answers to those questions aren't reassuring, you may have to let someone scoop you on your brilliant inspiration or golden opportunity. This time. But have confidence in yourself that another inspiration, another opportunity for growth, will come to you in the future, hopefully at a more propitious time in your life.

That said, it's important to also know that not all opportunities come with a second chance. A close friend and physician colleague recently called to get my opinion on a significant position he was offered, one that would be the pinnacle of an already-distinguished career but would come with the significant risk of a very high-profile post. He and his actions would constantly be under the microscope and, for political reasons, many would be hoping for his failure—but success in the position could benefit the lives and health of thousands. Although healthy, at sixty-five years old, my colleague wondered if the risks of public scrutiny and potential failure were too great at this stage in his life. Should he should step back rather than step up? I told him about a similar decision faced by another colleague, someone we both know. Also given a once-in-a-lifetime opportunity for a high-profile position, she declined. I don't know her reasons, but I do know her regrets. I urged my colleague to project ahead a few years, envisioning the regrets of potential failure in the position compared with the regrets of passing it up. He took the job; time will tell if it was the right decision. *No Regrets Living* gives us a valuable mechanism for weighing the risks of once-in-a-lifetime opportunities, challenging us to foresee which decisions will result in fewer regrets.

The COVID-19 pandemic amplified the act of taking risks to become a matter of life and death—for individuals, for communities, and for nations. Many of the decisions we faced during the pandemic had no risk-free solutions. Sometimes those decisions had to be made instantly: whether it was safe to go to the grocery store when the milk ran out for your family, or to the pharmacy for your medicines, or to the doctor's office for important appointments, or to the emergency room for chest pain. Other decisions weighed on us longer: Could we visit our aged parents or grandparents in their home? In the hospital? Should we send our kids back to school when it reopens? Should we get on an airplane for an important family or work commitment? Or, the heartbreaking decision facing the family friend I mentioned earlier—is it safe to go to her husband's funeral?

Some of the actions we took to reduce the risk of infection had unintended consequences. We know of a man who attended his grandmother's funeral after she died of COVID-19. The funeral director limited the number of cars allowed into the cemetery with the goal of limiting the number of attendees—so this man, the grandson, squeezed into an overpacked car whose passengers ultimately all developed the infection, likely caught from the grandson who had visited his grandmother when she was dying. Grocery stores and other retail outlets established senior hours in hopes of protecting that vulnerable group from the risk of exposure to millennial and other shoppers. However, senior hours resulted in long waits to enter the store and in the checkout aisles, exposing seniors for long periods of time to others who may have been infected. July 4 saw traditional fireworks displays canceled across the country, with communities hoping to limit large gatherings of viewers. As a result, the number of fireworks injuries from fireworks used by individuals skyrocketed like the bottle rockets they were igniting. Even the best intended decisions can be risky.

The riskiest decision faced by our communities and by communities and nations around the world during the pandemic involved how long to stay locked down. There was no doubt that social distancing and stay-at-home policies slowed the pandemic, flattened the curve, prevented hospitals from being overrun and lifesaving equipment from running short, and saved lives. But the same policies decimated the economy and shuttered small businesses. And it also became clear that the issue of reopening was not a simple decision of risking health versus risking the economy. The economy has a significant effect on people's health and well-being and, in turn, illnesses and deaths threaten the economy. Lives and livelihoods are intimately related. Ethicists will argue that controversy for years to come.

Ethicists will also debate other weighty issues the pandemic evoked. How does the imperative for lockdowns impact the rights to religious freedom? And to freedom of speech and assembly, for example, the right to gather in protests or celebrations? Is contact tracing a violation of the right to privacy? Although these issues took on unfortunate political overtones, they do go to a core ethical dilemma of how to protect the health of our people while still protecting the health of our democracy.

I hope ethicists also argue, and resolve, the issues surrounding what I believe are the greatest risks exposed by the pandemic—the risks faced before, during, and after the pandemic by the most vulnerable members in our society. Those are risks we can no longer afford to take if we are to continue to move forward and upward as a society.

LIVE LIKE YOU ARE DYING

To conclude Key #7 and my prescription for growth, I'm borrowing from a country hit that touches me deeply, Tim McGraw's "Live Like You Were Dying." Given a terminal diagnosis, what does the man in the song do? He loved more deeply, spoke more sweetly, became a better husband and friend, gave forgiveness. And then he leaves us his wish that we get the chance to live as he did, as if we are dying.

It reminds me of a patient I met as a medical student many years ago who told me he had put off too much for the future, a future he would never have because of the terminal diagnosis he faced in his mid-fifties. He had so many regrets. Yes, part of living like you're dying is a carpe diem approach to life: making the most of each day, appreciating the wonders and blessings all around, taking advantage of good health to do the things you'll wish you would have done should health fail you.

But my idea of No Regrets Living is not just about carpe diem or smelling the roses. It's also about the way we treat people, the relationships we form, the legacy we hope to leave. If tomorrow was suddenly and unexpectedly the last day of your life, would you die owing apologies? Would there be people you didn't say I love you to enough?

And didn't the countless hours in our homes during the pandemic force us to ask those questions—and act on them?! We reconnected with friends and family and said, "I miss you," "I'm thinking about you," "I love you." And if we didn't take that opportunity then, shouldn't we take it now?

During the pandemic, social psychologists asked if we would ever be able to return to the type of intimacy of human connection we had previously. Will we feel comfortable hugging our friends, kissing our loved ones, walking arm in arm, holding hands, making love? Will we allow our kids to kiss and hug their grandparents? Will we shake hands with colleagues at work? Give high fives to kids in hospitals, schools, and down the block?

The answer to all of these questions must be a resounding YES! As I wrote in Key #3, we have been aware of germs and their risks since the days of Louis Pasteur in the mid-nineteenth century. Germs are indeed passed from person to person by kissing and handshakes, but we don't live in a bubble and we shouldn't create one because of the pandemic. Exposure to germs actually boosts our immune systems, protecting us from other more dangerous infections and other diseases. Not long ago I wrote a book about that for parents, *Germ Proof Your Kids: The Complete Guide to Protecting (Without Overprotecting) Your Kids from Infections.*[59] The key is in the parentheses: without overprotecting. We should never live in a world devoid of intimacy and warmth. I believe that rather than making us fear physical connection, COVID-19 should leave us with a renewed appreciation of the value and beauty of physical connection. Once we've done enough social distancing, it's time for social nearness.

And toward that end, remember that COVID-19 was by no means the first pandemic we have faced in modern times. Also in Key #3, I described how the Asian, Hong Kong, and Swine Flu pandemics came and went during the past seventy years, and, despite the tragedy of the millions who died across the world, including hundreds of thousands in the United States, we emerged still able to shake hands and hold hands, eat in restaurants, fly on airplanes, and even vacation on cruise ships. When the fear of COVID-19 has passed, we will again be able to live life to the fullest or, as the song says, live like we are dying. And we should.

As I wrote each section of this book, I repeatedly asked myself, "Do I regret any of the choices I've made or the actions I've taken in any of my life's roles, and, if so, can I still correct them?" Have I done enough as a physician, as a scientist, as a husband, father, and grandfather? Have I done enough for my community? For society as a whole? Have I volunteered enough, donated enough, educated others enough? Have I lived like I was dying?

No, not yet. There's more I know I could have—should have—done in many aspects of my life. There's no such thing as a perfect person, a person who doesn't wish he had chosen different paths or that some things had turned out differently. As I confessed in the Introduction to this book, there's really no such thing as *No Regrets Living*. Accepting that we all have some regrets is part of our growth as human beings. But my goal for all of you, and for myself, is to move closer to being able to look back at life someday with much more satisfaction than remorse. To experience wonder and feel contentment. We needn't wait for that someday to look back—the past is available to us now, and, thankfully, so is the future.

And it starts with these 7 Keys:

Believe. Discover. Heal. Appreciate. Accept. Seek. Grow.

Appendix A

ℒ

This is my updated take on Edwin A. Abbott's famous nineteenth century novella, *Flatland: A Romance of Many Dimensions.*[7]

"THE MIRACULOUS EVENT"

The TWO-DIMENSIONAL planet known as Planar had night and day, seasons of heat and cold and warm and cool. But the source of these natural phenomena was unknown to the geometric Shapes who inhabited Planar. There was no up or down on Planar, only length and width. Shapes were all flat, like on an endless sheet of paper, but without even the thickness of the paper itself. Shapes were born and Shapes died. Scientists on Planar had hypotheses for all of these occurrences that could not be proven. Believers on Planar had spiritual explanations that reflected their faith. Yet every day, despite the qualms of the scientists and the quandaries of the believers, the light came to Planar, and every night the light left. It was warmer when the light was present, and the light was present longer during the season of heat than during the season of cold. What preceded birth and what followed death remained unsolved.

The Shapes had colonized Planar for as long as history had been recorded, and it was assumed that Shapes were present even before they knew to record their own history. What was known to the Shapes was that every Shape starts out as a dot, growing over a long period of time to resemble a mixture of its parents. In the beginning, it is written in the ancient texts of Planar, the Shapes were all distinctly geometric. The dots of circle parents grew into circles, the dots of rectangle parents into rectangles; triangular Shapes grew from dots of triangular parents. But today on Planar, there are few Shapes that even remotely resemble perfect geometric shapes. Over the eons of mixing and mating on Planar, Shapes of every form and size had emerged. The Shapes of Planar fit together like a beautifully designed puzzle.

But, "The Miraculous Event" changed everything.

· · · ·

Midday in Town Center, everyone rushing back and forth from lunch, edging past one another, as always, along their flat routes. Amidst the daily din, no one noticed when the Dot first appeared.

Dots were commonly seen with their parent Shapes, being pushed and nudged along on errands. Cute collections of dots could always be found at nurseries and dot day care centers, but, outside those contexts, dots were always with parent Shapes or dot-sitters.

This particular Dot on this particular day in this particular Town Center was at first only remarkable for the fact that it seemingly came out of nowhere. It wasn't being pushed or nudged by a parent Shape toward the general store or the fast food restaurant or the schoolhouse. It was suddenly just there. Had anyone been paying attention during this busy lunch hour in the hectic Town Center, the spontaneous appearance of a dot would have generated great curiosity at least, perhaps even panic. Where did it come from?! Is it lost?! Abandoned?! But the flow of Shapes was heavy in that place at that time, with everyone hurrying about, looking ahead toward their next destination and only conscious of the throng of other Shapes around them by how snugly they were pressed against one another. It was not surprising that no one noticed that this new Dot suddenly materialized. Later, there would be great debate and discord regarding the genesis of the original Dot.

The Shapes in Town Center that day only took notice of the nascent Dot when it began changing. Dots growing into Shapes was a normal and natural biological occurrence. Gradually, over many years, dots matured into adult Shapes. But there was no precedent for what happened next in Town Center. When this Dot began changing, those Shapes closest to it stopped in their tracks and stared. Within moments, the Dot became a small Circle, then a larger Circle, and then a very large Circle. As the Circle grew to become gigantic, its span pushed back the onlookers. The Shapes in any one area could only see a small segment of the Circle, a moving arc in their immediate vicinity, forcing them backward. Only when the news reports emerged of other Shapes all around the Town Center backing away at the same time did everyone realize the enormity of the unfolding Event. It would later be determined, through careful interviewing of hundreds of witnesses, that all the arcs were connected, forming a gigantic perfect Circle shape.

Within mere moments, the space cleared by the Circle ultimately reached nearly the size of the Town Center itself, threatening to displace everything in its wake. At the zenith of the Circle's growth, the crowd collectively held their breath; some Shapes who witnessed the Event fainted, others screamed, many prayed. Just when it seemed as though the Circle might push aside the entire town, destroying structures and squashing Shapes in its wake, the Circle stopped growing. It stayed at its gargantuan, maximum size for just a moment before shrinking away to a smaller and smaller Circle as quickly as it had grown. At last, the Circle was again a Dot. The Shapes watched, spellbound with a mixture of fear and awe, until the Dot disappeared entirely. Gone, without a trace.

Of course, all newborn dots on Planar *eventually* grow to adult-size Shapes but over years, not seconds. Dots don't emerge from nothingness or vanish into nothingness. Dots never grow to the size of an entire Town Center. Shapes never shrink! And it had been many generations on Planar since anyone had seen a perfect geometric Shape, circle or otherwise.

The Event was unnatural and unprecedented, perhaps miraculous.

The Event impacted every aspect of Planar life for many years to come. It dominated the news media; inspired the arts and scientific study; created new specialties in medicine and law; prompted the hasty formation of a military (in case this heralded an impending foreign invasion); forced the rewriting of history books; caused the emergence of new political parties; and dramatically changed religious observances throughout the planet.

All of these changes were accompanied by important and often contentious discussions in the writings and teachings of Planar in the years following the Event. In the absence of any real evidence to explain it, disparate theories among the scientists gradually began to coalesce, as did diverse philosophies among the believers. Ultimately, most Shapes on Planar found themselves aligning with one of two prevailing ideologies: the Genesists, made up mostly of believers, or the Naturalists, those who took a more scientific approach to explaining the Event. Some Shapes allowed for both possibilities, putting themselves squarely in the middle of the debate and therefore suspect to both sides.

The Genesists interpreted the Event as a spiritual revelation from a Supreme Being who used the miraculous Dot to awaken the

Shapes from their mundane and meaningless existence and, even more important, to reveal their own origins to them. The Dot, they believed, represented the genesis of all Shapes, emerging from nothingness as a living entity capable of great things, and returning to nothingness. From dot to dot. The initial appearance of the Dot was called the Creation Vision, an immaculate demonstration by a Supreme Being. This Creation Vision, it was said by the believers, mimicked the creation of Planar itself, with the rapid growth of the Circle reflecting the actual creation of Planar. Hence, the Genesists argued, the Supreme Being must have created Planar spontaneously, a dot suddenly appearing in the midst of nothingness, emerging from a void, before expanding infinitely into the universe the Shapes now inhabited, and stretching to the outer fringes of the planet where no Shape had ever been. The Genesists opined this original dot somehow contained in its infinitesimal structure all the matter and energy that would comprise Planar and its Shapes. The Supreme Being, the believers continued, used the shrinking Circle that day in Town Center to give the Shapes a future vision, wherein Planar would gradually contract until it became nothing more than a dot once again and finally becoming nothing at all, just as it had started. The Genesists believed the Supreme Being blessed those many witnesses in the Town Center that day with these visions so that they might go forth, spreading the word and the prophesy.

The Naturalists explained the Event very differently using established and proven natural laws and, where those were found to be wanting, devising new scientific formulas to accommodate the observations. The Event was not a revelation from a supreme being, nor was it evidence for the existence of a supreme being, nor was it a vision of Planar's past or future. Rather, the Naturalists opined, the Event was simply a heretofore unseen and extreme manifestation of the natural laws of Planar. The appearance of the Dot, the

Naturalists reasoned, was consistent with the first appearance of all Shapes at birth and not in of itself surprising except that no parent Shapes were ever identified for this Dot. The growth of the Dot into the enormous Circle was consistent with known Shape growth except in three ways: the speed of growth, the perfect geometric form that had not been known on Planar for many generations, and the ultimate maximum size reached by the Circle. The Naturalists argued that two of these deviations from known Planar processes, although quite remarkable, were nevertheless still consistent with natural law. Perfect geometry had been part of Planar history and therefore allowable by the laws of nature. And size was likely a simple mutation of the expected size of Shapes.

But the Naturalists had difficulty explaining, by any known phenomena, the chronology of the Event: the spontaneous appearance of the Dot, the rapidity of its growth into the giant Circle, the equal rapidity of the Circle's shrinkage, and the disappearance of the Dot. Indeed, the shrinkage and disappearance of the Dot were both unnatural, regardless of speed. When old Shapes died, their size was nearly the same as their maximum adult dimensions, allowing for slight shrinkage at the margins, and they certainly did not simply disappear at the time of death.

It was in these unnatural areas that new Naturalist theories emerged, none lending themselves to rigorous scientific proof. The Theory of Relativism, for example, posited that the observations of the growth speed were the result of a simultaneous slowing (some said simultaneous speeding up) of normal Planar processes during the time of the Event, making the growth of the Circle seem relatively faster when compared with simultaneous occurrences. No one could explain how or why the normal processes slowed (or sped up) during those precise moments. Time had inexplicably been altered, the Theory of Relativism argued, to allow the normal life cycle of a

Shape to grow unimaginably fast, from a Dot to a gigantic Circle. And then, just as inexplicably, time altered to allow the gigantic Circle to shrink back to a Dot, leaving Planar just as it had been before the disruption. Thereafter, time resumed its normal behavior.

In contrast, there were Naturalists who held to the Illusion Theory, which concluded that the daylight at the time of the Event was actually warped to create the appearance of rapid growth and enormous size while, in fact, this was merely the passing through the Town Center of a standard-size (albeit perfect) circle Shape. Since the source of Planar's daylight was unknown to the Shapes, warping of the light was a difficult concept to embrace for many scientists.

Still other Naturalists combined the concepts of the Relativism and Illusion theories and spoke of the warping of time-space. Although time and space had never before been thought of as part of a continuum, the invention of new formulas seemed to justify such a composite construct. Time-space could not be seen, or tested, or even modeled by researchers, but those limitations seemed to make some Naturalists even more resolute in the accuracy of the formulas. Theoretical physicists on Planar suggested that perhaps time-space represented a third dimension.

When asked how they reconciled the unnatural aspects of the Event with a Naturalist philosophy, particularly the spontaneous appearance of the Dot and its subsequent disappearance, the Naturalists simply explained that there were natural laws yet to be identified and that time and research would ultimately uncover new, still-obscure scientific truths. The Naturalists referred to the appearance and disappearance of the Dot as the original Singularity and the final Singularity, concepts to be explained in the future when Shapes were more sophisticated scientifically.

The Genesists had an easier time, reveling in the absence of a scientific Unifying Theory. They felt their theories of intervention by a

Supreme Being were strengthened with each passing day wherein no new scientific evidence emerged. The Genesists did not accept the natural explanations for any aspect of the Event. They argued that the appearance, rapidity of growth, size, shrinkage, rapidity of the shrinkage, and disappearance of the Circle all defied Planar laws of nature and, therefore, were manifestations of a divine miracle. The Genesists argued that no single moment of the Event was scientifically reasonable, much less the totality of the Event.

And so it would remain. The Event polarized the Shapes along the most fundamental of issues: their very creation and existence.

On one and only one aspect of the Event, could all agree...somehow, *time* was involved. For the Shapes of Planar, time was an intangible, a way of putting all occurrences into context as either before, during, or after this moment. The concepts of before and after depended on the long-entrenched dogma that time was linear and traveled in only one direction—forward. The Shapes had tools for measuring time based upon the coming and going of light each day. They knew they aged as each day passed and that their age determined their abilities and their fertility. Until the Event, Shapes believed the passing of time could not be changed. After the Event, many questioned the traditional concept of time, but nothing new was learned regarding how time might be controlled.

Time remained a powerful and unknowable force in the lives of the Shapes.

THE TRUTH ·

The laws of nature, as Shapes knew them to be, had been broken, and no single, Unifying Theory could explain this cataclysmic Event to two-dimensional Shapes.

On a planet in which there was no above and no below, no height and no depth, how could the inhabitants possibly understand…a Sphere?

When the Sphere touched down on the surface of Planar, it first appeared to the Shapes as a tiny Dot. As the Sphere began to pass through the planet, it grew in the eyes of the Shapes to become a series of tiny arcs connected to form a tiny circle, and then quickly became a larger and larger circle. It reached its zenith as the equator of the Sphere passed through Planar, and then shrank as fast as it had grown, finally exiting as it had entered, a tiny Dot. And then, nothing.

The best and most reasonable explanation the two-dimensional Shapes could posit at the time was that the Event was a Dot that changed over time. As amorphous as the concept of time might be, it would have to suffice. Time, moving from past to present to future. A dot became a circle that became a large circle and then shrunk back to a dot—all in matter of moments, moments measured in the only terms Shapes knew, moments of time.

Yet a sphere is a very tangible and comprehensible object to those in three-dimensional worlds—those who live in such worlds would never confuse a sphere with time. A sphere is not linear and doesn't have direction; it doesn't contain a before, during, or after. The entirety of two-dimensional time, from its beginning to its end, can easily be grasped and manipulated in a three-dimensional universe as easily as one might hold a sphere.

In a two-dimensional world, the third dimension is called time. In a three-dimensional world, a sphere is just a sphere.

Appendix B

ʃ

THE "MIRACLE" OF COLONOSCOPY

Let's take a look at one of the most unheralded medical advances, and underappreciated medical miracles, of our time—colonoscopy. Stay with me here (or if the idea makes you a bit queasy, come back to this after you've finished dinner).

I've come to admire colonoscopy as a remarkable testimony to the ingenuity of modern medicine, to our ability to heal, to the miracle of the human body, and to the power of prepared minds. For those of you too young to have needed one of these procedures yet, I'll elaborate (I've just had my third, so I'm something of an authority). A colonoscopy procedure inspects the large intestine, or colon, for any worrisome signs of cancer or pre-cancer. The procedure involves inserting a long, flexible fiberoptic hose-like device, the colonoscope, into the rectum and navigating "backwards" (from bottom up) through the five-foot-long colon all the way to where the small intestine joins the colon.

While "steering" the scope, the gastroenterologist (a physician specializing in gastrointestinal diseases) carefully visualizes the entirety of the colon and can determine if there are any suspicious areas for colorectal cancer, the third most common (non-skin) cancer among both men and women in the US. At the tip of the colonoscope is a camera, which the doctor uses to document any worrisome areas (and send the patient home with souvenir photographs!). This wondrous colonoscope also has at its end a snipper device with which the gastroenterologist can perform biopsies of any areas he or she is concerned about. Following gentle sedation, the procedure is performed completely painlessly in about twenty minutes. Compare that to what preceded the advent of the flexible colonoscope—a rigid "proctoscope" (manipulated by a "proctologist," now an obsolete medical term), which was terribly uncomfortable and only visualized the rectum (six or seven inches of the entire colon), followed by a barium enema to visualize the rest of the colon. In those days of proctoscopy and barium enemas, many cancers were missed.

There are 150,000 cases of colorectal cancer diagnosed each year in the US, but since colonoscopy has become a routine screening procedure, the incidence has been steadily falling. Colonoscopy saves lives, which is further evidence of the enormous potential of modern medicine, and the ingenuity with which we've been imbued to advance the field. But it's not just the lifesaving quality of this procedure and the cool colonoscope device that merit discussion in the context of No Regrets Living. Indeed, as I wrote in Key #3, many advances in medicine have saved lives and given me reason to believe in the nearly limitless potential of the human mind to heal. Colonoscopy, though, is much more than just another important medical advance—it is also an invaluable window into the design of our wondrous human body, as I'll explain in a moment.

The enormous benefits of colonoscopy come at a price—and I don't mean the price your insurance may or may not cover. Although the procedure itself is painless, the preparation for the procedure is anything but pleasant. Actually, it's pretty horrible. (If you haven't already taken a break for dinner, this would be a good place to do so before reading on.) Over a period of a few hours, the patient drinks a full gallon of a salt solution that acts like Drano on the intestine. It cleans out everything inside. A complete purge. The salt solution tastes terrible and the cleansing means hours and hours of quality time in the bathroom evacuating all that's been in your gastrointestinal system for days. Although the colon is five feet long, that's nothing compared to the small intestine that empties into it, which is more than twenty feet long and is filled with undigested and partially digested food. The distribution of labor between the small intestine and the colon is pretty straightforward—the small intestine absorbs all the nutrients the body needs from the food we eat, while the large intestine absorbs water from the remnants to create formed stool (bowel movements). Too much information? Why am I telling you all this? Because in the preparation for the colonoscopy, the gallon of salt solution the patient drinks enters the mouth, passes through the esophagus to the stomach, empties into the small intestine, which in turn empties into the colon. In passing, this Drano-like concoction treats our entire thirty-seven-foot-long digestive tract as if it's merely PVC tubing draining a plumbing fixture in our home. Our gastrointestinal tract is a marvelous single-tube, multifunctional system that drinks in this vile salt solution at one end and evacuates it (and everything it brings with it) at the other end. The salt solution isn't absorbed, it just pours straight through until your entire gastrointestinal tract is cleansed and all that comes out from the rectum are the final ounces of the salt solution, leaving no evidence of your past week's culinary indulgences. Our other organs—heart, lungs, liver, spleen, brain, etc.—are unaffected. Even our kidneys have little to do with the gallon of salt solution because the precise salt balance is such that the water in it isn't absorbed—it just comes out the other end, whoosh! Imagine a long plastic straw passing through a balloon from one end to the other (without popping the balloon). In that image, the straw is our intestinal tract and the balloon is the rest of our body. The salt solution flowing through the straw never enters the body, yet when the procedure is all finished and it's time for lunch, our "inner straw" (our gastrointestinal tract), returns to absorbing everything we need to live without allowing the waste that comes with it to enter our body. Miraculous!. Nowhere is the miraculous nature of that system in clearer view than when sitting on the toilet during the pre-colonoscopy purge. Sure, the colonoscopy preparation is pretty disgusting—but what it tells us about our bodies is worthy of wonder. And . . . following the purge, the colonoscopy procedure itself, seemingly anti-climactic after all those hours on the toilet, prevents cancer!

Screening for preventable and curable diseases, much like getting vaccines, is exemplary *No Regrets Living,* of course, and colonoscopy is yet another reason for optimism that we can continue to improve the human condition. I have no doubt that in the near future, simpler tests, with much less awful preparation, will be shown to be equally or even more effective than colonoscopy,* much as colonoscopy has been so much more effective than the proctoscopies and barium enemas of the past. But even when colonoscopies are a thing of the past, we shouldn't lose the sense of wonder they have given us about the miraculous design of our bodies.

*There are already less-invasive tests available to screen for colon cancer that are being studied in comparison to colonoscopy for effectiveness. Which test is right for you is something to discuss with your physician—but screening is not optional; it is recommended at forty-five years of age for all adults who are not at high risk for colorectal cancer; high-risk individuals (e.g., those with a family history of colorectal cancer), should be screened even earlier.

Appendix C

⌒

ZADIE'S PTSD

As I wrote earlier, my father was an Auschwitz concentration camp survivor, but I don't know as much about what he went through as I would have liked to. He didn't readily share, and I didn't readily ask—both common patterns among survivors and their kids. I regret not asking more. That said, however, I have a vivid memory of my grandfather's devastating reaction to retelling *his* past.

As a child, Zadie, my grandfather, my mom's dad, watched his mother and sister die at the hands of the Cossacks, set afire along with his house during the Russian pogroms. He escaped with the help of a cousin. That story stayed buried deep within Zadie for more than eighty years until a reporter for a local paper heard of a special prayer book Zadie brought with him when he came to America from Russia around 1920. The reporter came to my grandfather's home and, with Zadie's great-grandchildren (my kids) sitting by his side, the reporter asked Zadie to tell her his story of the prayer book and that led to her asking to hear the story of his survival during the pogroms.

Zadie, posing with our kids, his great-grandchildren, for the story about him in the local newspaper. Author's personal collection.

The resulting newspaper story was beautifully done and is a lasting memory for our family. But so is what happened to Zadie the following day. He became suddenly catatonic, unable to speak or respond. His doctors thought it was a type of stroke; I now recognize it as an induced PTSD episode, the result of his reliving the horror of his childhood. It took him several days to return to normal.

Recalling the real and powerful mental anguish Zadie experienced in rekindling repressed and painful memories comforts me somewhat in not having asked my father for the details of his Auschwitz experience. I don't know what reliving those experiences might have done to him.

Notes

𝒮

1 Helen Epstein, *Children of the Holocaust* (New York: G. P. Putnam's Sons, 1979).

2 *Natural History of Infectious Disease*, Frank Macfarlane Burnet, Natural History of Infectious Diseases 4th Edition (Cambridge University Press, 1972).

3 https://www.skyandtelescope.com/astronomy-resources/how-many-stars-are-there/.

4 https://www.nytimes.com/2020/07/10/science/astronomy-galaxies-attractor-universe.html.

5 https://www.nytimes.com/2020/07/10/science/astronomy-galaxies-attractor-universe.html.

6 Albert Einstein, *The World as I See It* (New York: Philosophical Library, 1949).

7 Edwin Abbott, *Flatland: A Romance of Many Dimensions* (London: Seeley and Company, 1884).

8 https://www.npr.org/2020/10/15/923915545/filmmaker-finds-an-unlikely-underwater-friend-in-my-octopus-teacher.

9 https://www.washingtonpost.com/news/wonk/wp/2014/12/08/no-really-there-is-a-scientific-explanation-for-the-parting-of-the-red-sea-in-exodus/?noredirect=on&utm_term=.105c7f40dbef.

10 http://www.pontecorboli.com/digital/he_archive_articles/he122018/1_Stockle_Thaler.pdf.

11 https://www.nytimes.com/1984/10/31/garden/when-quail-come-back-to-alex andria.html.

12 https://www.theguardian.com/environment/nature-up/2013/jul/19/jonathan -franzen-egypt-migratory-bird.

13 https://www.nydailynews.com/news/world/locusts-swarm-egypt-israel-passover -article-1.1281267.

14 https://www.cnn.com/videos/world/2020/01/24/locust-swarms-east-africa- kenya-jba-lon-orig.cnn).

15 https://abcnews.go.com/Technology/evidence-suggests-biblical-great-flood -noahs-time-happened/story?id=17884533.

16 https://www.nytimes.com/2019/10/24/science/fossils-mammals-dinosaurs -colorado.html?smid=nytcore-ios-share.

16a Harley A. Rotbart, MD, *Miracles We Have Seen: America's leading Physicians Share Stories They Can't Forget* (Deerfield Beach: Health Communications, Inc., 2016)

17 https://www.uspto.gov/web/offices/ac/ido/oeip/taf/us_stat.htm.

18 https://www.psychologytoday.com/us/blog/excellent-beauty/201504/why-are -there-so-many-religions.

19 https://www.linguisticsociety.org/content/how-many-languages-are-there-world.

20 https://www.youtube.com/watch?v=p6pEcgDmEUk.

21 https://www.cnn.com/2020/03/02/health/surgeon-general-coronavirus-masks -risk-trnd/index.html.

22 https://www.cbsnews.com/news/coronavirus-surgeon-general-jerome-adams -wearing-masks-face-the-nation/.

23 https://www.businessinsider.com/fauci-mask-advice-was-because-doctors-short- ages-from-the-start-2020-6.

24 https://www.scientificamerican.com/article/caterpillar-butterfly-metamorphosis -explainer.

25 http://aeropx.com/collection/frontier-airlines-fleet.

26 https://video.nationalgeographic.com/video/short-film-showcase/00000149-6694 -d0c2-afef-e696773b0000.

27 Bernard Beitman, *Connecting with Coincidence: The New Science for Using Syn- chronicity and Serendipity in Your Life* (Deerfield Beach, FL: HCI Books, 2016).

28 Judith Leventhal and Yitta Halberstam, *Small Miracles: Extraordinary Coincidences from Everyday Life* (MA: Adams Media Corp, 1997), and numerous additional titles.

29 https://www.politico.eu/article/coronavirus-isis-terrorists-europe/.

30 https://www.cdc.gov/flu/pandemic-resources/basics/past-pandemics.html.

31 https://www.ncbi.nlm.nih.gov/pmc/articles/PMC4520913/.

32 https://www.nbcnews.com/politics/2020-election/poll-less-half-americans-say-they-ll-get-coronavirus-vaccine-n1236971.

33 https://www.usgs.gov/faqs/can-you-predict-earthquakes?qt-news_science_products=0#qt-news_science_products.

34 https://www.nhtsa.gov/.

35 https://aviation-safety.net/.

36 Dagmar Schroeder-Hildebrand and Peter W. Schroeder, *Six Million Paper Clips: The Making of a Children's Holocaust Memorial* (Minneapolis, MN: Kar-Ben Publishing, 2004).

37 *Paper Clips*, dir. Joe Fab, 2004.

38 https://www.timesfreepress.com/news/chatter/story/2018/jan/01/whitwell-tenn essees-unlikely-legacy-childrens/459602/.

39 https://services.aap.org/en/news-room/news-releases/aap/2020/pediatricians-educators-and-superintendents-urge-a-safe-return-to-school-this-fall/).

40 https://www.wsj.com/articles/the-science-of-prayer-11589720400.

41 Harley A. Rotbart, *No Regrets Parenting* (Kansas City, MO: Andrews-McMeel, 2012).

42 Isaac Asimov, *Understanding Physics* (1966) pp. 4–5

43 https://www.google.com/search?q=fudging+the+facts+for+peace+of+mind+rotb art+nyt&oq=fudging+the+facts+for+peace+of+mind+rotbart+nyt&aqs=chrome. .69i57.9431j1j4&sourceid=chrome&ie=UTF-8.

44 https://www.cnn.com/2020/05/04/us/retired-colorado-paramedic-obit/index. html.

45 Harold Kushner, *When Bad Things Happen to Good People*, Schocken Books, 1981.

46 https://www.torahcafe.com/rabbi-lord-jonathan-sacks/9-why-do-bad-things-happen-to-good-people-video_722d8db6e.html).

47 Yechiel Michel Tucazinsky, *The Bridge of Life: Life as a Bridge between Past and Future* (New York: Moznaim Pub Corp, 1983).

48 Viktor Frankl, *From Death-Camp to Existentialism* [Man's Search for Meaning] (Boston, MA: Beacon Press, 1959).

49 https://psycnet.apa.org/manuscript/2015-22642-001.pdf.

50 https://wellbeingtrust.org/areas-of-focus/policy-and-advocacy/reports/projected -deaths-of-despair-during-covid-19/.

51 https://pubmed.ncbi.nlm.nih.gov/31564187/.

52 https://www.nytimes.com/2013/05/21/booming/for-an-auschwitz-survivor-his-sons-graduation-spelled-freedom.html.

53 https://www.ncbi.nlm.nih.gov/pmc/articles/PMC3166409/.

54 https://www.reuters.com/article/us-zoom-video-commn-encryption/zoom-users -top-300-million-as-ban-list-grows-idUSKCN22420R.

55 https://www.cnbc.com/2020/04/03/how-zoom-rose-to-the-top-during-the -coronavirus-pandemic.html.

56 https://www.independent.co.uk/life-style/fashion/news/screen-time-average -lifetime-years-phone-laptop-tv-a9508751.html,

57 Peggy Anderson, *Children's Hospital*, Harper and Rowe, 1985

58 Ibid. pp. 1–23.

59 Harley A. Rotbart, *Germ Proof Your Kids: The Complete Guide to Protecting* (Without Overprotecting) Your Kids from Infections (Washington, DC: ASM Press, 2008).

60 Edwin A. Abbott, *Flatland: A Romance of Many Dimensions* (London: Seeley and Company, 1884).

About the Author

Dr. Harley Rotbart has been a nationally renowned infectious diseases specialist, pediatrician, parenting expert, speaker, and educator for nearly four decades. He is professor and vice chair emeritus of pediatrics at the University of Colorado School of Medicine and Children's Hospital Colorado. He is the author of more than 175 medical and scientific publications, and five previous books for general audiences: *Miracles We Have Seen; 940 Saturdays; No Regrets Parenting; Germ Proof Your Kids;* and *The On Deck Circle of Life,* which was endorsed by National Baseball Hall of Famer Cal Ripken, Jr.

Dr. Rotbart was named to *Best Doctors in America* for eighteen consecutive years, as well as receiving numerous other national and local awards for research, teaching, and clinical work. He serves on the advisory boards of *Parents Magazine* and *Parents.com* and makes numerous media appearances every year, including two media tours with *American Idol* finalists to promote influenza prevention, and two appearances on the *Dr. Oz Show* to discuss medical miracles. Dr. Rotbart is a regular contributor to *Parents Magazine,* has written numerous pieces for the *New York Times,* is a consultant to national and local media outlets, and writes his own blog at *www. harleyrotbart.com.* "Coach Harley" coached youth baseball and basketball for sixteen years, including eight years at the high school level.

Dr. Rotbart and his wife, Sara, live in Denver, Colorado, and are the parents of three big kids and the grandparents of three little kids.